A Stranger's Neighborhood

Emerging Writers in Creative Nonfiction

General Editor: Lee Gutkind

Donald Morrill

A Stranger's Neighborhood

EMERGING WRITERS IN CREATIVE NONFICTION

DUQUESNE
UNIVERSITY PRESS
PITTSBURGH, PA

This book is published by
Duquesne University Press
600 Forbes Avenue
Pittsburgh, Pennsylvania 15282

Library of Congress Cataloging-in-Publication Data

Morrill, Donald, 1955–
    A stranger's neighborhood / by Donald Morrill.
        p.   cm. — (Emerging writers in creative nonfiction)
    ISBN 0–8207–0280–3 (cloth: alk. paper). — ISBN 0–8207–0281–1
    (paper: alk. paper)
            I. Title.   II. Series.
    AC8.M69 1997
        081—dc21   97–21157
                                                                        CIP

PN
6071
,T7
m67
1998

Portions of this manuscript, in slightly different versions, originally appeared in the following
publications and are used with permission: *The Bellingham Review:* "White Horse Flame and
Shadow"; *Creative Nonfiction:* "I Give Up Smiling" and "Original Friend"; *Five Points:* "Once in the
Treehouse, Later in the Garden"; *Grand Tour:* "Encountering Time" and "Hitchhiker's Hat";
Manoa: "Migration of Wonder"; *The Missouri Review:* "The One Strong Flower I Am"; *New
Virginia Review:* "My Millionaire Life"; *Northwest Review:* "Shoes at Giverny"; *The MacGuffin:*
Part 3 of "Encountering Time" as "Gauges: A Memoir of a Crossing"; *Quarter After Eight:*
"Sleeping on a Door"; *Southwest Review:* "Never Wanting to Go Back."

In a few instances, names have been changed and details substituted to protect the privacy of
individuals.

Design by Jennifer Matesa.
This book is printed on acid-free paper.

My heartfelt thanks to the following people and organizations:

Virginia Benson, my student,
whose interest first inspired me to write this book

Richard Chess,
for his early and sustained encouragement

Abe and Kathleen Lerner,
and Debbie Frederick,
my literary family

Lee Gutkind,
for his editorial support

The Virginia Center for the Creative Arts,
The Arts Council of Hillsborough County, Florida,
The Dana Foundation

Lisa Birnbaum,
without whose skilled eye and ear
this book could not be

for Lisa

Contents

Sleeping
on a Door

In Gyantse, Tibet, an ancient woman approached me as I gawked at an old man napping in a temple courtyard. At first, I thought she might chastise me for my rudeness. But she spoke softly, in a language unintelligible to me, and her eyes were exceptionally kind and wet, made so, perhaps, by illness. With hands as wrinkled and smooth as shell, she led me onward, and I—with the traveler's unjustifiable trust—followed. Why did I think she might be trying to show me some special part of the temple rather than deliver me to a pair of waiting robbers?

Around the corner of the building we ambled, and almost as quickly as she had appeared, she drifted away, leaving me in the company of a half dozen begging urchins. Like most of the children I'd seen in Tibet, they were ragged—with runny noses and the snare drum cough. I distributed the cookies in my knapsack. Then I sat on a stone and wrote a note in my journal. In recurring wonder, the children ran their hands up and down my forearm hair. They also strained over the mysterious words on my page.

Finally, one of them held out his hand, and I drew a letter on his open palm. He leapt back and squealed happily. Soon, each child mustered the courage to receive a mark.

Later, in the town's crowded truckstop-hostel, I lay on the only bed available—a door across two sawhorses—and gazed at stars through the broken pane of a latticed window. I'd been in the country a few weeks, most of them in and around the capital Lasa. Now I was heading cross country—to the Nepal border—with a hodge-podge of other roamers in a city bus we had secured through a fidgety black-marketeer called "Secret Steve." The stars elated me because I saw them framed by a land famously forbidden to outsiders, jealous of its remoteness, a place which had briefly allowed me entrance. I had been drawn to Tibet more by its myth of inaccessibility than its myth of spiritual uniqueness. I'd also come because I'd been teaching at a university in Changchun, in the northeast of China, and summer recess had permitted me to escape the routine there.

That old woman at the temple and those children were provincials, I thought, like myself. And, of course, they were so much unlike me. One of the children had written in my journal, and I, too, had peered confusedly at a page. How mystified my Chinese friends in Changchun had been by my wish to visit this distant domain! To them—citizens of the nation occupying Tibet militarily for the last four decades—it seemed vacant and dreary. Why not go to Beijing? they asked. Or maybe Shanghai!

Thinking of them, I recalled that surveyor-spy who in the last century had traversed a closed Tibet by posing as an ordinary pilgrim, recording his survey by tallying his footsteps on a string of prayerbeads. How much had his purpose been altered by his journey? How much had he tried to maintain an unvaried stride, as uniform, say, as the length of a supplicant's body crossing the land one prostration at a time?

Thus I lay, with a doorknob gouging my hip, a kink confidently investing my shoulder, supine on some rigid, ambiguous plane.

Sleeping on a door. While this seemed to me then an ideal image of a stranger in a strange land, it seems now an even more apt embodiment of one's relation to the first home place—in my case, Iowa, a place existing, for me, increasingly in memory only. On that door in Gyantse, I was as far from Iowa as I could be and yet no distance at all. I had begun to realize that my hometown of Des Moines was a foreign land always near. I had left it years before. It had become forbidden to me inasmuch as the door to my time there could never be re-opened, though I might dream a way through that barrier and support. Still, I wondered then as now: *am I on the inside or outside?*

This is the quandary of being from somewhere that made you. There is a knocking on the door: is it something you want to let in . . . or lock out? Is such a choice possible?

Iowa, my intimate Tibet. So far from an ocean. Horizontal to anyone not on foot or bicycle. But, like the brain, crowded with obscure, intricate valleys, habitats of undiscovered species and undocumented life. No Shangri-la. No current army of occupation. This is the country of the accent erroneously called neutral, with its theology of dry humor and economics of sincere routine, where people make room for you in public, excusing themselves for passing within a foot. Territory of farms foreclosed upon, spawning ground of syndicated advice columnists and runaways to the glamorous, predatory metropolises.

Its dreamer and progeny, I still survey its monotonous grandeur, its full capacity to bore. Des Moines, for instance, which seems to symbolize for the rest of America the aspiring capital of humdrum; home of the dumb, appreciative audience; Stucksville. It greatly comforts those superior to its niceness. And in certain hearts it begets an anguish that beats metaphysically. But one is born lucky if simple repetitions—the sunset or the odor of snow—also please him, and I am lucky. Nothingness is everything in that landscape. I have loved it so often, and ignored it: the meager brook among the osage orange; the ripped-up rail line; the nighttime gleam of downtown's three proud office buildings. Why do I still leave it and try to make more of it than it is?

I have sometimes wanted to be one of them, the people who could stay there. I huddled with them in the southeast corner of our basements, sirens wailing overhead, the June sky green, knobby, and pendulous. We listened for the wind to ebb and that ominous quiet to settle on everything around us, that legendary silence before the roar of the tornado so often described as like a thousand railroad trains. That sound never swept over us, and we were grateful. Just as were oddly proud of the number of cows killed in a December freeze: the more fatalities the more memorable our weather. I failed to belong irrevocably to this huddling, to that climate of a spirit one must endure long after one leaves it, though that has been my greatest success. No one there knows how clean he is, how plentiful his uncomplicated, unwholesome food. Some part of me still longs to belong there, and this could happen someday—though I'm also proud of my exile and call it my belonging.

Like those children in Gyantse, touching me in amazement, I sometimes recall those encounters, however brief, which impressed themselves on my growing up. I study the mark I received. I see, for instance, a neighbor, Mr. Mills, who as a teenager in the 1930's worked at the medical dispensary in Dexter, Iowa. There police brought in the blasted body of Buck Barrows and his wife Blanche blinded in the ambush at the Dexfield Park campground. Buck's more famous brother, Clyde, and Clyde's lover, Bonnie Parker, had escaped the posse. Nonetheless, Mr. Mills could hold up his hand before me as a child and claim it had touched the bullet wounds of a notorious villain, an evil nature actually among us. Or maybe I see again Lanita Connett—to whom I never spoke—just as our eighth grade teacher, Mr. Simonson, whispered to her the news that her father had died suddenly. I see that utter change as the horribly unforeseeable swept into her features, for the first time, surely. She wept while she awaited the car coming for her, and the class looked at her for a long, purgatorial minute before she was at last excused.

Or, maybe, I happen upon someone like Dorothy, the painter, who pursued me in my first year of college, intrigued by my whiteness. She was, I think, collecting exotic experience, as I imagined I was. Her beauty and her blackness fascinated me (how could they be separate?), but the latter frightened me. I ran from her, still in the age when people like my parents referred openly to blacks as "coloreds," when Italians on the south side of Des Moines made up *the* town ethnic group in Anglo minds and eating in a tratorria there was thought a daring excursion.

Who, or what, led such beings to me then? Among them and so many others, I carved, in relief, on a redwood plank: *Be What You Can Be, Not What You Are.* Words not mine but from a pop song. Words not outlined on the plank by my hand but by another more skilled. Words, however, that I worshiped for their permission, in all the complacency of the youthfully desperate, who cannot stop to wonder if their capacity might render anything but good. I bestowed them, as a birthday gift, upon my high-school girlfriend, who knew I was leaving before I did, who sensed better than I what could hold her well. Such are the materials and terms out of which one may urge oneself, by turns reckless and timid, toward what one cannot imagine. Such, too, is a door to dream upon.

"A threshold is a sacred thing," wrote Polybus. The cemeteries

of the east side of Des Moines have begun to house stones bearing names unpronounceable—and sometimes illegible—to the
natives of midwestern English, itself an immigrant language.
Sleepers of a different sort, these dead bore their own Tibets to
Iowa and relinquished them for a more enigmatic journey, a
present they can't bring back to this second, or third, or fourth
homeland.

And what soil is this? Next door to my brother's house on the
west side, a Bosnian couple in their fifties, refugees from geno-
cide, planted tomatoes in a garden plot. A yellow, two-story colo-
nial fronts it, the residence of citizens who had donated the plot
as part of a resettlement program. The couple stooped over their
work, the man wearing an odd felt cap, a scarf wrapped tightly
around the woman's face almost like a habit—figures from the
generic old country, the former time which is somehow still ours.
They were—can this be?—new. My brother waved to them, respectful of the murder they had witnessed "over there," which he
had witnessed on television. My brother who, at twelve, had decided to escape by stealing our father's car. Barely able to see over
the steering wheel, he drove west until he ran out of money and
gas, at our grandmother's house in Omaha.

A preserved buffalo herd now roams Jester Park, north of
Des Moines. Teenage boys are smoking their first public cigars
in Younkers Tea Room. The bookmobile teems with grade school-
ers on Dubuque Avenue, one of them checking out volumes
of Sartre she cannot possibly comprehend. Old Dominic at the
kiln on the south side gains local fame through the remarkable
number of bricks he can stack on his head. His picture graces the
newspaper, but the copy doesn't mention his encounter with the
Virgin Mother among the pallets stacked in the warehouse.

In the life of my starting place, they are a few beads in a suspect pilgrim's hand. Trivial, perhaps, in isolation; in aggregate,

part of a summing up of self lost in the secret one tries to tell of the person he has become. My stride has varied, helplessly. The world is round but one never really comes back. Character moves through us, between us. Iowa, where a youngest son drives a tractor all one summer day in only his BVDs. Des Moines, where a mother honks her car horn for her children as they pass through the tunnel south of the capitol and later plays a loud Medea at the community theater. In Gyantse, I awoke at dawn with them and others like the birds fluttering in and out through the missing windowpanes. Strangers rose all around me, some shy about rummaging through their belongings, others quick to the mirror, each of us bearing necessary and unintended confidences.

Autobio

Who is this boy roving through the yards and alleys, the play-grounds and grocery stores of east Des Moines, 1969? In some determined trance, he slaloms between lilac bushes and displays of canned goods, apparently humming to himself. But that sound is not a hum. It is the song of rpm's, a whining up and down and further up the fretboard of horsepower's slide guitar. It is his engine talking to him under his breath. For he is a car, a car with a driver in it, often a racing driver—nipping through the esses and chicanes of an inner speedway, blasting from its hairpin turns and banked sweeps to ride inches from the wall of catastrophe and onto the next lap. He is a sweet street machine, cruising his mind's downtown glitter and chrome in low gear, never popping the gas for show and, by this, tempting anyone to try him. He knows what he is about, this boy, though he doesn't know that an era in the evolution of life on earth is ending, that a brief glory in the human fiction of mutating technology is reaching its climax. The last year of muscle cars approaches, and it will be the last year of this kind of self for him, as well.

I see him—this boy-car like a man-horse—and wonder how I could have been he. Too old even then to pretend to be such a thing as a car, I knew my imaginings were somehow immature. After all, I was almost past the point of fighting invisible foes from barroom punch-outs on TV, flinging myself backward in the living room, face whacked sidewise and stupefied by each blow, yet scanning—as I took the *coup de grace* squarely in the chops—for a soft place to crash down in defeat. But when fantasy came upon me, I was enveloped by it, and I possessed no intimation of what this daydreaming indicated about my character or what it might later demand of me. I did not wonder where it began.

A car holds one of my earliest memories. On the old gravel road leading from Highway 5 to my mother's home town of Pershing, Iowa, the front doors of my Uncle Tony's '56 Ford stand wide to a night of bugs. Its engine idles *na-na-na-na-na*, and I sit in the middle of its front seat, not quite able to see over the dashboard which gleams softly green. I cannot see out toward where the headlights point, toward where my father and Uncle Tony have gone, and from where a red light pulses. *Na-na-na-na-na*: primal wreck. Excitement swirls within me like the bugs in the light beyond the side doors, but I don't try to discover what is happening over the dashboard—perhaps I've been told to stay put. Instead, I gaze at the gravel glowing lunarly amid shredded shadows. I stare into the dark field beyond. Many years later, Tony and my father do not remember that night. And I wonder if the red lights emanated from the wreck that paralyzed a local man from the neck down: a man who then took up art to support his family, who, with a ballpoint pen clamped between his teeth, drew thousands of minute interlocking circles, making rural scenes of them, a man who eventually had one of his pictures hanging in the governor's office.

No one can tell me what happened on that road. I stare into the dark field: *Na-na-na-na-na*. . . .

Growing up, however, I lay through summer nights in front of a floor fan and navigated dark turnpikes in a sportscar of my own conjuring, snug and solitary and bound to an unnamed destination. In middle age, I am still seduced by driving—or riding—at night, the thrum of hot metals in concert, talk and then the end of talk, perhaps radio music, always the center line reflectors like golden cat eyes receding into blackness. And even now, late in bed, craving a trusted soporific, I return to roads from those childhood reveries. I put myself behind that steering wheel.

Muscle cars. In 1969, the neighborhood around my street, Garfield Avenue, rumbled with their mythic passages. Their owners gathered after work at the far end of the soda fountain of Strait's Drugstore—each machine like a superhero's uniform, his unique power. Kelly Reinhardt in a silver Plymouth GTX with smoky purple trim, towed by a 426 Hemi beneath a breather as broad as a bass drum: seven miles to a gallon. And Art Dunagan in a competition orange SS 396 Nova with a 4-ll rear end and wrinkle slicks. And the bruised red '63 Chevy Impala of Big Jimmy Padgett, its demure stock hubcaps belied by beefy headers writhing from behind its front wheels—headers bolted to 435 horses, uncapped only on Friday night for the illegal drags down Vandalia Road.

There was also Allan Delpierre's 429 Mach One, and Charlie Brinkerhoff's suave yellow Vette convertible with the aluminum block 454, and John Padgett's Superbee, its pistol grip shifter shivering like some diviner's stick when he turned the key. And—comic relief—Timmy Tollason's green Mustang 301, a weasely sidekick rod barely able to lay rubber but allowed sometimes to tag after the group.

One day a Chevy man, another day a Chrysler, I could slouch four stools down from these personages, imbibing their talk and a lime phosphate, waiting for my bundle of afternoon newspapers to be chucked from the delivery truck. They worked construction, or at the rail yard, or on the line at John Deere, and they were older—18 to 24. They manned or moused a poker hand at a party last week; they punched a biker at a kegger near the Saylorville spillway; they pissed on someone's windshield. Readying for weekend nights laden with women they could always get laid by— imagine it!—they battened themselves into starched button-down Gant shirts and slipped sockless feet into penny loafers; they stopped at the drugstore for cigarettes and mints, and a little bantering display for Mrs. Strait behind the counter.

No doubt as I listened to them I overestimated their glamor and cohesion as a group. I could still imagine that friends wanted to spend night and day together, though more and more evidence in my own life denied that premise. People understood things differently. One night, my best friends, Tom and Sam, and I climbed through the boarded windows of Mr. Larson's abandoned house to smoke the cigarettes Tom had filched from his mother's purse. Later, John Padgett said he had seen us climbing out of the window. At that moment, I thought of Art Dunagan parked with his girlfriend in the drugstore lot at 3 A.M. on a Sunday morning— Dunagan, whose hair boasted the swoop across the forehead which had proven irreproducible, even with setting spray. So cool. I assumed, wordlessly, that John would think Tom and I and the rest had been making out with girls in Mr. Larson's place—something more advanced, anyway, than smoking. I was about to imply such a story when John laughed, "So, were you boys having a little circle jerk in there?"

Down Garfield Avenue, other images of power beckoned futilely. At my cousins' house, mounted deer and antelope stared soulfully from the walls, past the bar and the Hamm's beer sign, toward the racked rifles and photographs of my cousins in the backs of Wyoming pickup trucks, lifting the horned heads of their quarry like barbells or the handlebars of a bicycle. Their father demanded a daily steak—because he worked—and ate it alone from a TV tray; he drove a lumbering camper to and from the factory until the following year's vacation allowed him to go west again.

I motored past this hunting, farther down Garfield Avenue to the Saturday night races on the half-mile dirt oval set before the grandstand at the state fairgrounds. Different from the snap-shifting spectacles of the drugstore gods or the sophisticated calibrations of the Grand Prix—which I had discovered in maga-zines—the stock car battles rattled through the chests of those standing trackside, of which I was one. These cars, too, were go-ing nowhere, but with what style! Through six eight-lap heats, a fifteen-lap semi-main, and a thirty-lap feature, they dipped and nicked and swung sidewise through the corners, casting gooey plumes of black earth into the air. They spun and bumped. There were those drivers who came to run hard and those who came to display a pretty car, and some who came to do both. Against the dirt, each wore a bandanna tied across his face, like a bandit, and the winner of each race paraded before the grandstand, bearing the American flag and a kiss from Miss Snap-On Tools.

Dave Chase, Bob Hilmer, Lennie Funk, Lem Blankenship, Ernie Derr and his nemesis, Ramo Stott—another set of deities arose, replacing those at the drugstore, like Roman gods superim-posed on Greek. These, however, were almost wholly silhouettes booming past the grandstand; or a figure, in souvenir photo-graphs, crouching beside the dented number on his car door; or the sweat-shiny center of fan attention in the ringing silence of the pits after the last checkered flag. They tore holes in the night like none of the others could; they pitched their machines into the fastest groove with apt recklessness, knowing their grip would hold. Yet it was the interior of their cars that most commanded my fascination, interiors gutted of all pretensions to ordinary luxury. They contained only criss-crossing tubular steel, to provide sturdiness should the world flip; a fire extinguisher bolted to the floor; an oil pressure gauge and tachometer on the dashboard; and a bucket seat which curled around to cup—and often bruise—the right side of the driver's rib cage during those wrenching left turns. A rigorous space, for the practice of a discipline—like a room, it seems now, occupied only by a mat, a notebook and a pen. What happened in such a place? I envisioned myself there, inside that completeness. At other times, I sheathed myself in the snug lines of a Ferrari or Lotus, though sometimes images of fatal crashes rose before my mind's eye—Fireball Roberts, Lorenzo Bandini—with burned remains pinned inside a fiery explosion by impact, the strew of injured parts. And there was my own crash, the tumble from my Stingray bike in a heat race against Tom and Sam on the oval we had laid out on the Stowe School playground: an entire summer with my kneecaps shredded, cracking open, oozing and itching, bandaged unsuccessfully in hopes that I could wear dress pants to a distant cousin's wedding.

I did not distinguish between the blue-collar ram-jam of the fairground stockers and the refinements of weight and handling demanded at the Grand Prix. I longed to drive and then—often the compromiser—decided that I might actually fit better as part of the pit crew. As much as speed and danger seduced me, I craved more the charisma of the equipment, though I understood its greased and whirring intimacies, its fine tolerances, only as a generalist might.

What then occurred in the more available and commonplace interiors, after I acquired the learner's permit, and later, the license? I had imagined myself by that time through many cars, not all of them muscled, and the lives I might possess through each model. I had sat in the back of the family station wagon—that drab fate—and pretended it was a Triumph Spitfire and I the envied bachelor, heading toward a holiday reunion. I had become the cool, prudent presence beneath the dark cloth headliner of my Uncle Clark's mint-condition '50 Dodge sedan. I had spent days in the prim existence of the neighbor's white Plymouth Valiant with no radio, powered by a tubercular slant-six.

I began to dream differently, however, with a real wheel in my hands. On the only long family trip, Des Moines to Denver, I guided my parents and grandmother and siblings through the hours, their fortunes in my supremely confident and inexperienced control—and this recognition did not then occur to me. My first car was a VW Beetle, simple, dependable, cheap—a counter to the big-block musclers which Detroit finally stopped making and which disappeared like the dinosaurs whose bodies had fermented into the suddenly expensive fuel once burned with impunity by the drugstore gods. Talk of superchargers and bleach burnouts and acceleration rates entertained my attention less and less. Terms of automotive endearment such as *wicked* and *cherry* receded into the dusty corners of my lexicon.

The highway, rather than the street or the racetrack, became my new language. Up from the pavement, summer heat wriggled like a transparent genie beckoning me to catch it and make wishes. American Sinbad, I roamed a grid of Iowa two-laners, green tunnels through August cornfields, gray tapes measuring the skull of winter. I roamed with Tom and Sam, nothing defined, no questions yet articulated—not capable, really, of asking the question that would send us toward what we might become elsewhere. And I drove alone, nomad clouds somehow within me pushing against my ribs, the horizon surprisingly with me, like dirt again under my nails—all the going that must be accomplished, and the destinations a body in our time could attain.

I went and came back, and then went, unforgivably, for good— like those relatives who abandoned their town's ambitions and became "hard," it was said, in some California or New York, who rarely wrote, and returned only for a death, or compelled by the epiphany of too much time lost. In the going lay myriad textures, malleable days, lives. There unfolded a testing, an indulgence. Battered towns, proud and prosperous towns, pathetic towns approached from the vanishing point ahead and retreated behind on command. I arrived and was surrounded by characters who were people in other eyes. Truths passed my window: *Venison, The Natural Food of the Twenty-first Century, Range-raised in the Garden of Eden; Mississippi Welcomes You, Only Positive Mississippi Spoken Here; Bail Bonds—Let Us Help You Plan Your Jail Break!* And sights flickered, becoming ambiguities. Did that sign say *Sanctuary*, or *Mortuary?* Was that man back there actually chopping a roll of carpet with an ax?

Small roads swirled through ravines and undulated like a vast train of hammocks. The interstate spread across the windshield like an epic drive-in movie, calming the contours of terrain, providing a familiar, ceremonial plotline—past military bases and swamps, past local arts and crafts, the shredded recaps splayed on the shoulder like monstrous, pummeled arachnids, the hideous billboards. Driving became a litany of naming performed by the eye: valley speckled with trailers; fence galloping toward the mountain; mascot painted on the village water tower; telephone poles, like vacated crucifixes, shrinking into the distance. The boredom and repetition agitated for romantic sensation, for some new knowledge, perhaps at the next exit, the next turn.

At some point in the years, I discovered the stillness of sixty miles per hour, perhaps the first stillness of adult life. At the wheel, I could sit quietly as nowhere else, the *slap-slap-slap* of my tires on the caulked seams below. A voice within me, my own, gathered like a mist. Unable to banish itself with the usual heat of busyness or obedience to a group, it began a scattered, ineffable monologue, an intermittent whisper at times dopey, trite, questioning, inescapably frank. Its presence could allow a nourishing solitude which rendered the insight of feeling and crucial utterings for which I would always be unprepared.

And then the voice could evaporate, almost without notice, and leave me with a meditative blankness, receptive as never before. I was then motionless and present like a stone or chair—or even a car during most of its existence. This, while wet asphalt marbled the rocker panels or dust dimmed taillights ahead, between stops for hotcakes at midnight, between guitar strumming and tent pitching, between debates about bliss with friends and girlfriends, between famous sites and toll booths—in a Dodge Dart humming over Wyoming, in a Chevy towing a U-Haul across Ohio.

When the car broke down, as was its wont at the ripe moment, I encountered my ongoing presumptuousness, my foolish faith. Stranded: that elemental, instructive condition—the itinerary interrupted, the story digressing without clear outline; let down and powerless according to the old terms of my journeying. I and my friend Mark shoved our thumbs out over the macadam, and people—people just like we once were—surged past, seated, staring. Exhaust and grit gusted over us, the dimensions of the roadworld unfitted, almost hostile, to any vehicle so soft and slow as flesh.

But a ride finally came, and soon Mark and I sat over diner coffee a 4 A.M. in Presho, South Dakota, awaiting dawn, so we could walk up the street to Merle Fuller's house. *Merle drives an old Beetle and he might have the part you need. Otherwise, it's 120 miles to the nearest auto store, which would be closed until Tuesday, anyway, because of the holiday weekend.* The coffee went down and was refilled and sat longer and longer, cooling into a stale pond over which Mark and I pondered the essence of a sheared fan belt pulley and the inclinations of the residents of Presho, who grew slightly sinister in the light of a stranger's fatigue and anxiety. Waiting: another stillness. Who was this man we would meet, Merle Fuller, who had not existed for us two hours before?

At dawn, we found him in his kitchen, his head and face a cue ball silvered by a few days' growth. And with him at the wheel of his ancient Beetle—colored the whitish-red of sun-bleached plastic—we rumbled across the wind-shocked prairie to his farm. Mark, in the front seat, chatted aimlessly and with gusto, fueled by *esprit de corps* and an excess of No-Doz tablets. In the back seat, I suspected the old man's eye for parts. I was also mildly afraid, though I would not admit that to myself—my fear an element of the cowardice I would confront on every journey thereafter, itself a reason for wandering.

We drew up to a white farmhouse, got out and sauntered toward the barn, where Merle stopped, unzipped his pants and let go a languorous steaming stream. "I don't have the power I used to," he said wryly over his shoulder. Mark and I shivered slightly in the bright chill, my suspicion giving over a little to the sudden elation at simply being in that place.

Eventually, we rolled back the barn door. In the dirt before us, in the middle of South Dakota, lay 20 or more VW engines variously intact. As though comparing signatures or fingerprints, Merle held the broken pulley next to the pulleys of the engines, settling finally on one. It did not, I thought, resemble the shattered part; it would never fit.

Of course it did, perfectly—also as its wont—and remained dependably there, recognized each time I opened the hood: Merle's part, the touch of the master, for which he refused to name a price and at last accepted ten dollars as a token. Driving back to town from the farm, Merle had talked about a journey he had taken as a young man: "I'd been driving for hours and was worn out, but I kept going, I can't remember why now. Suddenly,

I swerved to avoid a herd of horses galloping across the road, a whole bunch of them. I almost ended up in the ditch. Then I realized there were no horses there at all. I must have been dreaming."

Mark and I sped out of Presho among a herd of Merle's dream horses toward some more refined notion of destination, with the highway, for the first time, more ready for us than we for it.

There would be other cars in succeeding years. By increments, however, those vehicles grew strange to me, no longer the conveyance of spirit. Other objects undertook that transit, as much as objects do. Yet now, years after, new lacquered street machines appear, their undercarriages festooned with tubular neon—something the drugstore gods would not have envisioned—and in them I imagine a continuity, however absurd, a passion that pleases, despite its limits. Too soon these models will pass out of date and leave their owners with the complex knowledge of a former life, a previous self, almost wholly unknown and unrequired by others, perhaps unrequired even by themselves. They will then begin to encounter what age must be: an ongoing relegation of what is to what was, the cultivation of a unique junkyard which one day vanishes like mist. And they may also return there, as souls do, for the salvage they need: the telling which veers and races and breaks down, and which also keeps between the lines.

Never
Wanting to
Go Back

Dimly and romantically, I assumed that I would be the lone Westerner in Changchun, China. Instead, I was assigned quarters within the walled compound on 13 Zhonghua Road, a foreigner among foreigners—14 from New Zealand, Great Britain, Canada and the U.S., and four from Japan.

As a group, we were like a giant mobile of mood, the balance and configuration of which shifted as one of us shifted emotionally, or arrived, or departed. We were married and with spouse, unmarried and indifferent to—or hungry for—the lover back home, unmarried and unloved, divorced and unsure, monastic and occupied, horny and thwarted. We'd come for employment, direction, escape, love, study . . . or because we had nowhere else to go.

And, of course, we were not alone. Around us were the two gatemen, the assigned maids, the cooks in the kitchen, the handyman, and the office manager—some of whom seemed to live, at times, in the compound's back rooms and storage areas, sleeping where they could clear a place.

For the foreigners, the compound was a haven and a test-site, a cluster of cells variously permeable. There, as on the street, Inside and Outside were not always distinct properties. Humor, forbearance, compliance, supple intimacy, and forgivable reserve defined each relationship. For me, the days, the months spun slowly into a luscious rhythm of the predictable and the unforeseen, repetition and variation—interrupted by brief cycles of inner blackness, exhausted sympathy, or grace. Changchun rose early for its exercise and closed early for lack of amusements. Often, I awakened at 5 A.M., jogged, and then worked at my desk for a couple of hours before morning classes. Then lunch at the compound and the midday nap—followed by afternoon classes, errands, or a walk around town. In the evening, we read or played cards or drank, turning in by nine or ten, the whistles clear and small from the engines at the train station several miles away.

Yet I could never be certain what I would discover beyond my door. Privacy was a shifting condition, as was possession. Once, I headed out for class, only to find a horse—leashed to a cart of roofing tar—standing in my hallway. Another time, when I answered a knock, the office manager and three workmen fanned out across the room, immediately ripping at the heating pipes in three corners. Because materials were scarce after the Cultural Revolution—when these buildings were erected—the pipes installed previously were too narrow to carry enough hot water to heat the room in winter to more than 58 degrees. I sat at my desk, plaster dropping like sugary plumes, thankful for the heat I would have in the coming winter, wondering how many nights I would be visited by rats until the holes the workmen were chopping in the floor would be refilled.

Sometimes, there was no knock on the door. My required maid, Xiao Wei, would often enter unannounced, to sweep or change the bedding—until she caught me naked from the bath.

After that, she tapped lightly, and I sang out a friendly "O.K.!" Slightly younger than I, she insisted on calling me "big brother," and I was supposed to call her "little sister." She was married and had a son of three. Once I happened upon her fingering the keys of my manual typewriter. I pecked out the alphabet, and suddenly, softly, she sang the alphabet song. Snooping among the papers on my desk, she found a snapshot of me with four of my nieces and nephews, and could not be swayed from her conviction that they were my children. She was sad for me—so far from my progeny—and warmed slightly to me thereafter. On those mornings I was at my desk when she came to sweep the room, I would try to assuage my uneasiness at having a maid by moving the furniture for her. Other times, I would return to my rooms to find her—and other women—boiling pots of chicken for their families on what I thought was my gas ring. I am tempted to believe, still, that when I was out of town, some Chinese person slept in my bed.

According to my students, privacy for most Chinese depends on a psychological rather than a spatial domain. Living quarters are often so cramped that people "take a walk" to give a married couple in the family opportunity to make love. Nightly, you could find young people, alone, reading under a dim street lamp. You could find people in the park, alone, regarding a single willow tree around which not a single blade of grass grew—it representing all of nature (always sentimentalized) in a country where urban culture, terraced farming, and toxic waste now relegate most remote, untrammeled lands to T'ang Dynasty poems.

I never grew accustomed to making room in my spirit for what I lacked in territory. Perhaps this results from a national history leaning for so long on the reality—and then the metaphor—of the frontier. Perhaps it is Henry Ford's dubious gift to me; Des Moines and Tampa (where I live now) are cities made horizontal by the car. Perhaps my longing for space merely derives from growing up in a moderately large family, where the televisions always chattered and siblings battled, and there was no way to sequester myself from distraction except to get out.

Few of the Westerners adjusted to their fragile privacy and frustrated territorial imperatives, though married couples seemed more successful at establishing boundaries. Apparently, our quarters (and persons) were an ambiguous zone—public *and* intimate. The Chinese people I came to know were impeccably courteous. But people on the street—schooled by the norms of deprivation or barnyard curiosity—could be rude and grasping. Like some freeway drivers in the U.S., people would cut you off obliviously or race to the head of a line. On jammed sidewalks, pedestrians routinely bumped into each other without acknowledging it. I finally stopped excusing myself.

Still, on ancient, beleaguered buses jammed like a packager's maximizing dream, fares would be passed politely through a half-dozen hands to the cashier and the tissue-sheer ticket issued the same way. How much of modern Chinese history—its mass catastrophes and self-annihilations—emanated from these tectonic counterpressures? Some people seemed smoothed and pacified by exhaustion; others, jittery or vibrant. On the shelf in one of my student's quarters—a space shared with five others—I found a book on structuralist literary criticism and Virginia Woolf's *A Room of One's Own*. My neighbor, Mrs. Gang, said, "Chinese people are like thermos bottles full of boiling water. Cool on the outside."

The Westerners came together most regularly at parties and lunch—the parties more frequent as winter extended itself, and lunch our ceremony of *esprit de corps*. Sometimes the parties brought us together with the foreigners at other universities in town—young men from Benin studying geology or Palestinians pursuing a major in auto design. Many of these spoke several

languages—a history of imperialist occupation in their mouths—
and all spent the first of several years in Changchun learning
Chinese, just to take the classes for which their governments
sponsored them. Some were married and visited home every other
year, some less frequently if their native countries were especially
poor or stingy. Some seemed wholly bereft. For others, like a number of the Africans (all of whom faced constant discrimination
from the local population), the time in China was a kind of penal
servitude they dared not acknowledge as such to themselves, if
they were to endure it.

At the compound dining hall, our group of 14 met daily. Over
the usual lunchtime rice, we swooned before imagined shopping
sprees sponsored by homesickness. We lavished upon each other
vast caresses of sexual innuendo. We bestowed world (Western)
news, such as it came—through VOA or BBC World Service . . . or
the Chinese newspapers, which generally devoted their copy to
dam projects on the Yang-tze, model husbands, the visits of foreign
leaders to Beijing, and the World Badminton Finals in Jakarta.

Overwhelmingly, we talked of China—what we'd read, and
what Changchun had shown or told us that day. Odd sights ob-
sessed us, as did the constancy of want surrounding us, the utter
fragility and cheapness of individual life in impoverished circumstances; and sometimes lack brushed against us, inviting us into
the realm of desperate risk and no choice.

Many knew more than I of the country, and of travel in general. Monica spoke Mandarin and Russian. Doug, a Minneso-
tan, spent hours before dawn translating the Chinese newspapers
into German. Brigid and Simon—British subjects born in remote
regions of the empire—were wandering scholars of exceptional
experience. All of us, however, seemed possessed by intelligent
enthusiasm. For that hour each day, we became fourteen sets of

lucky eyes and ears relaying to our communal mind, inventing our China.

By necessity, we also found ourselves interested by—and intimate with—Westerners we would not have met at home. Rex and Sylvia (with nothing apparently in common but loneliness and British citizenship) became lovers. Neither brought birth control, so the luncheon group would anticipate the daily post, hoping it would contain a letter from one of their friends with a condom or two. On those good days, they would adjourn early for the midday nap. Often, Mr. Du from the Foreign Affairs Office delivered our mail—to capture rare stamps and envelopes for his collection, about which he said he was "mad, quite mad." With our general permission, he opened envelopes enough to clip away the stamps. One day, he appeared in the dining hall with a large letter, the corner of which was scissored away. He dropped it before Sylvia's plate, and condoms spilled forth like doubloons from a strongbox. Mr. Du grinned, displaying proudly the stamp that had been affixed to the envelope, his prize.

Despite our retreats and solitudes, people in the compound knew whose turn it was with the *Playboy* smuggled from the States and passed, during one cold snap, among the single men and women. For the group, we made cheese expeditions to Harbin—the only place it could be bought, the Chinese disliking it, believing it makes for unpleasant body odor. We purchased imported almond roca and handed the can around for general snacking and found, a few days later, fly larvae inside the wrappers of remaining pieces. We invented Christmas—which was just another Wednesday in Changchun—our feast featuring paper crowns for the diners and chicken we roasted despite the Chinese cooks turning down the oven for fear the birds would explode. On the dining hall roof one spring night, we strained to sight Halley's Comet, which was wholly obscured by dust storms off the Gobi Desert. For a number of wintry Tuesday evenings we played basketball at the gym with missing boards in its floor—until "culture shock" splintered nerves and the games grew embarrassingly rough. At the local Korean restaurant, we savored dog soup and listened as Monica told of her conversation with a middle-aged Chinese woman in the neighborhood, who'd said that she'd never had an orgasm and Western women must be very weak to think them important.

In our cold rooms, we made an art of cursing the world made gray while our heels turned to chilled glass. We praised the rusty yellow water when it steamed twice a week into our bathtubs. We dodged mudslides of unrequited love and fell in muted wars. We counseled each other when necessary, our woes at home remote and highlighted.

Besides Doug, my most frequent traveling companion, I grew closest to the family in the apartment above mine, the Correards: Rita and Lance, and their sons, Gilbert and Stephen, aged twelve and fourteen. From a small town near Chicago, they had come to China, it seems, for the most American of reasons—the possibility of new opportunity. Lance was a recently unemployed businessman who thought that since China was opening to the West, he might make contacts in the import-export trade. He'd convinced Rita that it would also be worthwhile to take the boys, and herself, out of school for a year and join the adventure. As the weeks and months passed in China and his business aspirations grew unlikely, he concentrated himself more on adapting to Chinese ways, learning the language, knowing his way around all things—a hopeless enterprise for which he was ill-equipped, though he fended remarkably well.

"Lance doesn't love being in China," Rita once observed, "He loves China."

Undoubtedly, imagination and courage had inspired him to

bring his family to China. Yet, I think he was engaged in a titanic struggle with his past and with the American notion of success. He was a dutiful, insecure provider, a retractable, worried soul who said he'd spent most of his adolescence sitting at a window, waiting for someone to come along and issue directions—which is what Rita did when she proposed marriage to him.

In his mid-thirties, Lance had almost made it as a middle manager in a modest, surburban way—only to have the ranch home life of decent comforts recede repeatedly on pink slips. His father, who came to see them in China, had made his pile and retired comfortably, and Lance could not forget it. A man of little deals and weekend triumphs, Lance could have been happy to run a small town hardware store, to proudly introduce a curious customer to his universe of three-prong plugs and ten-penny nails and the right drill bit for the job. Instead, he was a frustrated son deluded by the blessings he craved, haunting Changchun relentlessly to discover where every product could be gotten, making himself expert at that.

But this wasn't the only thing on his mind. He and Rita had married as teens. A couple of years after their sons had started elementary school, she'd gone off to the local college, and he'd approved of her quest—to quell whatever threat rippled within. She was hungry and discovering that she'd always been hungry. For a year or more, she'd been having an affair with a sweet, constricted philosophy professor who talked of leaving his wife but never would. Perhaps Lance knew of the professor. He was the only other lover Rita had then known. Undoubtedly, he sensed his marriage besieged, regrouping or unraveling.

Rita was like a nervous chairperson determined to accomplish something, one who'd watched closely 16 years of marriage pass through the tree outside her kitchen window and was uncomfortable with an afternoon in the house alone, with no husband or sons needing food or first aid. A reader of poetry and Kant, the eldest of four daughters, child of a father who said that "they get better as they get younger," she was dogged by Catholic guilt and a moneyed notion of self-sacrifice instilled by her mother, as well as her own keenness. After a couple of polite months, we became friends, talking for hours on long walks. Eventually, we became lovers.

I had left a woman in the States—Winifred. She'd encouraged me to go to China. We broke up when I left but within weeks were corresponding regularly and sending audio cassette "letters"—assuming a reunion that allowed us to circumscribe any current love arrangements. Her arrangement was named Dwight.

Rita and I agreed to limitations as lovers, and despite vacillations and melodramatics, we stayed within them. I massaged away any sense of wrongdoing by reminding myself that she and I were both needy, and that I might be good for her confidence and she for my emotional maturation. Also, it seemed that Lance somehow sensed our congruency and made room for it—almost encouraged it. Among other things, Rita was just coming to imagine the possibility of life ahead as an unmarried person. I was learning about the complexities of care and responsibility. She knew about Win, about most of the women I'd left behind. Through her stories, I heard about bonds deeper than I had fathomed. Together, we thought aloud about our lives; and despite our public discretion, several in the compound detected a stronger connection than friendship, disapproving openly just before they departed from China permanently.

Through it all, Lance and I remained friendly—for reasons beyond the demands of living in close quarters. Rita insisted that I was the first man in years with whom he seemed comfortable. I liked him, genuinely, perhaps because I had to like him.

Gilbert and Stephen were my other intimate influences. At times, they became my roughhousing younger brothers . . . or my bewildered nephews . . . or my sons. An unfamiliar, captivating species, their presence introduced me to my own vanished adolescence and to an older maleness previously unavailable to me. They were glib, sometimes dopey shape-shifters in a world of adult forms. By the week, their arms and necks seemed to lengthen visibly. Their voices popped and deepened. Like odd, delectable fruit, they were handled frequently in public by Chinese adults—who worship children and sentimentalize childhood because it seems a brief, woefully fragile refuge. Playing soccer with neighbor children in the street, Gilbert and Stephen picked up Chinese. Among the Westerners, they sometimes said adult things—things they couldn't fully understand—and watched for a response.

I played catch or cards with them, or walked the town. On those rare mornings after a package had arrived from relatives in the States, they shouted down the stairwell an invitation to pancakes whipped by their mother from powdered mixes.

Gilbert—a master of charming self-deprecation, a forthright subaccomplisher—struggled for his independence, his younger brother disarmingly cute and often more attended. An authority on boredom for which he blamed no one, he kicked a soccer ball for hours against the compound wall. He discovered that his mother was a woman, one day telling her, "You know, you're not bad looking, for a mom." At the dance parties for the Chinese students, he triumphed over the classic geekiness that marked him in Illinois—standing tall and stooped and shaggy-topped, like a royal palm tree, encircled by twenty supremely rapt girls.

When I think of that "era" of Gilbert, I remember the day I found him gazing off blankly, pulling his hair straight up and snipping it with the index and middle finger of his other hand.

"What are you doing?" I asked.

"Oh . . ." he said, snapping back to the present, "this is how I pray."

The more introverted of the two, Stephen sometimes spoke with the foreclosing moral tone of a nineteenth century American industrialist. At other moments, he was a witty, gregarious boy wanting to be held. I once mentioned that his beauty empowered him in a special way. His reposte: "Yeah, but you're not a kid forever." He worried incessantly about his place among the adults— not wanting to bore. He believed Gilbert would be haunted in Illinois by his crushes and social victories in China. He thought his father deluded about the import-export trade. Prescient and craving the detachment that sometimes seemed to possess him, he knew that somehow all of us should descend from the ether of foolish assessments to reliable, dead-level earth. This, at the age of 11.

In the days before he left China, he announced that some day he would return, perhaps to study and wander more. Years later, he told his mother, in passing, "I cried every day in China."

The Stephen I remember was given a harmonica for his birthday, on which I blew a ditty, letting him believe I could actually play. Later, he asked me if I would teach him, and I gave one or two suggestions, nothing more. It was a disappointment to him but not a surprise. Adults, he knew, were full of promises, pretending to skills and authority they didn't possess.

Another time, I tried on his coolie hat, and he worried that I would ruin it. I told him that I respected things.

"Yeah, but you don't respect some things," he said.

We looked at each other, me still wearing the hat. I understood then how adults can fall into hopeless conflict with a child they love and who has wounded them, or who seems to have some secret insight into them which they want to recover. Maybe he knew about his mother and me. Maybe.

Yet another time, at a party, we wrestled, and suddenly my big-brotherly half-nelson slipped into a hug and frightened us both. Fleeing, he paused at the archway in the dining hall—to keep me from following him with words. Often, he'd been mistaken for a girl by the streetmarket women, and he detested their attention until it got him the gift of extra peanuts. I'd seen him on several occasions sneak out the back door of the dining hall with bottles which the cooks had saved especially for him to exchange for chocolate at the corner kiosk.

As he vanished from the archway, I thought of how much he resembled his mother, and how one morning when he took off his glasses to play she discovered a young man, soon to be too handsome; and how she hoped a decade would pass before he found out about "us," his recollection of China somehow more important to her than her own.

I think now of how she swore the country was ruining him. Pretentious, I mentioned *human flexibility*, and reminded her of the change she underwent in those minutes between tucking him in and our rendezvous. And what about my hat-buying trips with her husband, whom I didn't know the year before?

At lunch on the day after the party, without asking, Stephen fetched himself and me the usual disposable chopsticks, and we ate without mentioning what had happened the evening before, both knowing our favor was required.

Since returning to the U.S., I've often wished to be the game traveler on my own street. I've longed to journey through my days with the wanderer's estrangement from local certainty and re-spectability, hoping to discover what I cannot otherwise discover when all goes as planned. This stratagem works sometimes, though I believe now it's my disguised nostalgia for those years on the road—that "second childhood"—and I should probably resist it.

Before she came back home from Changchun, my colleague Monica begged her father to visit her in China, where he had worked as a surgeon for several years during World War II. He refused, declaring that he didn't need his memory of a lovely country altered by new views of the place disfigured. While this rationale might not withstand an accusation of sentimental cowering in the past, I'm struck by its dry-eyed acknowledgment that all is unrepeatable. He was saying: I can't replicate my experience, and I don't need to have the experience of seeing things changed.

Not only did he not want to go back to China, I believe he didn't want to have the desire to go back.

This last assertion says more about me, of course, than him. My years in China were irrevocably defining. For some time afterward, it seemed crucial to put them behind me, to move on to other things. I found myself caught between wanting those times charged with the contours and intensities that give us our vision, and yet not wanting them to dominate me, the present, or other pasts to come.

In this, I think about Gilbert and Stephen, my fleeting nephew-sons in the compound in Changchun, now grown up.

"China made both of them dissatisfied with what is," Rita said to me one night on the phone, "but that's probably just my own excuse, given the divorce and other failures."

Restless when they turned of age, Gilbert and Stephen followed the Grateful Dead on the band's concert tours throughout the U.S.; they mined crystals in Arkansas; they traveled with a group of druggie-artisans. Gilbert, now 22, soon wearied of the road and returned to the small town just outside of Chicago where he grew up, and moved back in with his mother. Feeling guilty but hoping for the best, Rita later evicted him, since it was clear to her that he didn't intend to find work. At present, he lives nearby in an abandoned house with a shit pit and no lights.

"He's completely surrendered his cares. Absolutely dysfunctional," Rita said. "He wants what he's doing to appear Zen-like, because that would make it more respectable.

"But he's just a user of people. He knows how to say the things to get himself into the car going to the party, though he has no money or beer. He's changed—unlike Stephen.

Stephen—that grave little boy in the coolie hat who may have suspected that his mother and I were lovers—also came home. One day in the backyard, he buried a tin box containing crystals, a bird's nest, beads, coins, and a lock of hair from Lana, the girl-friend he'd gotten pregnant several years before, who had an abortion and moved away, eventually, with no further word. Later, he fell in love with an airbrush artist named Terri, and they moved out West to the mountains.

"He sent good, long letters from there," Rita said.

Then Terri returned with a new boyfriend from a weekend camping trip, and Stephen ended up at Rita's again, briefly.

"He told me," Rita said, "that if he stayed here, he'd just become like his brother—getting stoned with friends and hanging out at the mall, looking at girls.

"He turned to me one day and asked, 'Does this empty feeling ever go away?' and what else could I say but, 'Sometimes we have losses that don't leave us.'

"He decided to go to Belize, to study homeopathic medicine at a Mayan farming commune. He thought that with those skills he could make his way back to China and become a barefoot doctor. I think he'd become a Chinese citizen if he could.

"One night he left, hitchhiking to Austin. My little boy."

Stephen worked for Greenpeace in Austin for a while and had his money for Belize stolen by a companion who turned out to have jumped parole in Nevada. One night months later, he appeared at Rita's door with nothing but a walking stick from which an American flag dangled.

He'd returned to renew his driver's license.

Before leaving a day or two later, he went out to the backyard and stood over the buried shrine. He also promised Rita that he'd return in May for her wedding.

"His letters are short now," Rita said, "Blood poisoning in Tulsa. Gathering food with the Diggers in California and giving it to the poor. . . .

"My son might be turning into one of those people you don't know the whereabouts of—only that they're *out there*, somewhere."

My
Millionaire
Life

During family holidays in Omaha, Grandpa Morrill would approach me, the oldest at the kids' table.

"Who is this?" he would mutter from the side of his mouth, leaning in and pointing to George Washington on a dollar bill folded into the palm of his cupped hand.

When I answered correctly, he would press the note into my palm and fold my fingers into a little fist around The Father of Our Country.

"Save some," he would whisper, and walk away regally, ignoring any questions or protests from the other children about what had gone between us. At the time, he was in his sixties. He had worked with his hands—for the railroad, the grain mill, and then the makers of cornflakes—since dropping out of the fourth grade in 1910. Ceremonies such as the Washington quiz (replaced by Lincoln when I reached puberty) exhibited his hindered craving for purposeless pleasure. He was justly proud of having gone from a boyhood on a farm with empty pockets to a modestly prosperous retirement—which a fatal heart attack would terminate in its fourth year.

These were not my first encounters with money, but they were my introduction to a lifetime course in the mystery of its faiths. My grandfather's ritual pleased me most in its exclusion of my siblings and cousins. It also taught me that one could receive cash for knowing something prized by the payers—even without understanding that knowledge or why it was esteemed—and that it was profitable to flatter the banker. All lessons in the ways of the adult world.

Though our family reaped the working-class benefits of post-World War II American empire, though we never wanted materially, we were provincials of consumption, peasants far from the capitol of capital. All the responsible adults I'd known viewed money as something you could acquire if you were willing to work—and you parted with it rationally. It possessed a power you needed but distrusted in others. It also provided the proper holding pen for many imaginations.

As a marginally impoverished graduate student (buying groceries at the gas station with my credit card) I rarely envisioned going abroad because I assumed it would cost a fortune. In thinking this, I had never really escaped my childhood on Garfield Avenue, where the only world-wanderers had been men, like my father, cast overseas for one hitch in the military. Ultimately, when I took a teaching job in China in the mid-eighties, I had to borrow my plane fare. My younger, more entrepreneurial brother instructed me in the ways of obtaining funds after I had approached my father with a sheepish, somewhat nervous request—which he had rejected as though I were still 12 years old and wanting to buy a pony for the backyard.

"You don't ask Dad for money," Mike said, "You *tell* him that you need it for a specific project and that if he won't loan it, you will get it elsewhere . . . and then let him think about how guilty he'll feel when you do what you say. He's afraid of money, of doing anything with it. Just give him confidence."

My neighborhood travel agent looked askance when I requested a one-way ticket to Beijing. She booked expensive group tours of three weeks' duration. My light pockets excluded me from the respectable cosmology of those round-trips . . . and included me among the bottom-end travelers—those who've discovered the graces in going cheap and make a proud personal cult of humping around, say, Africa for a year or two on a few hundred pounds sterling. Of course, with a job waiting and a thousand in hand, I didn't expect to be wholly roughing it in China—an assumption nursed into the bones by an America where the average yearly income of a newspaper carrier exceeded that of a Chinese peasant. Each month at the university where I taught in Changchun, several workers looked on as the bursar at the Foreign Affairs Office counted out my pay, 12 times that of my Chinese colleagues. The relatively small maximum denomination of "peoples' currency" heightened the disparity, resulting in thick, colorful stacks of bills, worthless outside the country.

"We know you are not familiar with our ways," said the bursar once, perhaps sensing my unease with the sums and the audience, "so you must have more . . . for your mistakes."

And so—slightly awed and embarrassed, should my Chinese friends see—I kept a brown bag jammed with bills in my bottom drawer, the equivalent of years of a worker's income, legally inconvertible, except into the experience acquired by spending it on the road.

Yet, any place where foreign tourists could be found, one encountered the means to transform funds on the black market. Near the Beijing Hotel, for instance, scrawny young hoodlums skulked in sunglasses behind even scrawnier trees, whispering

"Change money?" as one passed by. Many worked for the variously corrupt authorities trying to generate "hard" cash to purchase products from abroad. With this in mind, it was sometimes difficult to remember that such activity was illegal, or simply risky—one could end up with, say, a wad of blank papers through a bait-and-switch tactic. Sometimes pocket calculators acted as the translator, and this made it more difficult to control the pace of the transaction, since the changer often wanted to hurry things along. Ultimately, we were all amateurs. In Tibet, once, I followed a Khampa tribesman into a dry goods shop. Bearing the regal countenance of a Geronimo blended with a Lord Byron, he wore a red and silver turban and a coral earring, a dagger with a crescent hilt slung in his belt. I counted his hundreds of bills—all ones—before passing him my few greenbacks, the prerogative of the seller of the more expensive, and coveted, money. During the eternity of the deal, his detachment crumbled, and his eyes began to squinch like someone trying not to show pain at having his arm twisted. He kept glancing out the window anxiously, a son who knows that any minute Dad will be home from work to exact the promised whipping. Impressed by the incongruity of his majestic appearance and demeanor, I became all Garfield Avenue, thinking, *Can you believe what we're doing? Wow!*

A couple of years later, while working in Poland—another land with a closed currency system—I confronted a black market under different, more chaotic, circumstances. The Polish zloty had once been convertible, and Poles could legally possess foreign money. Many received cash subsidies from relatives in the U.S. and elsewhere. In 1989, the Polish economy was in collapse, and the only hope of escaping the jaws of inflation was to hold foreign notes. No matter how much the zloty declined in value, dollars and deutschmarks remained unperturbable. During my time in Poland, the zloty declined from 1,300 to the dollar to 16,000, and experts estimated that as many as five billion U.S. dollars lay secreted in Polish mattresses and coffee cans—the value of which exceeded all zloties in circulation. Though officially encouraged to avoid the black market, non-Polish workers changed money routinely, since our pay in zloties—again, several times that of our Polish colleagues—wouldn't carry anyone past the first week of the month. Academic cartels, looking for dollars to purchase computer equipment from abroad, approached us, and we did business. The authorities finally realized that they couldn't regulate the activity and opened a "premium exchange" window at the bank—where they offered a rate ten times higher than the official exchange rate window beside it, but slightly lower than the black market changers just outside the front door. One day in Warsaw, I decided to bypass the changers and try the premium window, just to be legal. The teller, a woman in her forties, looked up incredulously from my documents.

"Sir," she said, leaning forward slightly, "you needn't do this. I, personally, can give you a better rate."

It was a glorious, in-between time for those with entrepreneurial means and a lucky position. Regular tourists could pay in black market zloties for minor items and services, but for anything more costly, they had to present documents which proved that they were spending zloties purchased at the more expensive official rate—making such prices nearly as high for them as in the West. Preoccupied with the general economic mayhem, however, the authorities allowed non-Polish workers the privilege of spending even our black market zloties, rather than dollars, for everything. We needed no exchange documents, only the cash. In effect, this condition (which was terminated just after I left the country) allowed me what will probably be my only experience as a millionaire—albeit a zloty millionaire.

So I could stay at the Intercontinental Hotel in Warsaw for

ten dollars in black market zloties a night, while other foreign guests paid 200. I would fly to Budapest for the weekend, round-trip, for the equivalent of 20 dollars, in zloties. Each month, I paid million zloty phone bills—approximately 100 dollars—for hours of late-night, transatlantic handholding.

In China, I somehow expected my privilege, as I had been schooled to expect—and appallingly accept—the surrounding privation; but because Poland lay closer to Western consumer culture, the power of acquisition expressed itself in more familiar terms. Stores offered few products that visitors might covet (most fine things being exported for hard currency), but they displayed enough that I had to confront again what money and imagination mean to each other. One day in Changchun, I found a ten fen bill on Zhonghua Road, not far from our neighborhood streetmarket. The Chinese mint issued both coins and paper notes of its lowest denominations. Ten fen had roughly the same status in most Chinese eyes as a few pennies in those of most North Americans. This ten fen bill, however, had been ripped in two, and it had been sewn—laced—together, with a thick string made up of three differently colored bits. In Poland, I sometimes thought of that bill—of the desperation of its tailor—as I stood before a rack of men's leather jackets or a display of silver jewelry, all of which I could purchase with impunity. It was not guilt that inspired me in such moments, but the incapacity to envision want in its particulars, from the inside out.

Over and over, I came to see that no matter how hard I tried to be sensitive to the struggles of my Polish friends to make ends meet, I failed. A student's unguarded remark about bribery, or a colleague's anecdote about ration cards, and the ground of my understanding fell away, leaving me afloat in the pleasant, undemanding clouds, remotely affluent. My American friend, Woody, contended that many Poles, including his relatives in the south of the country, skillfully exaggerated their woes to court sympathy—and this disturbed me not only because I wanted to believe him but also because it cast another mist of ambiguity over daily events; though the Poles appeared so much more like me than the Chinese, I thought it might be a mistake for me to assume I understood them better, at least in these matters. Despite Woody's assertion, I saw most precisely in those moments when my footing fell away how easily the prosperous lose touch with the reality of material need—even if they wish to understand basic want or alleviate it. Money invites the imagination to entertain different vistas and honor other objects than does privation, and it gently turns the head of its newest accumulators and executors. Comfort becomes a warm room in winter which, over time, seems not warm at all but normal; one's memory of the cold one suffered and cursed is now slowly transformed into an unconvincing moral fable. Of course, money's power vanishes most immediately with the last shilling or franc or dollar, and one could be again cast out; but that cold, too, becomes difficult to fathom.

My Polish friends laughed at me when I mentioned such thoughts. "Bargain hard," I was advised, "Or people will think you are stupid. No one will respect you."

I sometimes remembered those words when I made my weekly trips to Warsaw for mail. Among snowflakes like coin-sized wafers, on days when wind yanked umbrellas inside-out, crowds lined up before the U.S. embassy, hoping for visas to the dreamland of equal opportunity advertised in glass displays mounted on the high, barbed fence. I would wriggle through the mass pressed around the Polish gateman. At the thick bars, I held out my passport, and he pulled back the iron and let me pass. I never looked at him, or at the people in the crowd, and only rarely at the people on their knees before the huge concrete planters in the courtyard, filling out visa applications—almost all of which would be denied.

The moment of passing through the throng, of entering with ease the door it longed to enter, seemed a scene from an ancient, absurd drama of exclusion, especially since the embassy remained a foreign land to me.

One winter night, for instance, the embassy marines (bored young men far from home) threw open their pub on the pretense of welcoming select American ex-patriates to the post. I stood happily sipping my American beer and munching American peanuts, gawking at the latest, shipped-in American rock videos emanating from the multiple TV monitors. A marine from Kansas was break-dancing, spinning on his head in front of the bar. The room looked and smelled and sounded like home, and I preferred it to any other place in Warsaw that night. Still, it felt strange, and even stranger when one of the GI bartenders burned out a brand-new electric hot-air popcorn popper. He looked untroubled, I thought, because two poppers were already at work; but he put the defective device back into its packing material and opened the cabinet behind the bar, and removed another new popper from the half dozen there still in boxes.

Just then the break-dancer came up for a drink. We chatted about the difficulties of his being so far from home.

"Is it true," I asked, "that embassy personnel are forbidden to fraternize with Polish nationals?"

"Yeah," he said, "We can't even date 'em."

Long before I went to China, I sometimes mused on writing a study of lines in the twentieth century—those we are compelled to stand in, or from which we are excluded; those we have the means to avoid or join; those that characterize a life or a place. Breadlines, picket lines, battle lines. Processions, parades, police line-ups, freeway jams. In its fantasies of consumerist individuation, the U.S. hopes to deny these most obvious features of mass existence. *No Waiting!* the sign says. Yet even if we have the cash, we wait—for a few minutes, say, at the automated bank machine late on a Friday afternoon, or in a partying queue for concert tickets.

I don't think I've yet stood in a difficult—or frightening—line, or been excluded from one I hungered to join. My millionaire life further spared me many unpleasant assemblies. More important, however, it opened my little fist clenched so tightly around the dollar—and its symbolism—which my grandfather gave me.

Currency. The word suits what it names. Notes and coins are the ineffable, recurring present made palpable, in a reduced form. For all our speculation, all our futures, their value is now.

Yet, with that dollar in hand, my grandfather and I were ancient Romans, believers—as citizens of empire—in enduring orders. Our money was good, and would be good, always. You could found your hopes, your ambitions, your soul on it—like assuming without question that people will always speak Latin.

In one sense, then, all money is "play" money—even that which we call "real"—and the play is serious. What kind of world would we inhabit if everybody won the lottery and, thus, we were forced to define our desires without the handy harness and blinders of Providing? What would we think of property if we were required to spend the whole pot? All of us should find ourselves at least once in a country where our money is worshiped . . . or laughable . . . or unrecognized.

The Alhambra, Sancta Sophia, the Piazza San Marcos, the Hermitage, Chartres Cathedral, Carthage—I circulated, courtesy of my zloty millions, on a grand tour of famous paintings and tyrant tombs and literary locations that grew to seem senseless and almost genuinely humdrum. Having sold most of my worldly goods before leaving the U.S., I wondered what kind of possession this purchased exposure was, or might become. People on trains seemed sometimes to stare at my waist, looking—I believed, in my paranoid moments—at the moneybelt secreted under my shirt. Occasionally, my Polish friends would ask me how much a U.S. green card would cost and whom they might contact to purchase one. I had no answers to such questions and was too eagerly embarrassed by my ignorance. When the Communist epoch ended quickly after many of the *nomenklatura* decided that their most lucrative futures lay in heading the new regime of Capitalism, crowds of dream-desperate visa applicants grew huge and sometimes restive before the embassy, and Marines came forth in battle dress to meet them. I kept passing through those people to my mail.

I Give Up
Smiling

Before I went to live in Changchun, what I knew of thronged street life derived from a few gyrating days in Manhattan. On Garfield Avenue, the only crowd—if it could be called that—gathered on ten consecutive August nights, drawn by the first booms of fireworks which concluded the grandstand show at the State Fair nearby. Mostly mothers and children, we watched the colors spray and then droop into heavy mops of smoke over the poplar trees, the women talking in the quiet interludes between displays and for a few minutes after the finale, parting, at last, to put the younger children to bed.

Other than this—and a few porch sitters and occasional barbecuers—I and best friends Tom and Sam were mostly the street life of the neighborhood. We delivered morning and evening newspaper routes, often camping out in each other's backyards in summer or mapping elaborate projects around the pot-bellied stove in our clubhouse converted from a gardener's shed. We lounged on the curb in front of Andy and Bill's Grocery, hungry for its racks of fruit pies and 16-ounce Cokes opened to us at 6 A.M. We bombed buses with snowballs and shot baskets in slushy twilights. We nursed soda fountain cocktails at Strait's Pharmacy, eager to be teased by our half-dozen idols who gathered there after their day shifts at factories, each of them coolly 21, getting laid and making payments on cars that could put down rubber in four gears. Vandals of the garden hose, adventurers in smuggled six packs of warm beer, we knew in the dark the whereabouts of every clothesline and merciless watchdog for blocks in all directions.

The only other person with whom we truly shared the territory was Mrs. Whittenhall.

10.16.85, Changchun

Most mornings, a young man in an olive greatcoat practices his trumpet on the lawn of the Geological college, not far from where an unmarked mass grave from the Cultural Revolution is said to lie. On the broad sidewalk in front of the main building, legions perform Tai Chi at dawn, and stooped ancients chat, hands folded behind their backs cradling a loud transistor radio.

Yesterday, the rationing of cabbages for winter began. Floods, I'm told, reduced this year's crop, yet most people can still afford to buy supplies beyond their government allotment. On corners around the city, people queue before green heaps, leaves splayed and twisting this way and that. Rumpled women in white cotton caps weigh each party's load, which is then strapped to the back fender of a bicycle, or stacked on a push cart. Everywhere the chosen stalks lie side by side on the pavements and roofs and garden walls, the heart of each pointing in the same direction, a pale green root in pale autumn sunlight.

The women weigh all day long, though the wind stings cheeks and temperatures dip into the 50s F. They wear white smocks and the customary five layers of underwear, standing in our street with hands on hips or sitting down with legs flat out, leaning with their tea against the cadre's wall next door. Their faces are worn but not brittle-looking like the women selling tofu in the streetmarket, women who stand outside winter or summer, sounding more hoarse each day.

And then a young woman arrives—one of the new, fashionable women with long, curled hair and earrings dangling. She's outfitted in stubby-heeled shoes, black stretch pants, the ubiquitous dull brown blazer (but taken in more daringly at the waist) and the equally ubiquitous black silk gloves. Too thin to provide much warmth, elegant, sexy—and incongruous as she grips the handle of a cart empty but ready for greens.

Once in the morning, once in the evening, Mrs. Whittenhall walked the six blocks from her house on Dubuque Avenue to Andy and Bill's Grocery. She purchased a few items—a bar of soap, a loaf of bread—and always a large bottle of Pepsi, which she sipped on her walk back. For the neighborhood, this routine was as much a gauge of the hour as sunlight on leaves. Dependable, too, were her sweat-darkened, floral dresses, her slippers, and the windbreaker she wore only on the most frigid days. A blocky, ruddy woman with long, straight, graying hair, she always clutched a round, styrene plastic case in which you could see a swaddled Barbie doll—her child who had died years before, it was said.

My friends and I called her "Smiley," but it seems now that her unvarying expression was more of a wince stalled at its inception. She seemed always to be looking ahead, which made passing her on the sidewalk more excruciating. Once, without provocation, she said "hi" to me. A soft, tight bleep, it shook and baffled me like a door in the night blowing shut.

She lived alone in a small white house nested in high weeds replete with butterflies. A man who said he was her husband once stopped me on the street to inquire about subscribing to the newspaper, but I never saw him again. Evidently, Andy and Bill fulfilled some guardianship role. When I saw her, or when I passed her place on my paper route, I wondered what she did during all the hours she wasn't going to and from the store. I wondered what her house looked like inside.

We wandered into a restaurant a few blocks from the Changbiashan Hotel and found ourselves opposite three round tables occupied by a wedding party. The bride and groom, probably in their thirties, were dressed in blue Mao suits. The bride wore earrings and make-up, both of which suggested how plain she must usually look. On the back of the groom's head, a half-erect cowlick wagged. All through his and her hair multi-colored confetti glittered. Though only 11 A.M., he grinned a little wider from toasting with bai jiu (white spirits), and he insisted that my colleagues, Monica and Doug, and I smoke with our lunch. We accepted the lights, though Doug has taken three puffs in his life, and I'm still nursing a burned epiglottis. Another man about his own age kept sweeping the groom away from our table with the arm-around-the-shoulder technique. I kept watching the bride, who would have seemed homelier had the groom been more handsome. Traditionally, the daughter-in-law occupied the most tenuous position in the family—subordinate to husband, father, and older women. Unless she came with a dowry, she was an extra occupier of space and a belly, and had to earn her way doubly. No wonder the suicide of the daughter-in-law is so prevalent in the Chinese literature I've been reading. How much has changed under the Communists? She sat at the end of the table with the other women and all the children.

We finished our meal with only a few more interruptions. Another drunken reveler showed Doug how to use chopsticks to eat the large biscuit Doug had been holding in his hand. Certain foods are too large to manage with chopsticks, this biscuit among them. It's an engineering disaster. Yet Doug listened as the man held the biscuit gracefully betwixt the sticks. To eat with the hands, say the Chinese, is vulgar. When one sees the state of most hands here, one must agree.

Later, on the restaurant doorstep, Monica found the red ribbon worn by the groom. Heading the list of embossed characters on it was the sign for "double happiness." Monica decided to save it, a little bit of a stranger's life in her pocket.

Remembering the regularity with which I saw Mrs. Whittenhall, I wonder how much I really see now of my five-minute commute to and from work along Bayshore Boulevard in Tampa. One of my friends says that a few weeks of driving the same streets to the office and she feels "wildly trapped" by the repetition, with its intimation that her life is going nowhere else. She then changes her route. But why should a known way, a routine way, be any less new and full of possibility than a path on which one has never ventured? I like to believe that imagination nudges repetition into gratifying deviations. I like to believe that when I notice Hillsborough Bay is a powdery brown tipped with silver—like the color of mink fur—I've recognized the constant change, the inimitable condition of each moment among our shifting continents. Of course, this strategy aims for the same state of expanding potential, of collectable experience, that my friend craves. It's only another wish to be immortal.

One of the beauties of sojourning is that in just walking to the post office and back, day after day, one can feel how fleeting things are, and are not. In Changchun, I could see a man on a streetcorner holding a chest x-ray toward the sun, a large pentagon shadowing the left lung. I could see a boy, alone on a soccer field at dusk, kicking a ball through eight inches of fresh snow. I could see a woman wearing a sweater with the word *hovering* woven across its front. Though I often roamed Changchun for hours—aimless except to consider what I came upon—I just as often followed the same paths. Perhaps this gave me the same comfort Mrs. Whittenhall took from her walks. It echoed those pleasurable family trips from Des Moines to Pershing down Highway 5—that road I knew best as a child.

It was always late spring or full summer on Highway 5 because our family went to Pershing on Memorial Day, the 4th of July, and for an occasional reunion picnic. A two-lane road through corn fields, it was uneventfully straight except for several hills and dips—and a few sudden, pinched curves which elicited from my father a repeated diatribe on dangerous attempts to pass farm vehicles and the sadism of highway planners. A passenger, I could stare out the side window at the powerlines rising and falling hypnotically as we passed pole after pole set along the shoulder. Cows and sheep and hogs in barnyards seemed still as statuary. A pollen-heavy haze hung over the crops, and the wind pulled my hair back flat and made such white noise that any remark from my parents in the front seat startled me.

The Chinese now welcome Japanese capital and technology, though a collective hatred burns under the surface, at least in this part of the country. We visited the provincial museum today specifically to view the wing devoted to maintaining the memory of Japanese atrocities during World War II. It's housed in the former palace of Pu Ye, the last Qing Emperor who was deposed and then made the puppet monarch of the Japanese-controlled state during the thirties. Young girls in white cotton dresses oversee each room of memorabilia, and through one of the windows we watched a man whack a horse in the belly repeatedly with a pipe because it couldn't pull the overloaded cart out of a rut. This was after he'd whipped it and then pounded its flanks with a long, heavy-gauge wire. Inside, as I strolled past photos of severed heads dangling from spikes, and skeletons in mass graves, past models of detention camps and the diorama depicting a Japanese soldier breaking a peasant's leg with bricks, I could hear the cry of the Jews, "Never again!"

Cottonwoods—planted by the Japanese occupying Changchun during the thirties—now broadcast their seeds, making the central part of town into a nauseatingly languid snow-scene. This "June Snow" gathers in the gutters, and I saw a small boy pile it up and put a match to some fist-sized, gauzy pyres. The stuff is a curse now not only for the memories it brings. It so suffuses some avenues, you can hardly breathe without having to brush it away from your nose and mouth. Many women wrap their hair in sheer nylon scarves, but the flakes still catch.

Changchun's life is in its trees. Its willows are beautiful but more well-known for their strength, which is attributed to difficult winters—willows woven into hard hats and decorative baskets for export. And its poplars, slim, straight, were planted after the decimation of nature during the Communists' various programs to modernize, trees planted because they are quick-growing, trees which are now young like most of the population.

I want to believe that I knew every tree and gas station along Highway 5. The electric powerplant with green windows overlooking the Des Moines river; the Knoxville high school mascot—a black panther—painted on a yellow watertower; the Uncle Sam mailbox post at the head of a dirt road winding to a white farmhouse: each thing I remember now seems a monument animated by desperate nostalgia. I want to believe that I knew where I was on Highway 5, what would appear ahead next and what had just vanished behind, and how long it would all take. It was a world dependent on our passing through for its orderliness—right and rhythmical, even in its contingencies.

For instance, no matter how agitated or incommunicative the family might be, we nearly always came together—leaning up in our seats and looking forward—as the car glided down a long slope a few miles beyond Knoxville. At the bottom, a narrow, metal suspension bridge spanned a creek. Given the traffic, we wondered if we would be forced to pass an oncoming car or truck on that bridge. Though Dad refused even a drop of alcohol if he was to have the family in the car, he seemed harried by the vision that a drunk driver would kill us all. Perhaps it was that the driver would be like his veering, lesser self that made him especially vigilant at the narrow bridge. As a camper or tilt-cab semi approached and the gusts of the noncollision rocked our car, my mother's lined cheeks plumped into daubs of white shortening. She always exhaled quietly, packing away fear with a curt clearing of the throat.

Beyond the bridge, the road ascended a long slope bordered on both sides by woods uncharacteristically dense and large for championship farm country. Halfway up, no matter how hot the weather, we passed through a zone of utter, sweet coolness—always a forgiving shade. There, below the south side of the road, stretched a glade in which stood a sizable, shacky house propped on blocks and sided with fake-brick asphalt panels. A fern of smoke rose from its chimney, and a creek wound past its front porch—past the gravid clothesline and the chopping stump and the junk cars. We seemed to sail through this "cool spot," always marveling at its dependable grace. It made us agreeable; our hot weather subsided for a moment, and the narrow bridge lay behind. That is probably why we named the place and looked forward to it, and why it is symbolic to me of those unburdening places we come to with others. In those days, of course, I peered down the glade at the house and imagined—no, *knew*—that the people who lived there were happy, that they had peace, if nothing else. At the top of the slope—as the road flattened and the woods retired into distance—I sometimes would gaze unblinkingly into a cloudless sky until snake-like blotches seethed and whirled before my eyes, images which I thought secretly only I could see, images which I believed were atoms.

Sun flickers through yellowing leaves. The flies have slowed down. An indistinct voice blares at the sports field two blocks away. In the street

*nearby, the junkman, seeking bottles, bangs his cymbals and yowls. Later,
a man cranks an iron cylinder on a spit over hot coals until the temperature is just right; then with a bar, he pops open the end of the cylinder:
BOOM! Basins of fluffy corn or rice blast into his mesh trap.*

*With three balls, three bowls and weary patter, a small, grubby boy
performed tricks for a crowd in front of the #5 Department Store. A girl (his
sister?) performed excruciating backbends and then—with the help of the
boy—wound a heavy-gauge wire tightly around her neck. In one motion,
he wound it and she turned toward the crowd with her hands cupped,
outstretched in supplication, her eyes clouded by disease.*

*I asked an old man in front of the Changchun Restaurant to pose
for a photo. With his cane, he pushed another old man—twice—out of
what he determined would be the area within the picture. The other fellow,
purple-red in the face, grinned—a single safety pin laced through his breast
pocket and a white wicker basket full of scavenged beer cans. I took pictures of each.*

*In one, the pushed man stands with the white sun casting a metallic
sheen on his eyelids—like eye shadow.*

*In the other, the shover grins, his teeth so many scattered nubs they
look like blisters on his gums, his beard a triangular wisp that seems glued
to his chin.*

Were these their first photos alone, or at all?

Named after the World War I general called "BlackJack,"
Pershing lay at the end of an asphalt strip branching from Highway 5. Its grid of a dozen tromped-gravel streets still constitutes
the remains of the somewhat larger company-owned mining town
that flourished during the earlier decades of this century when,
presumably, demand made it more profitable to burrow under the
land for soft coal than to farm. Legend says our family started
there in the late teens or early twenties when my grandfather
Albert Marshall gave up a shot at pitching in the majors to marry

my grandmother Fay Cauldenburg and work in the mines. The reason given for his choice is the same my father gave for exchanging his theatrical ambitions for a steady spot on the assembly line: he didn't like the travel and the being away from home.

Growing up, I often believed Dad regretted his decision, that he felt he had betrayed his dream by forsaking it before it might have proved beyond him. My grandfather—who died just before I was born—appears to me in a single photograph, clad in a baseball uniform, the shade from the bill of his cap shadowing his eyes. Through my mother's reverent taciturnity, he speaks only in calm, patient tones, and I imagine her—a middle child of eight—loving him from her place among the faces. I once believed that because he and I were left-handed and I was her first born, I was her favorite child. He died of heart disease encouraged, no doubt, by the same coal dust that sometimes befogged Changchun like gaslit London. Perhaps his forsaken major league prospect was a soothing substitute for talent, or possibility. I can only verify that my mother—who resembles her mother—played baseball as a youth and taught me the basics of the game.

Pershing could be roamed like the streets I shared with my three best friends and Mrs. Whittenhall. There, my cousins and I whipped Nazi commandos in Dracula Woods and careened at the steering wheels of cars rusting among weeds. On trampolines sunken like swimming pools in a lot called "Recreation Center," I bounced and romped until the glands in my throat ached. Using a ditch, I learned one day how to get on my cousin Jim's 26-inch bike—and rode and rode and rode, proudly waving at my relatives as I pedaled past on another town circuit, weary but perplexed as to how to get off the thing without injury.

During one family reunion, I watched men somehow get into the casual play of secretly passing around a twisted, muddy, bald baby doll. On finding it in his front seat or on his dashboard, each man would avenge himself by putting it on another man's hood or tacklebox, or in his cooler—where the latter would surely find it and pass it on, hoping to spy the next man when he discovered it.

That night, back home in Des Moines, my father found the doll as he unpacked the station wagon. He chuckled like a mother bewildered by a made-up game in which her children have included her. He took it into the house, and nothing more was said about it until one winter Sunday when he open the sewing machine. He cleaned and straightened the doll's limbs and dressed it in a smock and bonnet fashioned from remnant satin. With rouge and mascara, he gave it back its eyes and the flush of infant health.

He also transformed it in some other way I may never be able to articulate. Now, I see the doll as having suffered more than the men through whose hands it had passed, the doll as the unfortunate world into which we press our imaginings—another case of making too much of things.

In a box outfitted with supple white paper, my father sent the doll back to one of my uncles in Pershing—no return address, just a note pinned to its smock, "I've come back."

When we visited the next time, no one asked my father if he knew about it. People just remarked on the incident with amusement and amazement, and some of the men looked at my father.

Pershing smelled of well water and blacktop. Its residents then, as now, went off to work at the VA in Knoxville, Rollscreen in Pella, or Maytag in Newton—or somewhere else. Mustard jars and breadwrappers and stacked plates cluttered its kitchen counters, and a sun-bleached plastic deer stood shyly in the yard. Pershing was my Aunt Myrna wet-nursing all of us kids—she had so much milk. It was vast husbands with deep bellybuttons recumbent in the shade, sipping Grain Belt beer and smoking Camel straights. Land of the double negative and the double entendre; of my cousin-in-law Walt plucking a string bass propped on a long, rubber-tipped screwdriver; of a fast-pitch softball team which in night games played rival towns: Attica, Bussey, Lovilia. Pershing was pride and formidable limitation, farm-pond fishing, and the dowdy gray stone my Uncle Tony broke open in his rock shed to reveal to me its glittering crystals.

Most of all, for almost two decades, Pershing also seemed a place of immortality. No one in our family there died, and few went away, until recent years.

I sometimes hear my fellow provincials wish aloud for more street life in their cities, for places where one could promenade, or linger safely, and observe the day or night abounding with strangers. The summer sunlight in Tampa—which can split dashboards and jab the brow like a searing spike—discourages outdoor cafes, though they are now coming into fashion in some quarters. The city has its joggers and dog-walkers and lunch hour strollers, but like most North American towns—Des Moines included—the people who spend real time on its streets are mostly homeless, insane, or for sale. Our only crowds near the size of streetmarket throngs in any provincial Chinese city gather for annual parades, sidewalk art festivals, or musical beer bashes sponsored by local radio stations. Otherwise, we teem in enclosures.

Some years ago, in suburban New York state, I was dismayed to see parents shepherding their costumed children around shopping malls on Halloween, rather than around their neighborhoods, as was common when I was a child. For an ancient celebration acknowledging the darker spirits, these children dressed as cartoon versions of those monsters their parents took them to the mall to avoid. The treats dropped into their bags from the chain stores and anchor stores and food courts would contain no razor blades or poison, only positive community images, which is good for business.

Undoubtedly, this is one more sequestering from the immediate environment, one more exposure to the seamless display of the market. But then, what is the immediate environment? It was once common to refer to something that seemed wholly false as "plastic" as in, "This place is plastic." But isn't plastic just as much a real thing as any other thing? Isn't it "real" plastic? Only someone, I think, who is surrounded by too many goods rather than too few—someone not from Changchun—could see this as a crucial question.

Though the media in China never missed a chance to show disaster in the States, the Chinese I met who thought America a dangerous place pointed to the images the U.S. exports through popular film, which encourage visions of shootouts on every street corner, like gas stations and fast food. I also found a number of Europeans who wanted to believe in this violence, partly to stem their envy generated by the glamor of American publicity.

I am awakened occasionally by the newspaper's *plop!* on my porch at 3 A.M., a newspaper now delivered by an adult in a car. I sometimes lie in that dreamy darkness before receding into sleep and remember how 25 years ago, I walked my summer route, smoking Swisher Sweets, majestically nocturnal and somehow feeling in charge of the landscape.

Two old men, near the Stalin monument, play checkers on the curb until midnight, several other men squatting around them and smoking cigarettes, looking on.

Barbells and guitar-strumming in a dim alley.

Lovers in a dark lane, one couple in each space between a row of lilac bushes.

Nearby, trunks of trees are whitewashed around their bases. "Socked trees," my father called them when I was a boy. "They are considered beautiful in China," he said, painting the elms in our backyard.

My neighborhood was safer then, I imagine, than now, but how much? Once, just after picking up my papers at the drop point on East 33rd Street, I noticed a distant figure backlit by the glow from Strait's Pharmacy. It approached at a stroll; then it spied me and started marching faster. No news-carrier bag hung over its shoulder, so I turned and began walking in the opposite direction. I glanced back. It was charging after me. I raced around the corner, my load banging wildly against my legs, and had just enough time to scramble among the bushes in Mrs. Gardner's dark backyard before the figure appeared and sauntered up Dubuque Avenue, fists at its sides, searching.

It was Wendell Wallace, one of the tree-service Wallaces from the semirural area beyond the end of my route. In Andy and Bill's lot at the close of a summer day, you could find Wendell and four or five of his grimy brothers draped on the bed of a tree-trimming truck, sipping cokes, slit-eyed like cats facing a wind. He was 16 or 17 and had been in my eighth grade algebra class, intermittently, the year before. "Fuck" was the mortar of his speech, slapped between each block of three or four words. One time, he'd walked out of woods behind the softball diamonds at Stowe School, asking to join our pick-up game. Within minutes, he'd slugged my friend Sam and was baiting Sam to retaliate, so he could hurt him. Sam, who grew up to be a platoon honor man in the Marines, was no coward, but he was no fool, either. He gave Wendell no eye contact and no excuse to do more. He knew Wendell liked to hobble dogs and hang kittens.

From the bushes—perhaps the only time I was aware that I held my breath in fear—I watched Wendell pass. Recognizing me must have spurred his pursuit. Had he found me, I'm sure I would have learned something new about my will to survive. Who knows what fuel burned in Wendell?

I let him get far out of sight before emerging, and I waited until near daylight before finishing that part of my route near his turf. I never saw him again—which was fine—and several months later I heard that he'd blown his head off while cleaning a shotgun. The papers called it an accident.

Last evening, as I waited to purchase chocolate at one of the kiosks near the streetmarket, I was accosted by the same beggar woman who had followed me back to the compound last spring. As before, she focused entirely on me, driving me off and pursuing, talking after me in a loud, high-pitched voice. I turned to her once and said in my poor Chinese that I couldn't understand what she was saying, but that did not deter her. At the compound, the gateman drove her off—at least as far as the cottonwood trees across the street, among which she crouched for some time.

I have never felt endangered in China, and I have seen, as every pedestrian here has, suffering of every sort on the street, but this woman somehow threatened me more than any other human wreckage I've encountered here, maybe because I'm sick of my selfishness—me with my waxy chocolate from the local shop, pretending I don't know what she needs. It also occurs to me now that with her ragged, raw complexion, she looks uncannily like Mrs. Whittenhall.

In the years just after I left Iowa for good, I sentimentalized it as vigorously as I'd vilified it in order to leave. This response was like the mirthless grin we North Americans pony up for snapshots—believing as ever in packaging as content—not thinking that by this we exchange all the expressions that make up our faces for the meager record of a single gesture. I pinned that false smile

on my neighborhood, on Highway 5, on Pershing and the rest—
just as I affixed the nickname "Smiley" to Mrs. Whittenhall.

In China, I often found myself smiling dumbly in public,
reaching for the faith in universal gestures. I finally stopped. It
seemed condescending to all that transpires between people, between our narrow bridges and our cool spots. I look back on the
foreseeable routes and wayward wanderings of my sentences here
and think of the palm-size notebooks in which I tried to "get
everything down," at times going blind and deaf and dull. Entries
like *I walked with an anguished and ecstatic heart* and *Monica looked
celestial, panicked* gain no accomodation under the obligatory smile.
It imprisons our fairer history. Like our disposable horror at each
day's headlines, it excuses us falsely from all we are and do.

Ice
Swimming

Once, in the English-language edition of the *China Daily*, a full-page advertisement for a major Western hotel-restaurant declared, "Dine in Beijing as Though You Weren't There at All." Aimed at foreign residents, it explained that eating out in the capital could tax one's patience, but now one could enjoy the splendid cuisine of the emperors with, in essence, the convenience of a drive-through liquor store at home.

The ad never reappeared. It had nestled too snugly against an embarrassing expatriate truth: one tires of coping with strangeness, with variance. "Culture shock," say the experts, noting also that the sufferer may be unaware he is already in stage two.

The condition conjures a thousand metaphorical descriptions, as anybody who has endured it knows. One that still suits me best derives from a New Year's Holiday trip to the Chinese city of Harbin. There, in Stalin Park one evening, I walked with a group of Westerners among ziggurats, leaping fish, rockets, Great Walls—hundreds of forms, some of them 60 feet tall—all sculpted intricately of ice and glowing with electric Christmas bulbs. Throngs of Chinese visitors also strolled in the sub-zero temperatures. Young men rollicked down ice slides, sometimes charging too manically into line, whipped back by ushers brandishing belts.

Earlier that day, our handlers had herded us to the Songhua River, where workers sawed the ice for the displays, the blocks hauled up the hill by donkey and tractor. Near one of the large, square cuts in the ice, a port-a-shed had been pitched and a diving board arranged. We gathered at the edges in our furs. From the port-a-shed, steaming men and women in swimsuits and rubber bathing caps emerged one at a time. Each dived from the board—jackknife, swan, somersault—and pawed through the slush at our feet, wincing a little at the cold but also, it seemed, at having come to this.

At various times in China, I observed myself breaststroking through the ice of my circumstances, and I pretended I was neither swimmer nor watcher. To me, it seemed axiomatic that a sojourner should adapt and compensate, not brood like a brat over a little inner and outer difficulty. No one, after all, had compelled me to leave home. If I sensed the freezing river of foreignness and weariness and loneliness sucking the heat from me, I acknowledged only that I had to keep seeing and doing all I could abroad because I might not get another chance.

There were times in Changchun when I shouted at shopkeepers who had done nothing more than say *no* when I requested items not in stock. There were days when I fled openly from students who wished to practice their English, or snapped at my colleagues during lunch, or sequestered myself in my room. But my longest and hardest period of ice swimming came later while living in Lodz, Poland. Before going to Eastern Europe, I had attributed too much of my fellow feeling about China to my stamina, rather than to good fortune and China's kindnesses. So I had not given myself the chance to prepare mentally for this second long sojourn so soon after returning from the first.

Thus, I taught my classes at the university in Lodz and attended the qausi-diplomatic functions and made the weekend and holiday trips, but my stoic, ice-swimming self sat at the desk next to the window identical to those in Changchun, trying to take notes and write letters and poems, dissolving with the gray Lodz evenings into nights of dim downtown lights. The swimmer almost seemed an exterior presence, an "it"—not really part of me. On Lodz's few clear days, its gaze lingered on vaportrails of jets heading west out of the drab life. For entire weekends— when it couldn't get a ticket to anywhere interesting—it lay on the convertible couch-bed, reading quips by Noel Coward and Oscar Wilde in *The Little, Brown Book of Anecdotes*. Sometimes I muttered encouragements to it as I walked up Tuwima Street to my apartment, past the Pewex store where for the hard currency equivalent of two dollars, men who gathered there in late afternoon could purchase the night's fifth of vodka.

It was my gray pencil-point soul going dull, the impresario of my bathtub nights: the hand that poured the three fingers of whiskey, lighted the candle and the Cuban Corona, tuned the shortwave radio and eased me into the steaming water, to drift across the commentary of the BBC reporter on the scene in Eritrea, East Timor, Mauritania—anywhere but Lodz. It caused me to stop one day on the uneven cobbles of the busiest section of downtown, Piotrowska Street. In all directions at once, I could hear the clicking of the walkers' soles.

I wanted to understand why things in Lodz suddenly seemed distant and redundant, but my ice-swimming self didn't. Eventually, an obvious recognition at last came to me, and the breach between myself and the swimmer disappeared.

My lover Winifred and I had split up before I went to China

but soon reconciled through the mail. Given the situation, we had our necessary lovers, about which we made no secret, and we had our correspondence, through which we assured each other of the real future. I still believe her enthusiasm for my journeys was genuine. Since her childhood on the commune in California, she had invited experience, believing that engagement with people from different backgrounds enlarged one's world and increased one's capacity for virtue. In our years together, I could never be certain whom she might bring home for dinner: East Indian medical students she met in the line at the bank; militant Nicaraguan lesbians from the dance club. While I was in China, she took in a scrawny, crossdressing convict just released from the local penitentiary on drug charges: Tommy, who maxed her credit cards and broke into our apartment after she evicted him, stealing the few electronic items of value. Though chastened by such mistakes, Win steadfastly refused to become "cold" to the world as she saw it. An idealist, she was part Mother Teresa, part Lone Ranger—an ideal combination for a public interest attorney defending the homeless and those washing up on Florida's beaches in truck tire inner tubes from Cuba and Haiti.

I trusted Win and her instincts. I had admired her long before she persuaded me to love her. I had always rested secure in the knowledge of her spiritual allegiance. What then made me realize at 3 A.M. on a December morning that she was no longer a lover to the pool hustler she'd appropriated as a comforter when I left the country, but that she was in love with him?

On that night, I'd just returned to Lodz on the creeping, drunk train from my weekly evening with my colleague Woody and friends at the Kongresowa in Warsaw, a restaurant in the basement of the Palace of Culture built by Stalin after the War. The Kongresowa featured flaccid vegetables and glossy fries and occasional Hungarian champagne, but it was one of the few night spots in town. Its floor show boasted acrobats, sword balancers, husband and wife bicyclists (all most likely unemployed circus performers), and The Solid Gold Dancers, a troupe of two young women and one man in Barbarella furs or leather thongs, flexing through martialized cheerleading routines to a blasted recording of "What Have You Done for Me Lately?" As a finale to the general show, the pale pink lights came up, and a gorgeous blond woman in a gold lamé gown appeared to the strains of "Nothin's Gonna Stop Us Now." She strutted elegantly and studiously, as though modeling the dress, making two quick laps around the bubbling fountain in the middle of the presentation pit before unsnapping the single clasp that sent all of her garments to the floor in an instant. Voilà! The strip with no tease! Nude, with a blue vein faintly visible on her large, young breasts, she made one more lap around the fountain and then vanished.

As I walked up Tuwima Street that night, past the crates of empty milk bottles stacked in front of the corner grocery, I suddenly envisioned Win kissing her pool player, her lips wet. I imagined the husky breath of her pleasure as she took him into her mouth. I saw her on top of him. It was eight hours earlier in Florida than in Poland, and it occurred to me that it was the middle of the evening there; and yet, I thought, they could be home, in my bed, now . . . and I am here!

By the time I opened my apartment door, my arms felt as though a great weight had flowed into them. I stood at the window overlooking the distant downtown and then tumbled onto the living room floor in a bawling heap, my shuddering somehow shaking the room. In the morning, I awakened on the carpet identical to those in Changchun, its red fuzz flecking my shirt and hair.

In more sober moments, I considered Win's love for her pool player—rather than their sexual arrangement—as her infidelity, though both amounted to my exclusion from her life. It seemed a betrayal. In the past, with whomever I'd been intimate, I'd worn the inner harness, withholding a special part of myself: Win's part. Now, she had undone her leash and she was gone. My home, gone. I had been away too long. It was that deceptively simple.

Yet our correspondence continued, and we spent hours—and a small fortune—on the phone. Each time I wished to call, a Polish friend would have to place an order for a transatlantic line with the Lodz phone company. No matter what time of day the order was placed, my phone would ring me out of sleep at 3 A.M., a Polish voice would mutter something unintelligible to me, and Win would suddenly be on the line. We spoke as though nothing had changed between us, happily—until we drifted toward the subject of "him." Her halting reassurances of affection for me—reassurances I craved—cut me unavoidably.

Often, after a few minutes, the operator (or someone) decided that we had spoken long enough and disconnected us without warning. Sometimes, after being cut off, I would ring the operator to complain and try to get a line. It amounted to my shouting in a cold room. After that, I depended on Win to resume the call; she could dial me direct whenever she chose—the cheery convenience of the loved, it seemed. Over the months, she kept in touch, though sometimes it felt like her volunteer work "for the boy overseas." Most harrowing of all for my imagination was to order a call and get her answering machine. That voice, and she elsewhere!

Alone, I spoke aloud to Win like an old widower to his dead wife. In a hotel locker room during a visit to Moscow, I stopped toweling off and peered at my reflection in a far mirror, trying to imagine how she looked at her pool player that night she decided to love him. Sometimes, I thought of an ancient Chinese soldier at some post along the Great Wall, far from a home village to which he would never return. I remembered one of my friends from graduate school confessing that she went out for a haircut, just to be touched. One afternoon, as I dozed on the convertible couch, all the women I believe I had betrayed—or hurt—filed past, each absolving me with a nod of the head.

And I went blind to Poland. My letters and journals consumed themselves with loss and escape, and then they dwindled to a few daily scratches on an icy sheet of paper, the only sign of the swimmer beneath.

Looking back on my letters and notebooks, I can find myself now superior to my jolly, self-absorbed correspondence from China, and, thus, charmed by it. But I whistle and chuckle anxiously at the pages from Poland about Win; I hum to scare off embarrassment at my sorrow and to escape the lavish, small, and deeply sincere slush of my old words. In the black lacquer Chinese cabinet in my living room now, there are perhaps two dozen audio cassettes that Win sent to me in Changchun and Lodz. I dare not play them, nor am I yet able to throw them out, though I must, remembering enough of them to imagine the horror springing from what was their comforting intimacies, and her tone. And, of course, Win may still possess the cassettes preserving my hideous voice.

In Lodz, I sometimes could no longer take the strain of missing, or longing—of feeling utterly abandoned by the home place I had struggled so hard to leave—and, thus, I grew lighthearted. In those more buoyant times, I tried—like a good imperialist of the heart—to make the alien days flatter the flimsiest exonerations of my state.

It's difficult to mark exactly how we climb out of such trouble with our lives. I met Aprille, a teacher in Cracow. We traveled happily and awkwardly, both of us wearing the harness of "living for the moment," both of us trying to ignore the thin ice below, and above. Among many common, beloved moments together, I most often remember coming home from classes one day and discovering her in the bathtub where I had spent too many candlelit nights adrift. Between us, there was also much restless rummaging through museums and ruins. And spring came. The oppressive, gray sky at last descended and poured forth as frosty white blossoms from the apple trees, and even the maimed shut-in next door appeared on Lodz's streets in shiny shoes.

Encountering Time

1.

It is the year 2043, according to the Nepalese calendar, and I stand in a shoe shop doorway in Katmandu while the monsoon soaks all saris, and a young umbrella seller grins at me (I have just refused his final offer). The chaos of gaseous, crowded junk buses and the spectral shops with stale imported chocolates emanate a ridiculous and inadvertent good will, an averageness.

Later, I eat dal baht with Brian, a Peace Corps worker who teaches math in a buffalo shed two days on foot from the nearest landing strip.

"Want to see a living goddess?" he asks, trying to light a cigarette with brief sunlight through a magnifying glass.

We wind through the streets that seem to narrow at evening, past buildings that necessity and chance have stacked into inseparable layers of styles. We pass markets where men steady trees of carved flutes, and houseflies on bunches of bananas look like shifting spots. We pass the "Radiant Shorthand and Typewriting

Institute," and a man trimming his mustache with enormous tin snips, and a cow lying like a dog among cement girders. Tibetan handicrafts—produced by exiles—hang in store fronts. In grim cubbyholes, women are making the shirts one sees in upscale anchor stores across the U.S.—shirts one can buy here for three or four dollars, and at Oak Tree Mall for 50.

"They call her Kumari," Brian says, as we walk. "They choose her to be a goddess at the age of six, don't ask me how. But after that, her feet can never touch the ground. In fact, she's only allowed out of her house once a year, in September. They present her on a golden litter. Because so many people make offerings, her family becomes wealthy."

"Like a child star."

"Yeah, sort of. When she gets her first period, she's demoted to mortalhood, and another goddess is chosen."

We enter a courtyard among a jumble of ancient wooden structures. Several tributaries bearing flowers and tossing coins call upward to a dusty balcony banked with doors and windows of elaborate lattice work. They call and sing out for Kumari to show herself. After several minutes, we turn to go. Just then a girl adorned in snapping red silks and stacks of bracelets and jeweled studs—her eyes stunningly deepened and enlarged by make-up—springs to the balcony. She rests her chin on her hands spread across the rail and pouts mockingly. She giggles, throws a wave to her supplicants and races out of sight—all in seconds.

Appeased, the group in the courtyard disperses gradually.

Brian and I step back into the street among umbrellas opened then against sunshine. "And what happens to the deposed Kumari?" I ask.

"I don't know much more about it," Brian says, "except that no one can afford to put her up in the style she was raised in. So she becomes a spinster."

2.

My friend Woody and I share a sleeper compartment on the train from Leningrad to Warsaw with a Polish woman and her small son, and 15 boxes of housewares they're most likely bringing back for sale on the black market. Exhausted by the cold and our visits to Moscow, Tashkent, and Leningrad in the last nine days, Woody refuses to acknowledge that he speaks Polish. We smile obligatorily at the woman and child, and they smile back (territory and tone established), and we all settle down for the ride—which is drowsily monotonous until the train slows.

"The border," Woody says, somewhat ominously. Throughout this trip, he has been the facetious angel of trepidation, the jester of foreboding. Perhaps his Polish childhood in Chicago and his involvement with making photographic images of it and the Old Country feed his shifting anxiety about the Soviet Union. Maybe it's the way the man with the fountain pen at the Soviet embassy in Warsaw said, "We've been expecting you," when we arrived to pick up our visas. Despite *Glastnost* and *Perestroika*, Woody has been waiting for totalitarian injustice since we crossed into the country on the train and the fruit and vegetable inspector—a bale of a woman—pointed to our five oranges and commanded: "You must eat them now."

The trip has been variously wonderful and horrible, exhausting. Hanna, the Polish agent in Warsaw who booked this "A la Carte" tour did not conceal her judgment on our enterprise.

"You should go to Egypt," she said, giving us her smile for fools.

She later explained how under the new drive for foreign exchange and openness, we would be mostly left to our own initiative in each city, except for an escort to and from our assigned hotel.

"You will fly on Russian planes," she said, "but don't worry. They don't crash as often as people say."

Each of our tour guides was named Natasha. At the Pushkin Museum in Moscow, one Natasha—a woman with a faint, sweet body odor—unpinned her matted, golden hair among the voluptuous Bacchanals and Rubens nudes, and wept for the dead and suffering in the recent Armenian earthquake. At the Peter and Paul Fortress in Leningrad, another Natasha unconsciously stroked her new fox stole which gawked with eyes made of jade-green plastic buttons.

Everywhere in the country, one could see that the Soviets had the means to incinerate the world—computer terminals and such—but not to serve a digestible chicken dinner.

"New York prices," Woody said, "for sub-Polish standard goods."

The confusion of the times abounded. Our hotel, the Kosmos, looked like a tired dormitory; our room—identical to that for which a dentist from Denver paid $300 a night—featured furniture with desquamating veneer and sack cloth wall coverings in need of a tuck. In the lobby, slot machines rang, and a poster of Dumbo the elephant gazed over arrivals greeted by a muzak version of "Strangers in the Night."

Around town, street vendors offered carnations in glass cases heated by candles, and rotting apples sold from the backs of trailer trucks commanded a line of buyers. Sergei, "a poor Russian boy, trying to make a living," offered a full line of military souvenirs, and left us his number. From a gate in the Kremlin wall where guards for Lenin's tomb marched forth, limousines sped like frantic, riderless horses and vanished into the night—the larger the car, the faster its pace. During the more poignant portions of "Sleeping Beauty" at the Bolshoi, when a solo instrument carried the music forward, one could hear the patter and thud of the dancers' feet, the susurrus of satin, the squawk of the floorboards.

Yet the chrome in Moscow's bright subway cars shone like fittings in bygone barbershops, and chandeliers lit some of the older platforms. At one station, a woman approached us.

"Pardon me," she said with a British accent, "But I must tell you that you must tie up the ear flaps on your hat. You don't know how to wear it."

I saw by my reflection in the glass that the "ears" of my Deputy Dawg were pointing outward, askew, Chinese style. The woman giggled.

"If you tie them up," she said, a Russian undertone now apparent in her British, "you won't be so conspicuous. People won't look at you. I'm sorry. But we wear these hats here. It's so cold, you see."

I thought of relating to her the history of my hat, which I purchased in China, but thought better of it, thanked her, and tied up my flaps. . . .

Now the train stops at the border. It's quiet for a while. The Polish woman readies her papers for the Russian inspectors. Woody and I follow her lead.

We hear voices at the end of our car. A young man in uniform throws open our compartment door and moves on to the next compartment. The Polish woman sits straight-backed on the edge of her couchette, her hand on her son's knee. In a few minutes, we hear the voice of the inspector speaking in Polish in the next compartment, occupied by the Polish woman's friend and her two children. Woody is agitated, though he tries not reveal that he understands the inspector.

"What a bastard!" Woody mutters. "He just called her a 'pregnant Polish pig' and commanded her to stand up."

Suddenly, the young man in uniform stands outside our door,

and the border inspector enters. He is thirtyish, blond, handsomely elegant—a TV stereotype of ruthlessness. He glances at Woody and me, and then turns to the Polish woman. His tone is polite as he asks for her documents. She stands and looks up at him, eye to eye, determined not to turn her face from his. He smiles down at her, speaks softly and steps into the hallway. She leans down to her son seated on the couchette, whispers to him, and then follows the inspector. Another young man in uniform appears and takes her away.

The inspector returns to us. He glances at our passports and hands Woody's back. "What is this?" he says to me in English, pointing to my backpack on the floor. "Open it, please."

I unzip the main pockets. Interested most in the design of the pack, he examines the pouches and the easy-release snaps. He pulls back one of the flaps, revealing my underwear and a blue sweater. From beneath my wadded shirt, he brings forth an unsealed envelope plump with 54 pages from a yellow legal pad: a desperate, pathetic epistle to Winifred, most of which I wrote during a 15-hour blizzard, nauseated by the pink linoleum of the Moscow airport.

He starts to remove it from the envelope.

"It's just a letter to my girlfriend," I say, suddenly anxious that I'm now the bag unzipped for inspection.

In all the border crossings I've made, I've never felt so powerless, never realized how much unacknowledged faith I have in the "golden passport" about which my Polish friends teased me. Me, commonplace fool of empire.

The inspector looks down at the folded yellow pages, and then shoves them back into the envelope.

"Love?" he says with mock weariness, handing the envelope to me.

Over the next two hours, the train nudges ahead repeatedly.

At last, our car sits on the elevated platform. Out the window, smeared gangs in denim coveralls call to each other, and beneath our feet wrenches clack and bite on bolts as the width of the wheels is changed to fit the different gauge track in Poland. It was by this necessity, decades ago, that the Polish poet Alexander Wat confirmed his suspicion that his prison train was bound for the camps in Siberia.

Woody tells me that during the inspection, he overheard that the Polish woman in our compartment and her pregnant friend with two children next door are returning from a holiday with their husbands, who are on military assignment in Leningrad. The woman in our compartment wore an elaborate gold necklace, two gold bracelets, and several gold rings, which she told the inspector her husband had given her on this trip as anniversary presents. The gold, Woody thinks, is why they took her off the train.

Another half hour passes, and just before we depart from the border, the young man in uniform returns the Polish woman to our compartment. All of her jewelry is gone. She speaks quietly to her son and then to her friend, who appears at the compartment door. After we've rolled on into Poland for several minutes, the woman gestures inquiringly toward my pack of cigarettes on the table, takes two and adjourns with the other woman.

"From what I could gather," Woody says, "the inspectors told her that she didn't have the proper documents for the jewelry and that they would have to mail it all back to her husband. Of course, they'll just steal it, now that she's gone.

"I think she said they also did a body-cavity search on her."

After a few minutes, I walk to the bathroom at the end of the car. In the roaring vestibule over the coupling, the women smoke. The woman from our compartment cries now with as much vigor as when she thrust her poise into the face of the inspector, her dignity, it seemed, meant as a lesson for her son.

She looks at me emphatically. Mascara drools from her eyes. I nod as respectfully as I know how.

Later, she and her friend return to our compartment and arrange slabs of chicken and cheese and a bottle of vodka, all of which they won't let us decline. Woody, at last, speaks Polish, to their embarrassment and then delight. We eat and drink and sing. We part at Warsaw Central station with the drunken luster of friends who will see each other tomorrow. Woody and I walk the usual route to our hotel. Suddenly, his L.A. artist's sheath—with it farcical anxieties—splits and peels away, and the Polish immigrant's grandson from Chicago, which he fears and detests like kitsch, appears. He stops on the sidewalk, curses Russia for ever existing and spits fiercely toward the East.

3.

"I bet it's that German from the souvenir shop near Luxor Temple," Aprille says, "the one who was relieved to find prices marked so he didn't have to dicker for a postcard."

In the distance, a figure strides toward us through the undulating heat of the Nile Valley. We stand near the gate of the Mortuary Temple of Hatshepsut, the first female Pharaoh of ancient Egypt. The only other person in sight for miles is a ticket-taker curled around a nap beside a low wall offering the hour's only sliver of shade.

Before us, at the end of a long walkway, Hatshepsut's Temple looms like an enormous mouth organ set into the sheer cliff. Her stepson had to wait 20 years to assume the throne from her, she who always had herself depicted with a beard. In Karnak Temple, Aprille and I had encountered their honorific steles and arches, hers always somehow larger and grander than his—a psychosexual drama in architecture.

Now her temple, like a number of fabulous structures of ancient Thebes, is undergoing restoration by specialists from Poland.

"World War II," Aprille says, when I'd express surprise at this. "That surely qualifies the Poles as rebuilders. Look at Old Town in Warsaw."

The striding figure turns out to be the German, fit and pink in a black sleeveless tee shirt, shorts and walking boots. A canteen wags from his brisk hip. He seems to have come across the vast, vacant flats, up from the sugar cane fields which are reluctant to venture far from the river. He looks at us and we at him, because we can do nothing else. We assume he, too, has come to see the Temple. He slows as he approaches.

"Look at that lazy Egyptian," he says softly, shaking his head at the sleeping ticket-taker as he passes, his smile inviting us to offer one in return.

In a moment, he resumes his pace and soon becomes an absurd speck among a searing cosmos of gravel and sand. Where is he headed, we wonder, with such determination?

Determined as well, Aprille and I have treated the previous two weeks like a languorous felucca ride on the Nile of ambitions—our "denial," as we call it, of the past and future. It is the most recent destination in our buddy/lovers tour of Living-for-the-Moment. Through each of our flights, Aprille weeps convulsively with fright, and I hold her like an abusive husband hoping to appear decent to the surrounding starers and ignorers. She always stops crying when we land, a veteran of trips, bruised over several bygone years of international dating with a trader, Ray, and another man from South America whose name and nation she refuses, irritably, to reveal. Aprille is the kind who longs to appear blasé but always fails.

In the Valley of the Kings, not far from Hatshepsut's Temple, we descend into dozens of pharaonic tombs, the more secure and lengthy the reign of each resident, the more intricately painted and elaborate the catacombs. One of the most incomplete is that of an assassinated despot. When the place had been sealed, only the outlines of the elaborate drawings had been drafted along the vast slate walls. We also visit Tut's emptied tomb; its extravagant contents lie under guarded glass in Cairo, testimony to the boy-pharoah's obscurity, since robbers had not plundered his sepulcher as they had those of the great. At the end of a brief hallway, its unadorned walls enclose a space no larger than the child's bedroom in a suburban starter-home.

Among the more modest crypts in the Valley of the Queens nearby, we come upon the saddest of the vaults—that of a future pharaoh who died as a boy. Along the walls are painted scenes of the boy's father grooming his doomed son for the throne, including the boy's introductions to the gods. In both valleys, carved steps descend into holes hacked for the modern dreamers and searchers, holes filled with gravel when they proved false starts.

Later, we pause on a ridge overlooking the ruins of the Ramesseum. I read aloud Percy Shelley's "Ozymandias"—a poem reputedly written in 20 minutes—about the fallen colossus there. For Shelley, it symbolized the folly and arrogance of thirsting for timeless fame.

> I met a traveller from an antique land
> Who said: "Two vast and trunkless legs of stone
> Stand in the desert. Near them, on the sand,
> Half sunk, a shattered visage lies, whose frown,
> And wrinkled lips, and sneer of cold command,
> Tell that its sculptor well those passions read
> Which yet survive, stamped on these lifeless things,
> That hand that mocked them and the heart that fed:

And on the pedestal these words appear:
My name is Ozymandias, King of Kings:
Look on my works, ye mighty, and despair!
Nothing beside remains. Round the decay
Of that colossal wreck, boundless and bare
The lone and level sands stretch far away."

Through her binoculars, Aprille verifies that the tiny man now perched on the shoulder of that "colossal wreck" of pride is the German we had seen earlier.

Just then, a barefoot little girl and younger boy from the hovels near the cane fields approach us on the glass shards and gravel. They entreat us for coins, as dozens have this day, the boy sobbing skillfully, one hand out and the other rubbing his eye. Finally, the girl turns toward the boy and pokes him hard in the testicles, twice, to give his tears more conviction.

4.

In Turfan, in the far Northwest of China, Doug and I piece together part of a human skull from shards scattered among broken bottles at the foot of a padlocked mosque.

"Bones have a way of coming up," said one of the Brits with whom we share a room at the town guest house, "in a place as old as this."

True, Turfan is old. The Persians had built the wells from which the water now flows, steaming at dawn in shallow channels beside dirt streets—water which makes the dry steppe arable. And we have seen many bones. Two days ago, Doug and I visited the Atsana graves at Goachang, a ninth century ruin not far from town. There, a jowly, quizzical boy led us past a dead dog which was to be buried in one of the vineyards for which Turfan is known. We marched down an incline, as though to enter a root cellar. He unlocked the slatted door, and we stepped into a powdery dimness in which lay two mummies.

"This is the female," the boy said, pointing to the one whose feet, slightly unwrapped, looked like undone toe shoes. Her gut was a crushed, papery cave and held three milkweed seeds, like three stars.

The day before, we'd gone to the Flaming Mountains, a range which knuckles down on the horizon beyond Turfan. We'd climbed red dunes, hundreds of feet high, the sand so fine it splashed against car tires. We'd roamed through the Bezelick Caves, which date back to the Tang Dynasty and which were adorned with Buddhist frescoes until discovered by Ariel Stein La Coq, a German who had them razored out, crated and shipped to Berlin—only to be destroyed there by Allied bombing in World War II.

Turfan seems full of presentiments. Its windbreaks of poplars and the frank, measuring look of its inhabitants, and the bone-glow of late winter light remind me of Pershing, and something else I can't quite grasp.

Later, after dark, Doug and the Brits talk of Lady McCartney, who, in the nineteenth century, had her Cramer piano brought from Britain to Turkestan in a zinc-lined box which opened along the way, causing the instrument to arrive with swollen hammers.

"She stayed 17 years," Doug says, "so I guess they had time to dry out."

He goes on to tell about a statue we had seen in Bei Hai Park in Beijing. It was of a bronze man, rod-straight, who seemed cowed by a shallow bowl he steadied on his head, almost like a shield. An emperor, believing it would give him eternal life, drank the dew which gathered there.

"Talk about wills," Doug says, shaking his head.

We sit on the second lowest point of the Earth, and the Big Dipper pours the darkness from around itself.

At last, what has been eluding me comes. I think of my older cousin Jim, murdered in Pershing four years ago—how, on one of my childhood visits, he drew water for me, carefully avoiding the white worms at the bottom of an infested well. On another of my visits, we had to share a bed, and I wouldn't allow it unless he wore pajamas, which he did. And, of course, I think of his bicycle, the first I'd learned to ride, not knowing how to get off without a crash.

The darkness pours from the Dipper, and I try to envision the dumb, stained two-by-four with which he had been beaten; and the coroner's look when he told Jim's sister, a nurse, "You don't want to see him like this"; and the shattering acquittal of the man charged with the crime, a man who had murdered before and served his time.

All through my childhood no one I knew in Pershing had died. Yet I hadn't visited there for years. My last meeting with Jim—a quick beer on my parents' patio—offered its false consequence. Who was he—is he—to the man to whom he last turned his back?

The accused stayed on in Pershing for a while after the trial, and then moved. He's become talk scattered among relatives. And Jim's widow, needing a father for her son, has married another cousin. How many caves and stars?

In the darkness now, the braying of a donkey sounds like a rusted well pump, and I have no more taste for night than those who rise suddenly from nightmares to find its chilling traces glittering in dawn light, and then gone.

5.

Yousoof's postcard comes sealed in an envelope to my Warsaw mailbox. Perhaps discretion—or a fancied shyness—has urged him to package it this way, though its few lines of fair weather and wishes for my good health hardly merit such cover. I'd known him for little more than a week on my way to Poland the previous summer. We'd met at the check-in counter for a flight from Athens to Istanbul. He asked me to watch his bags while he went to the bathroom, which I did, somewhat nervous that he might be getting safely clear of explosives concealed in them. Later, in Istanbul, we split cab fare and the expense of a modest hotel room near the Blue Mosque. He was anxious among the dirt and crowds, and he seemed uneasy with the manner of travel he'd chosen—a good risk as a roommate, I believed, still troubled by the plight of two Swedish girls I'd met in Athens: on their first holiday from the chocolate works back home, they had been chloroformed and robbed down to their passports, most likely by a young American woman who had shared their train compartment and then disappeared.

On vacation from engineering school in Lyons, France, Yousoof carried a photocopy of a world map which he brought forth to each acquaintance, his homeland—the island of Mauritius—a daub of pink highlighter in the Indian Ocean. An animated, dull commentary on Mauritius, the center of the world, emanated with a French accent from beneath his dense mustache, accompanying all he did and saw. A Muslim of Indian and French descent, Yousoof despised France and all things French with the determination of one rejected by a club he longs to join. Yet when he spoke of the U.S.—which he enjoyed deriding often—he swooned with an imperious nostalgia for Paris, applying this show of personal glory like the slight contingent of hair dispatched to his bald crown from a part just above his ear.

Sprawling from the Bosporus into Asia and Europe, Istanbul seethed in the heat, its vast populace roiling around honking traffic gluts. The Galata pontoon bridge shuddered slightly under foot traffic. Ice cream vendors announced another sale by striking bells with a newly filled cone on the end of a holding stick, teasing each customer by yanking the cone away as he reached for it. Above salads and skewers and urban male smiles, pale chickens turned on rotisseries, glistening like glazed porcelain. On large shaded terraces, men smoked water pipes all day, adjusting their tobacco coals with tweezers, sipping sugary tea delivered by boys racing on appointed rounds.

In each carpet shop, young men quizzed me about the prices of things in Greece. They, unlike other Europeans I'd met, praised the U.S. When I mentioned that many Americans thought Turkey a dangerous place, they laughed in mock bewilderment.

"Oh yes," they said, "we know the movie, *Midnight Express.*"

I aimed for the main tourist sites and for general walking, and Yousoof seemed content to come along, though my lack of schedule irritated him. It soon became clear that he needed company in order to travel—hence, his ruse with the luggage in the Athens airport—but also he liked his days orderly. Every hour or so, he required food, and then there were the naps. Though he didn't dare say it, his tone implied that I should sit with him for two hours while he nibbled, and that we should turn back when he wearied.

While I, too, welcomed companionship after months alone on the road, I was unwilling to compromise. In this, I'm reminded of a friend in the U.S. whose roommate was so rigid in his vision of evenly shared chores that he divided a pool of dog vomit on the kitchen floor—halving it precisely—and cleaned up only his portion.

Yousoof napped at the hotel, and I lay on the stones of Sancta

Sophia—that grand, empty railway station of Islam and Christianity—and gazed at the glorious domes from which chandeliers hung like stupendous plumb bobs. It was the first interior in all my travels that tour groups could not belittle or fill with chatter.

I also visited the grand bazaar, that ancient shopping mall with miles of gold necklace unspooled in its windows and alleys nattering with tinsmiths' hammers. One day, I looked down a dry well and found a man sleeping. On a side street, a pigeon fell at my feet from a branch, dead.

When I mentioned the heat, Yousoof snickered, "White men sweat more than Indians . . . but less than blacks."

Eventually, I announced to Yousoof that I was heading around the country by bus the next day, assuming that at last we could part, without unpleasantness.

"But of course," he said, "we should go." The supplication in his eyes, like a little brother's fear of being left behind, persuaded me to capitulate.

Travelers' tales, it seems, lavish more attention on odious buses than any modern mode of transportation. Istanbul's terminal teemed with companies, its lot criss-crossed with myriad vehicles and informal traffic directors, all passengers seeming part of a group charter racing to depart before the Apocalypse. Yet the coaches Yousoof and I experienced—all of German manufacture—featured operative air conditioning and a waiter who anointed his hands with lemon oil, and distributed complimentary bottles of Urgup Spring Water—liquid silk—from a cooler onboard. About every two hours, the driver, needing more coffee to negotiate narrow highways at high velocity, pulled us into a roadside cafe, where even the snacks sufficed. My only displeasure lay in reboarding and finding that Yousoof had taken my seat because, as he explained, he could sleep more easily next to the window.

In Urgup, a boy at the station led us with hand gestures

through broad, quiet streets to his family pension. We sat outdoors at a table as he and his older teenage brother signed us in and prepared a room. Bees hovered over the jelly tins, and wind rattled in a bush of dry pods. Urgup lies in Cappadocia, an arid spread of geological rifts in Central Anatolia, similar in appearance to the Badlands of South Dakota. Once the domain of Hittites and Romans, it now is home to donkeycarts and shops amenable to Mastercard and chamber of commerce tribalism.

We'd come to see the fabulous valleys of Troglodyte dwellings. Led by John/Franz—the young Turkish hustler with the shifting American-British-Australian accent—we climbed narrow ladders to the Byzantine cave churches: the Church of the Buckle, the Church of the Sandal, and others. Some had ceilings carved elaborately; one bore a fresco of St. George Slaying the Dragon. Havens for persecuted Christians in the eleventh century, these intricate caverns contained stone banquet tables; the porous rock walls absorbed the smoke from their residents' fires.

Later that day, John/Franz took us to a pottery shop in Avanos, a routine promotional stop—except that the potter, Galip Korukcu, also had on display his cave of women's hair. A nine-year collection of locks snipped from female customers and visitors covered its arching walls and ceiling, a plush, dangling mat of the world-feminine. Affixed to each specimen was a business card signed by the donor.

"They are all close to me," Galip swooned, "All my girlfriends!"

Yousoof had me take his picture in front of each cave. His unexpected enthusiasm refreshed and encouraged me to forgive his whining about the sun and his increased rush to exert his pride by accentuating my tour-guide mistakes. Over the days, I'd found it more difficult to ignore his bathroom hawking and his ass-scratching while he brushed his teeth. Frequently, he'd speculated on what unfriendly dish had heaved within him the night before, though his appetite seemed undiminished. As a counter-measure, I had begun eating midday meals on my own and leaving the hotel before he arose.

Yousoof also had me take snapshots of him on the travertine terraces in Pamalkalle. He stood among bathers and dawdlers, each in one of the shallow, calcified basins brimming with warm spring water which trickles into the basins below, all the way down the mountainside. The scene resembled the first photographs of Mammoth Hot Springs in what is now Yellowstone National Park—a nineteenth century panorama, before management came to demand controlled access to such spectacles.

One night in Pamalkalle, I awakened to the soft thump and stifled pant of Yousoof masturbating in the bed across our darkened room. Later that day, we stood in the ruined amphitheater farther up the mountainside, not far from the little hotel where families on holiday frolicked in pools lined with fallen columns from an ancient Roman health spa abandoned after a local volcano erupted.

"Aren't you bored with this?" he asked. "Let's go look at video."

"That's it! Enough!" I replied, pouncing on each word, and I marched off. Yousoof tagged after me until it became clear I would not respond to his inquiries. Within an hour, I'd checked in to another hotel. I lay on the clean sheets and smoked one of the cigarettes I'd forsaken indoors for the sake of his delicate lungs. Why, I wondered, had I not ditched him much earlier, like a bad blind date? Why the foolish stoicism and the notion that I should adapt to his skillful helplessness?

When I left Pamalkalle, Yousoof took the same bus. He sat several rows behind me, and we did not speak. He took rooms not far from mine in Selcuk . . . and Kusadasi . . . and Izmir. I would see him from the corner of my eye among the crowds or out the window while I tried on shoes, or sat down to lunch, or leaned back as the barber pinched my nostrils shut to trim the hairs. We would pretend not to notice each other, though it was difficult not to laugh or charge, shrieking, at him.

He came and went through those days until we separated— with a quick handshake—in the Istanbul airport, my pathetic phantom, afraid to be among the wholly unfamiliar.

Now in Warsaw, seemingly years away from him, I look at the picture on his postcard—sunset among the ruins at Ephesus—and I think of him leaping onto the pedestal of a headless statue there. With a pouchy grin resting on the stone shoulders, he had replaced the vanished face of a maiden that once regarded the surrounding hills. He had me snap that picture of him, too.

6.

In a cafe, I strike up a conversation with Karen, who first came to Nepal in 1965, when she was 21. She stayed seven years, married, and had a baby. Now a painter and advocate of fly fishing as Zen practice, she returns when something in the nerves makes her "homesick" for the country.

"It's always an adventure getting here," she tells me. "I've flown in on World War II-vintage DC 3's, bolts in the wings jiggling. I've flown into valleys with farmers plowing above us. I've landed on grassy fields. One time a little old farmer talked to the pilot, and eventually the pilot let the man unscrew the cap from the fuel tank and fill a can.

"And then there's the Bangladesh Airlines flight from the States to Nepal. They always stop along the way, claiming to have engine trouble. Actually, the crew has already flown around the world and can't fly longer without sleep. Air safety regulations. But the airline can't afford to put passengers up in a hotel, so they say it will be a delay of two hours, then three hours, then several more hours . . . until the passengers remain in the terminal through the night. I've taken the flight six times, and it always breaks down at the same place, precisely."

After finishing our coffee, we decide there is time to have lunch before I catch my plane to Rangoon.

"I come back here," she says, "because I can sit at dinner with one of my Nepalese friends, and I can feel his life going on, at that moment, with me in it. I don't feel that in the States.

"There's something about the people here, an ingenuous charm, a sophistication that's almost childlike. For instance, I once had a housekeeper, a Tibetan woman of no more than 20. One day she revealed that she had been a paratrooper in the Tibetan military. She made ten jumps. On the first two jumps, she said, she and her female companions drifted downward, singing Tibetan songs together. On the third jump, she said, she thought to herself, as she sang, 'This really is dangerous.'"

Later, Karen asks me if I've done any trekking in Nepal, and I reply that I've been on vacation, nothing strenuous. She says, "I used to trek and sometimes still do, but it's too much like those people who come here to write trekking books—predictable, too much of a worn path, even at 16,000 feet. For instance, you come to a village with no food. It's a sacred experience, but it isn't a sacred place to me, though it's a sacred place.

"I mean, you can take a picture of that village, but your photo isn't of the villagers' village. The picture lies somewhere between what the village is for them and what it is for you. Maybe that's why the image is a spiritual space.

"One time, a village I lived in had a play in which there was an American character. I had an allergy and sneezed frequently. The actor who played the American saw this and, trying to be accurate in his portrayal, sneezed throughout the play."

Eventually, Karen finds out that I write poems, and this helps me get her on the subject of painting—which also returns us to the "homesickness" she feels for Nepal. From her pack, she takes a souvenir postcard from a show of her work in the States. On it is a painting of a hallway inhabited only by ochre light and the smoke of burning incense. Beautiful.

"I've been painting that hallway for twenty years," she says, "dozens of pieces, and I've never 'gotten' it. I sometimes wonder how it can be real, it's been on my mind so long."

She tells me that the place is close but too far for her to show me before I have to catch a taxi for the airport.

"One time," she says, smiling to herself, "I was sketching the hallway, and this boy monk sat next to me. We chatted in Nepalese, and I eventually gave him one of those postcards. The next day I came to sketch again. There, in the hallway, at the foot of the Buddha, was the postcard with the painting of my vision of the hallway."

Original
Friend

A year ago, one of my mother's rare, brief letters arrived, bearing in its folds the reason for its being: Tom's obituary. In two column inches of newsprint, I learned that, at 38, he had died at home of complications from diabetes; that he was a lifelong resident of Des Moines; that he was survived by a sister. My mother's letter said he had been cremated the week before, so I was spared a cross-country trip for the service. To be honest, I wouldn't have gone—would have told myself that I couldn't get away, or made some other excuse. Tom and I hadn't spoken in at least a decade, and we hadn't seen each other for longer than that. Yet, he had been my closest male companion through childhood, adolescence and beyond. He had been my original friend.

I thumbtacked the obit to the bulletin board near the desk in my study, among—and soon beneath—stalled drafts of poems, postcards, reminders of things to do. Sometimes I brought myself to find it, and I studied it, looking for some further insight among the few yellowing facts. Memorial contributions, it said, could be made to his church, though Tom had never attended any church in our years as friends. The home address given was not that of his family's house on East 33rd Street, two blocks from where I grew up, but of a residence across town, in a more urban, less prosperous neighborhood. When I had known him, he had two much older sisters and an older brother—a mythic brother, really—whose existence was demonstrated by a sepia-toned graduation photograph, and who had left behind a conflict with Tom's late father years before, never to return. Legend further asserted that this brother taught at the school back East attended by the Kennedy children. Had one of Tom's sisters and his brother died in the years since we had last talked? Or was this surviving sister the only sibling with whom he still had contact, given his history of familial conflicts?

There was also a photograph: Tom in his familiar aviator glasses, leaning into the frame, portrait-studio-style, and looking off toward some horizon beyond the words surrounding his image. There was the burry, bristly, enviably unmanageable hair tapered and parted. There were the faint pencilings of a mustache he had first tried to grow at 15, and the clear, satiny complexion—infant flesh—bearing the slight shadow on the cheek, no doubt his ineradicable red. He didn't smile. He never smiled in pictures, because he was cute and frail of frame, a runt, and had always been so. And he was desperate to be taken seriously—perhaps to take himself seriously—and to be seen as a man, worthy of his brother's legend. He might also have withheld his smile here because his diabetes had cost him several front teeth by his mid-twenties. It was impossible to tell how recently the picture had been taken. He had always looked like a boy.

Besides the gravity in the announcement of his death, I kept confronting the crucial absences outlined by these details. Had he died alone? Was it sudden? Had he really gotten religion? Why was he living in such reduced circumstances? Did he have *anyone* in his life? I envisioned a ramshackle, buff-brick rooming house surrounded by commercial parking lots on the fringe of downtown, and within it a dim, chilly apartment which housed stacked, grimy dishes and tossed clothes, the enduring shambles of a bachelorhood renewed by a divorce more than a decade before. The chill in that apartment clamped down and squeezed the pity up in me—an unjustifiable pity, of course, for a life I had no right to judge as pathetic and somehow failed, though it appeared so.

At the time of our last talk, Tom still lived at the East 33rd Street house. In fact, he had just inherited it after his mother's death from a fall we both knew—but would not say—vodka had encouraged. He was thinking of selling the place, and he'd called me to see about the prospects of moving to the town where I then lived in Florida. He sounded eager to start a new life. The county sheriff's office still employed him as a photographer and uniformed clerk—jobs he had always glorified by intimating that they also involved undercover work which had to be kept scrupulously vague. He thought the Sunshine State might be the place to pursue his long-held aspiration for a career as a real law enforcement officer.

He also sounded shy, nearly embarrassed, as he asked if it was possible to stay at my apartment for a few days. A graduate student, I shared a small, one bedroom unit in a refurbished carriage house with my girlfriend at the time. Though I was surprised and genuinely pleased to hear from him, the mild apprehension in my "sure, no problem" must have struck him square and fortified any reluctance he had felt in calling me. We joked and reminisced, and hung up after promising to talk at the end of the week, when he had made his travel arrangements to Florida. We never spoke again.

Why didn't I pick up the phone when the week passed with

no call? Why did neither of us make the gesture? I believed, somehow, that further contact with me would pain him—undoubtedly a rationalization for my own paralysis, or indifference. Yet, his silence testified to a distance neither of us could broach alone, solitary as we seemed to ourselves in the remains of our friendship, most of which lay in memory. Had he been as relieved—cruelly relieved—as I to be free of our contact?

The selling of the East 33rd Street house touched me as a poignant but inevitable farewell, a necessary transformation. When visiting my parents in the years after Tom and I did not call back, I often drove by it, noting, as in times past, that his car stood in the driveway or was absent—until one day I passed to see different cars parked there, new aluminum siding and window frames, and two children playing on a new swing set out front. Original friends don't choose each other so much as they are tossed together by fortune, and they stay together—even if they are not ideal mates—because their world is small and their alternatives few, and the possibility of questioning and choosing their places in life remains obscured by the naturalness of the way things seem. I don't remember where, or how, we met as children, though it must have been in the local public kindergarten. My first memories of Tom, however, occupy the East 33rd Street house and surrounding property. The place became the spiritual center of our friendship, where we learned about intimacy and limits.

That house was not so much my second home as a new world where I could escape the wrenching and embarrassing conflicts in my family. Though not appreciably larger than our two-story place, it seemed richer, more refined and exotic—with a stone fireplace in the living room and built-in, floor-to-ceiling, mahogany bookshelves jammed with forgotten hardback novels; wainscoting in the dining room and beveled glass in the doors; an enclosed front porch mystically called the *solarium*; and upstairs, a laundry chute.

According to Tom, his father had once headed a large construction company in the area before an associate betrayed and ousted
him; that was why Tom was born in Australia during a sojourn
at a building project and why the older neighbors called him
"dinkum," a nickname at which he scowled frequently. It was also
why his father then worked as a welder, he said, and why his parents had to sell off the large acreage that had once surrounded
the house, on which a school and some of the neighborhood
stood.

I was not a second son at Tom's house because Tom was not
so much a son himself as he was a late-arriving, "accidental" obli-
gation to an older, busy, troubled couple. His willfulness and their
weariness gradually removed him from the usual parental over-
sight. Thus, he and the house also embodied a kind of early freedom I might never have discovered on my own. For instance, Tom
introduced me to worldly pleasures on one of my innumerable
sleepovers. We must have been ten, perhaps 11 years old. His
siblings had long before grown up and moved out, and his parents were at work. We had watched "rassling" on television with
Tom's grandfather—a failing, crusty, genial man who drank
cough syrup and smoked crooked, rum-soaked cigars, and who
would die within the next year. Grandfather abed, Tom opened
the windows of his room, pulled out a crumpled pack of cigarettes
and three *Playboy* magazines. We sat drenched in the peeled white
glow of a bare light bulb. I declined the offer of a cigarette, as I
would for a few more years. Tom smoked lavishly on his bed, his
nose runny and glistening from manifold allergies, his fingernails
uncut and filthy as they would be into adulthood. He'd gazed
aplenty at the magazines and reclined in his sophistication. I had
never seen such things before, and I did not know they were supposed to be "dirty." I hovered over the images, somewhere in that
erotic zone of adolescence just before the first full-force erection

arrives with clear neural instructions. A pure, sweet urge held me in a fine mesh of fascination. I remember one image: a woman standing in a red Corvette, her blonde hair flying, bare breasted, wearing what I believe were white cotton panties. I turned back to her over and over, uncertain why I was drawn to her chest and that one cloaked region. I would look at other such images later, but never as I did on that night.

Tom relished these moments. He liked being the first and being in the know. His proud suavity crowned him like his cigarette smoke. He wore it the day he brought home his snare drum from his first lesson and instructed me in how to hold the sticks, casual about the ways of junior high school band members. He wore it when we hunched over cherry cokes at the soda fountain while the drugstore gods—who all knew him because of his sisters—talked about their cars and jobs and dates. He wore it partly because, like the smoke, it could not last long. He was too clumsy, too vulnerable. He didn't finish things. After a time as a thundering band member, he retired his drum. The drugstore gods sometimes gave us rides in their muscle cars, but they also called Tom "dinkum stink'm." He sensed I could see these debacles, yet he also perceived that part of me was a great fan of his posturings, his cool, however much it was incommensurate with his station in the world. A simple stability in me approved of his comical swagger, and inflated it and, at the same time, declared it harmless— though, at some level, Tom seemed always to have been harming himself.

We were partners of a sort, even when in the company of friends our age. After his day in the local public school and mine in the Catholic, we swept through imaginary adventures, pretending to be secret agents. We played pick-up football and playground baseball. We lolled through the summer, sitting on his porch in the night odor of cut grass and looking at downtown lights in the distance. Car crazy, we built model racers relentlessly, some in imitation of those on posters plastered across our bedroom walls, accumulating huge stocks of spare parts and customizing paraphernalia. In the old summer house behind the garage—a single oak room, with an attic, that once housed the acreage caretaker—we cleared away stored furniture and rubbish, and established a place to build and store our models. With a black marking pen, we drew a sign on a sheet of fiberboard and hung it above the door: *Tom & Don's Speed Shop.*

Some time after this, Tom turned to me and announced that his father had cancer and was going to die. He said it quickly, almost matter-of-factly—uneasily, it seems now. I accepted the news without more than a forgettable comment, probably because I didn't know what to say. At 12 or so, I had not known death, though Tom's grandfather had died the year before. A part of me also thought Tom might be lying about his father, to garner my sympathy—though I couldn't see why he would do that. The next several months witnessed his father's transformation from a tall, whiskey-flushed man in khaki coveralls to a stooped scarecrow sucking his last days through a milkshake straw, his few words popping and gargling from a tumorous throat. Remote in his health, he became, in his decline, our odd intimate, especially in his last summer during which Tom's mother worked days as an aide at a nursing home. We would accompany him on errands, he hunching over the steering wheel, barely able to raise his head. We would try to speak softly when in the house or playing at the speed shop, so as not to disturb his lengthening sleeps.

In those long months, Tom, too, began a transformation which seems obvious now but was then obscure. He grew more willful with his mother, more petulant, no doubt out of confusion and sorrow. Repeatedly, his fury sprang at the order of things as he discovered his new powers, often driving himself, and sometimes me, to precipitous emotional edges. For instance, I walked up the driveway one afternoon to rendezvous, as usual, before we began our newspaper routes. Tom and two of our friends stood in what had been the garage—a ramshackle structure with a rotted, gaping roof and sagging red tile walls. To the shock of all present, Tom had swung a sledgehammer at the supporting beams and bricks, toppling the walls. The others had taken whacks while he'd rested, and then he'd resumed. He pounded and pushed with a fierce concentration—the rest of us laughing nervously and glancing around for the trouble that was sure to arrive—until we all stood taller than the surrounding rubble. At nearly that moment, the back door opened and Tom's father appeared not in his robe but work clothes. In great agony, meager and barely able to move, he must have risen at the sound of the blows and struggled to dress during the wrecking. He shuffled, head down, mute until he stood before us.

"Goddamnit, Tom!" he mumbled almost inaudibly, breathless like a gutshot infantryman in a Hollywood epic. "What do you think you're doing?!"

Tom stared into his father's face. "Well," he replied, his tone oddly light, "we're going to rebuild the thing, but first we have clear away all this junk."

In the silence thereafter, we waited, stranded, hysterically still, until Tom's father turned and went back into the house.

Later that summer, Tom and I fought as we hadn't before. The circumstances of the conflict are no longer clear, but we ended up shouting at each other in the speed shop. Tom threw boxes of parts, and I broke some models and walked out. I had only marched 20 or so paces when I heard him call to me. I turned to see him pull down our *Tom & Don's Speed Shop* sign and break in it two.

Even now, that gesture pierces the boy I was, partly because I see that it introduced us to an adult truth. A few minutes later, Tom approached me on the front lawn of the nearby school. I had bounded off and sat and wept, ashamed of my tears but unable to restrain them. The breaking of the sign had astonished me. Only now do I have a word to name what I felt: betrayal, on the order of a lover's unfaithfulness. Tom and I talked, and looked at the sky and, eventually, reconciled. We had discovered the risk in our trust of one another. For some months, the speed shop remained in disrepair, until we finally packed up our model-building paraphernalia and took it home, and made the place into a clubhouse for all the friends in our circle.

In the fall after Tom's father died, my parents finally allowed me to transfer from the Catholic school to the public school Tom attended. This furthered the changes between us. Since kindergarten, what I knew of public school life derived from Tom's anecdotes and those of a few others. On the first day of class, I entered the seemingly vast junior high building with Tom in the lead. He introduced me to his friends, showed me around. It was vintage, big-time Dinkum, brimming with the *frisson* of adolescence and the determination to impress.

And I was impressed, though not as he might have wished. With time, it became clear that Tom did not belong to the most elite cliques, as his stories had implied. He was not the great glad-hander and universal mover and knower, but one on the margins of a cruel and utterly clear social structure. I, of course, was a newcomer and a nobody, which may have quickened these insights. Yet, in them, Tom and I also found ourselves in a familiar relationship. Eventually, we ceased any efforts to be with each other at school and saved our friendship for evenings and weekends and summers.

The following year, Tom decided to go out for the wrestling team. He talked of joining the Marines, of becoming a cop, and he thought that if he could excel at one of the lower weight classes, he could build himself up. Throughout the summer, he seemed to be weak and constantly sleepy. Heading for my paper route in the afternoons, I would enter the East 33rd Street house without knocking, since his mother was at work, and find him nearly comatose upstairs. I attributed it to his variable hours and general defiance of his mother's enfeebled rule, both of which I encouraged and shared. The required physical for the wrestling team offered a different explanation, however: a severe case of diabetes.

Just as at school, Tom attempted to show me around the hospital during the weeks of his stay there. It was the same facility in which his father had died. As we strolled the hallways, I remembered the night we stood outside his father's room, how when the door opened and his sister ushered him in, we could see his father's bony feet kicking as he thrashed for his last gasps. Tom seemed to have entered another realm that night, and his illness seemed yet another realm. It was beyond me and always present. In the kitchen after he returned home from his stay in the hospital, his mother instructed me and two other friends—all aged 14— in how to prepare and give Tom a special injection, should he lapse into a coma. The needle and the little brown vials stored in the refrigerator bestowed upon us a responsibility which, for the most part, I took seriously and was relieved to ignore.

Fortunately, I never had to administer that injection. I don't know if I would have been able, as cowardly as I am about needles. Once the glamor of his new condition ebbed, Tom carried his illness like arcane knowledge for everyone to esteem and for him to deny. In all the days and nights in the East 33rd Street house, I rarely saw him give himself his shots. Still, he sometimes used his burden as a means to make us verify our care—either by our asking if it was wise for him to eat a particular food or drink so much alcohol, or by our pretending not to notice. For him—the slightly built boy now facing an irrevocable slight—there would be no Marine Corps, so he cast himself, however questionably, into a future as a police officer. He also careened between being his body's ally and its vengeful punisher, until his abuses almost seemed the norm.

Tom's obvious vulnerability usually attracted girls, as did his good looks. Though he was sexually active by 15, he generally maintained a delicate silence about the particulars. In high school, for instance, I hitchhiked across town to his girlfriend's house a couple of times. Her parents were out, and she and Tom would occupy a bedroom upstairs for two or three hours, while I sipped gin and listened to music at the bar in the basement, so as not to hear the bedsprings. Afterward, thumbing back, without strain, we spoke of anything but what had transpired. At that time, I was excited and shy about girls, terrified of going even for that first kiss. Others in our group razzed me about it. Perhaps Tom suspected there might be something wrong with me, since I seemed almost catatonic with fear at the come-ons of his girlfriend's friends. He only mentioned the matter once or twice, tangentially. He sensed in me, I think, a fragility he understood, and left it alone.

Eventually, I found a girlfriend, though not a girl Tom knew. I had begun to roam in different arenas. Tom liked to play the rebel at school and rejected any involvement there. I'd been introduced to "popularity" and the system of gestures necessary to access and enhance it. I was becoming a joiner and doer, and a guy known for his wit—something like the figure Tom had once pretended to be—and I was hoping to learn how far I could go by being seen with the right people. Tom and I never discussed this split between us. I would circle back to the East 33rd Street house less frequently but with regularity, and we would smoke and drink and hang out, as always. We graduated. I enrolled at the local college. In the room where Tom's grandfather died, I finally cast off my virginity at 19 with an older friend of Tom's future wife.

His marriage that same year to Debbie, a hairdresser, proved ill-fated. He and Debbie moved into a minimalist apartment complex nearby and arranged their few belongings. Their early life there brimmed with TV evenings and decent homecooked dinners, and they exuded an enthusiasm which seemed to infect my girlfriend and me. For a short time, she and I talked seriously, and foolishly, of marrying, stimulated most by the thought of picking out furniture together. Tangled in such giddiness, it seems to me now that we most resembled our parents of the World War II generation.

For Tom, marriage was another first, and perhaps the product of a hungering for anchorage against the storms of his own existence. More mature and more reliable, Debbie had lived on her own since her middle teens. She'd worked hard for what she had: a paid-off car, some clothes, cookware, and a good sofa. As the months tumbled past, the role of mother and guardian to her young, reckless husband closed slowly around her. Nearly two years had to elapse before she began to realize how much she despised that embrace. By then, she and Tom had moved back to the East 33rd Street house, partly to cut expenses. He attended law enforcement classes at the community college and worked at the county jail. I had dropped out of college for a semester, and I paid rent on the room where Tom's grandfather had died and, technically, I'd given away my innocence. Debbie and I became pretty good friends. She was intelligent and talkative, and later she sought in me a confidant for the frustrations with Tom. Marriage had isolated her from old friends, and neither of us felt any connection with Tom's mother, who also lived in the house but who seemed to work night and day, when she wasn't drinking, and who was almost a ghost, when she was a presence at all.

Ultimately, I moved out of the East 33rd Street house after Tom, in a fury, accused Debbie and me of cheating on him. For some time, he had grown as petulant with Debbie as with his mother, and this incident marked a new level in the escalating conflict which continued until Debbie divorced him a few years later and eventually remarried. His indictment hurt not because I felt betrayal like that on the day he broke the old speed shop sign, but because his desperation awakened in me a pity that had lain dormant since childhood. I had to admit to myself, then, how much we had already left each other behind on our routes to elsewhere. A couple of years before, he had given me what was reputed to be his older brother's Princeton sweatshirt, and I had worn it often. I browsed and read the books lining those beautiful mahogany shelves in the living room, while he never did. Instead, he spoke lavishly about the dangers of his job at the jail, all of the details gleaned, it seemed, from cop shows, and because of this, embarrassing.

Here, my memory of Tom evaporates, except for images from a few late visits and his call to Florida. A blankness remains, on which I try to inscribe some further meaning. In his fantasies, in all his "firsts," Tom sought an outsized, perhaps even heroic life—though he wouldn't have used such terms to describe it. He confronted barriers he probably couldn't name, and neither of us asked many important questions of ourselves during our time together. Who, in those years, does? I turn now to survey the limits of my own life and its untenable, sometimes harmful, ordinary bargains. Among my failings and unrealizable dreams, Tom stands and stares back at me, another "first" for him. Alternately 18, 20, 13, 24, he offers no word about how unfairly or inaccurately I've represented him here, nor any word about the present or the future. Instead, he swaggers, as always, almost on tip-toes. His eyes well with tears from a smashing tackle on the playground. Or he adjusts the badge on his uniform. Though long out of contact with him, I could, while he was in the world, at least wonder what had become of him. The wondering must be different now.

Migration
of Wonder

Our ignorance of other languages is inevitable, however many tongues in our head. This is an ultimate equalizer and a mystery. Each language is a world that pretends to be *the* world. The multilingual know this better than the monolingual, but not much better. Sooner or later, even their worlds of words are shattered—perhaps charmingly—by a collision with another, unknown world of words.

And this shattering is always a matter of the heart, however sophisticated, because it is elemental, a matter of access and exclusion.

Unable to use my only language, I am more sentient, more attentive to my surroundings. I become a strategist of contact (when I'm up to it), and my body often becomes my translator. Charades. Improvisations. How many people toot like a train before someone who, they hope, will point the right way to the station? I remember a white-haired bus driver in Moscow trying to tell a Japanese woman that he was waiting for a tour group at the Bolshoi. He extended his arms delicately, fastidiously, like a swanning prima ballerina. The gist.

And is there any silence quite like that between two people who have learned where each is from and where each is going, who have exhausted what they know how to say and now will share a train compartment for two days? Yet there are those like the Warsaw cab driver who knew only *Bush, Reagan, Soviet, no, benzine, cigarette* and seemed to recombine them endlessly, laying down a cogent, manic patter for two hours. There is the Polish granny in Gdansk who for several blocks walked with my friend Mitch, chatting and lecturing, and not seeming to notice that his replies were in English.

Character and culture suffuse the permutations. In China, for instance, you can be assured your Mandarin is wretched if Chinese people commend you on it. Many assume it's just too hard to learn—unlike English. To know the language well is, of course, a compliment to China but also somewhat threatening to those who have always had the power of the tongue over their visitors. Doug—one of my Changchun colleagues—told of visiting the father of Liu, his university friend of three years. At dinner, though Doug and Liu's father conversed pleasantly and easily in Chinese, Liu kept trying to translate everything Doug said, even as his father admonished him for it. Another Westerner, George, reported phone conversations interrupted by surveillance personnel breaking in on the line to correct his Chinese grammar.

I remember the week I began to dream in Chinese, understanding it famously in that realm. Several of the other Westerners with whom I lived there also began about the same time. And there was, over weeks and months, the transformation of Chinese in my awake ear from a smear of sound to strings of discrete words and phrases, some of which were familiar, some I could repeat, a few I could comprehend. I remember Monica from Salt Lake City, drunk, speaking Russian and Chinese with the egg man, both of them switching back and forth with nearly each phrase. I remember Patty, a Chinese-American from California, who fled Changchun after a few months, unable to bear the hard expectation that since she looked like a native she should be treated like one. Patty, who spoke only Valley-girl.

My friend Rick says that he is more outgoing in Hebrew than in his native English, partly because a language acquired later doesn't carry the same psychological freight, at first; it will never be the tongue in which you were scolded or cheered at six. Ola, in Lodz, is a native speaker of Polish and English, but she prefers English, almost to the damnation of Polish. She feels weaker in the latter and stronger in the former, so much so that she taught her husband English, and they spoke only English at home. Suzie, a Korean-American from Seattle, told me that she always speaks English when dealing with men in Korea, because gender bias against women is built into Korean grammar, causing women to demur. Korean men laugh at American GIs with Korean wives, Suzie said, because they speak Korean "like women."

And this reminds me of John/Franz, who ran the small bus tours in Cappadocia. He'd acquired his English, in addition to other languages, from his customers. So he pronounced each word, or phrase, in the manner of the speaker from whom he'd learned it. One of his shortest sentences could careen and chime through U.S., Canadian, Australian and British accents. All natural—like those two students with Chinese faces from Vladivostok, their English percolating with a Russian accent; or the five young, local men sharing a Saturday night smoke from a waterpipe in a Tunisian fishing village, among them one as red-haired and freckled as a mythic Irish warrior.

I've heard it argued that we confront our ignorance of

character when we see a "foreign friend" speak in his native tongue to others for whom it is a first language. This reveals to us that much is hidden or deleted in translation. In these instances, people who seem dull can suddenly sparkle, or the gruff grow calescent. The moment of certainty and understanding cracks open and tumbles—yet another tower of Babel.

Of course, this can entice profoundly. My friend Alvin had an affair with a German precisely because neither could share a word. They had to attend to each other differently, he says—somewhat nostalgically—and with greater patience, and he adored his lover having an orgasm in German. . . .

When people ask how I managed abroad with only English, I recall some of these things. I also tell them how, in China, people sometimes assumed that I didn't understand what they were saying because I was one of the Muslim minorities from the far northwest of the country. So they wrote the words, in characters, on their palm or mine—since everyone can read Chinese.

Or I recall the little girl on the express train from Beijing, with whom I tried to speak. After chatting with Doug for some time, she asked him if I was retarded. She had never heard of anyone who could not speak Mandarin. I recall her astonished and skeptical look as Doug tried to explain.

STARING, *CIRCA* 1985

On my first morning in Changchun, I walked down Liberation Street, a main boulevard near the compound where I had been assigned living quarters. Everywhere, heads turned or waited until I passed to turn. Children pointed. At each step, I faced a throng neither hateful nor inviting—occasional grins but mostly blank, pannish gazes spawned by crowd interest and a momentary respite from routine. I kept walking, sometimes concentrating on the upper stories of the surrounding apartment houses, like an anxious arrival at a party who pretends he spots a friend calling to him from across the room. I tried to smile. Among the swirling faces, a woman of twenty or so—a lovely, scruffy woman—looked up from the curb, her hands in her pockets. She did a double-take and then spat into the gutter.

What did these people see? A provincial capital of several million, Changchun had a small foreigner population, perhaps one hundred—counting the 14 Westerners I lived with, the college students, and the engineers at the auto plant. And these were recent arrivals, part of the country's newest drive for Modernization. Yet even so close to the university, on Zhonghua Road, I encountered that fascinated and shocked fixity. From all sides, my presence pressed on me the weight of history, stereotype, deprivation. For many, I was the first "outsider" they had seen in years; for some I was the first ever, and I assumed that I represented much more of the U.S., of the West, than I wished. I felt my gestures becoming specimens. Never before had my face, it seemed, so little to do with me.

In this regard, though months passed, it was always my first morning in China. Even in what I came to call "my neighborhood," bicyclists gawked, sometimes crashing. Circles gathered and leaned to watch my left hand write a postcard. In Nong An, a small town near Changchun, crowds of 50 or 60 followed my companion and me through a department store (some loitering on the first floor as we went to the second and third, knowing we had to come down); 200 or more gathered around us on the railroad platform as we waited to depart.

Every Westerner faced this seemingly relentless attention. For instance, on a visit to the nearby city of Harbin, one of my British colleagues, Sylvia, went into the train station bathroom to change her tampon. Women congregated before the doorless stall while she squatted over a square hole in the concrete.

The staring decreased in intensity only in those more cosmopolitan places—like Beijing and Guangzhou. And even when such scrutiny wasn't readily apparent, I was reminded that *someone* was looking. In a neighborhood restaurant, for instance, I once prepared to light a Polar Bear cigarette—to test the taste of the cheapest brand the street vendors carried. A patron bounded from his table 20 feet away, blew out my match and offered me his brand from a long, gold pack—begging me to throw away those "dangerous" smokes.

Sometimes, I ignored the staring, trying to ignore the fact that I was ignoring. The unvaried gaze was only frightening, or eerie, on a nearly empty back lane. Occasionally, I berated the crowd, shouting nonsense or my culture-shocked frustrations—strutting, spinning like a lunatic. This delighted many. A few times, I performed the only song any Chinese requested of me, my one hit (which was every Westerner's one hit): "Take Me Home, Country Roads."

In this age—where no shore exists untouched by human action, where all beasts are penned, dependent on legislation or living only on film—the staring feeds some of the hunger for remoteness, for *terra incognita*. It is a worthy, ancient frontier to be encountered again and again for the first time; and this recurring newness, this potential for discovery, is not the same as reaching for that famous stream into which you cannot dip your hand twice.

The staring helped me appreciate the obscurity of dimly lit streets and, in winter, the bundling up that made everyone appear more generic. It also revealed something, I fancy, about fame—about finding yourself inescapable, publicly identifiable, and stupendously anonymous. Over the months, I grew accustomed to causing a stir wherever I went. Those few times it didn't happen, I was a little like that American TV actor who readied himself in his beach chair to be recognized by a friend of mine. She strolled past, seemingly oblivious, and he slumped back, crestfallen. I, too, had developed such a sugar thirst for being special.

And all this was temporary, surely. The staring would move to some other subject, in some other land and time, as it had for centuries. But when?

How much contact with Westerners would it take before, say, the old woman at the streetmarket no longer refused to sell me peanuts when she thought them too old and unfit? How long before she would hate the tourists and businesspeople the country sought to attract, and for good reason?

That first morning on Liberation street—on that recurring first morning—I was part of the migration of wonder, or at least I like to think so. It was my first morning abroad. What did I expect to see?

I remember waving to a man only wiping a window.

MISTAKEN

In my room in Changchun, seated at my desk in the final, rashy light of an autumn sunset, I opened the packet of photographs I'd just picked up at the kiosk—to savor the images from my summer trip across Tibet. As I looked through the prints, I grew peeved to find (aside from the blurriness and daft framing achieved by my own incompetence) squiggles and black flecks where the person who developed them had scratched and perforated the negatives. Having snapshots developed in the U.S. is a routine thing, part of the convenience industry. But in China things were not so simple—at least not in the small shop whose accessible location drew me. The proprietor's machinery or chemicals or expertise suffered no "quality control." Leafing further through the snapshots, I remembered how, upon entering the kiosk, I'd found the old man behind the counter handing three of the prints from what turned out to be my envelope to two girls warming by a knee-high stove. The girls had reviewed the prints with great interest as I'd fished out my receipt and waited for my glasses to defog, and this hadn't troubled me. I had accustomed myself to their curiosity about what the foreigner might have seen through his viewfinder. There in my room at the compound, envisioning no recourse for the damaged photos, I thought, *be satisfied that you have them at all*—in this, becoming a little bit Chinese.

It was then I came upon the photo of the charred man—several photos, in fact, also black and white. He sprawled prone, half on a bed and half on the floor, dressed in what appeared to be the pants of a uniform, perhaps military. What remained of his torso was naked. The burned end melded with the burned portion of the bed and the ashy clutter on the floor. The wall behind seemed clean, exceedingly bright.

No wonder the girls and old man at the kiosk showed such interest. Did they know this was a mixup? Or did they think me just a morbid stranger?

The stripe down the side of the dead man's pants whispered that perhaps I'd been dealt pieces of police or military business. Who was he? Where was he? And who took these pictures?

I scanned the negatives, finding none of him. A few negatives from my trip had no prints. They nestled in another photographer's packet, surely. But whose packet?

The whole street seemed then to stare into my darkened window. I felt oddly ashamed: everyone somehow must know I possess these appalling pictures. In the morning, I thought, I could return them to the kiosk, and after laboring to explain, after embarrassments and the mayhem of politeness, the matter would be done. I sat with this for a moment, and then burned them in the ashtray.

OLD HANDS, *CIRCA* 1989

On an afternoon in February, I stood with a dozen of my colleagues in the parking lot of St. Brygyda's Church in Gdansk, waiting for two Solidarity security men, dressed like longshoremen, to give the all-clear signal. When at last it arrived and we entered the side door of the rectory, one by one, we were met by an experienced handshake from Lech Walesa. He wore a gray tweed sportscoat like those made in Lodz, a Solidarity badge on one lapel, the Virgin Mary on the other. He was grayer, rounder, shorter than in photographs—a disarmingly formal uncle.

Cheesecake and coffee had been laid out on a side table with lavish china. At the end of the small conference room, Walesa sat on a wooden throne, his hands on the arm rests cupping the brows of carved lion heads. For an hour he answered our polite, aura-softened questions, baiting us, challenging us to be more pointed. Witty, charismatic, ego-happy, he spoke crisply, in segments measured for translation (though sometimes he continued too quickly, overrunning his translator). He was ready with an illustrative anecdote or metaphor, some drawn from the conversation at hand. Obviously, he had grown into his role as a world figure—labor activist, Nobel Laureate, and personification in the U.S. of anticommunism. Yet, on that day, Solidarity had not yet been re-legalized; the Communist regime had not yet crumbled; he had not yet been elected President of Poland. So as a favor to one of his translators, he met with us, nobodies.

It's him! I kept thinking, somewhat nonplussed. Resisting this,

I remembered Mr. Du, the mad stamp collector from the Foreign Affairs Office in Changchun. At my room one evening, he pointed to a postcard of Marilyn Monroe on my wall.

"She is beautiful," Du said. "Is she famous?"

After the interview, Walesa signed autographs and shook more hands. I went for a second slice of cheesecake and turned to find him and Louise—who met her husband in the dormitory during martial law in 1981—standing with their backs to me, posing for a snapshot. Just before the shutter snapped, Walesa pinched her on the behind.

Later, in the summer after the elections, I stood in line, in Warsaw, to pass through a metal detector at the American ambassador's residence. The President of the United States had come to Poland to celebrate the end of communism and offer some financial aid—much less aid, as it turned out, than some Poles had imagined. On his way to visit Walesa in Gdansk, the President would pay a brief thank you call on embassy personnel, including Polish nationals, gathered for morning coffee on the ambassador's lawn.

A few weeks before, the Chinese authorities had massacred unknown numbers of students peaceably demonstrating in Tiananmen Square for relatively mild democratic reforms and the opening of political dialogue. I wondered about my students in Changchun who had begun speaking of communism as "a false religion" and of the need for greater freedom. I thought of my friend Liu on the night before I left China, remarking wearily, "God gave people rights, but Chinese people don't have the right god." Where was he now? We'd exchanged several letters before his replies had ceased without warning. Perhaps the censors had intercepted my letters to him and he'd gotten into trouble for corresponding with a foreigner.

President Bush was an "old China hand," having served as a

diplomat in Beijing, but he seemed eager only to placate the Chinese camorra, still chasing the West's dream of opening the biggest target market on the planet.

Bush, the First Lady, Secretary of State Baker, and his wife arrived two hours late. Like stuffed debutantes with their escorts, they posed for photographs. Long before they had appeared, of course, the scene had been arranged by the not-so-Secret Service. A perimeter was set up around the patio of the house. If anyone crossed it, a spokesman said, "We'll move the President away, and you won't get to see him."

Still wet-headed from his shower, Bush thanked all present and commiserated with the group about hardship abroad, alluding to his years as a diplomat in China. He stripped to his shirtsleeves and moved toward the perimeter with the awkward good intentions of a CEO at an overly formal, overly large company picnic. Followed by Mrs. Bush, he worked his way down the line awaiting handshakes.

Maybe it was the general excitement, but I thought of the drunken soldiers on duty the night before at the Grave of the Unknown Soldier. They had been celebrating the evening with vodka, perhaps because they stood so close to the Victoria Hotel, which swarmed festively with the media and various diplomatic staffs. One of the soldiers, approximately twenty years of age, glanced over his shoulder after he and his fellow guard had downed a shot. From the military headquarters across the broad, concrete piazza, a senior officer marched toward them. Both scrambled to their stations, stumbling to attention, rigid and swaying.

Suddenly, Bush paused before me. As I shook the old China hand's hand, I was overcome by the deepest desire to laugh—to let fly a silly roar at the power which swallowed the man and those, like me, impressed by its trappings. It would be an unforgiving, self-protective *haw-haw* at the portable satellite dishes, the press corps planes, the fleet of staff cars shipped in from Berlin, the parade route plotted so that no hospital, with his blood type, lay more than a few minutes away, the secreted gunsights leveled on me at that moment.

I nodded politely at the President.

SHEPHERD

On the train back to Lodz from a shopping trip to Warsaw, Ola, my assigned shepherd from the university, lamented that the country and people will never change.

"Just read the accounts of Poland by English visitors in the seventeenth and eighteenth centuries," she said, slouching and staring out the window. "They all say the same thing, and it's true today. *The Poles are a laughing and morose lot—with fetching women.*"

We sat quietly for a while, watching the passing fields.

"So," I finally asked, "Where did you get this chip on your shoulder about Poland?"

She guffawed, and then looked at me, slightly bewildered, as though she had never pondered such a question.

"I don't know, exactly," she said. "When I got back from Canada after high school, I felt like a real outsider. I knew I needed to get involved and make the best of things. All that stuff. And I did, eventually. In 1980, the students here went on strike and occupied the main building of the university. It was a high time all over the country. People were optimistic about Solidarity and throwing the Communists out, about getting control of things again.

"I didn't really care about Solidarity or the Communists or any of that. I'm not political. But I joined my classmates in the main building. I wanted to feel some sense of belonging.

"After a while, it didn't seem right somehow. I mean, emotionally right. One of my friends convinced me that it was okay to go home. So after two days, I did.

"My father is a Party man, a total company man, who's never stood for anything in his life. But when I came home, he was furious that I 'quit.' That was the word he used. He may as well have told me I had betrayed him. It was obvious that's what he felt.

"Anyway, I went back to the strikers, but they wouldn't let me in the building."

We sat quietly again, but some channel had been opened. Later, Ola spoke at length of how her parents badgered her about why she hadn't had a child, like her younger sister.

"I've got nothing in common with my sister. She spends her time gossiping and standing in meat queues. She doesn't read. She doesn't think. If I had a baby, that would be it. I'd never get out of Lodz. Maybe that's just what I should do and forget everything else."

She then drifted onto her husband Marek's problems at work. Local party leaders were pressuring him to spy and report on his colleagues. He had resisted thus far, but he might lose his job if he didn't cooperate. The stress, she thought, might be causing his heart arrhythmia.

"I asked my mother for advice," Ola said, "and she told me, 'A wife must support her husband in everything. It's a wife's duty.'"

Ola then explained that she and Marek first became lovers because she wanted to help him end a relationship he didn't have the courage to finish, a relationship with her best friend, also named Ola.

She claimed that Marek is "sentimental and cruel." She sees herself as the activist in their marriage—all the while praising him for his "surgical mind," his "down-to-earth perspective," and his ability to "cut through things."

"In a way, I made him," she said. "I taught him English."

As summer approached—with the date of my departure from Poland—Ola and I had regular lunches at the semi-Chinese restaurant in Lodz. Through it all, she maintained a strained chipperness. Finally, she announced that she and Marek had agreed to divorce, though they had not yet filed. He had moved in with his mistress from the British Council. The general change in the country, the opening of things, it seemed, had inspired them to act.

Despite these political and personal liberations, however, Ola found herself constricted. Her colleagues at the university pressured her to join Solidarity now that it was in power. At one of our lunches, she waved the application form they had sent to her office mailbox.

"I'm not political," she said, "Nobody I work with understands this. Nobody will allow it."

More important, Ola said that she could tell no one at the university—or elsewhere—about her separation from Marek.

"I just say everything is fine at home when they ask," she explained, wearily. "They're not going to sponsor a divorcee for a visa abroad. If I want out of Lodz, it's best now for me to appear nonchalant and play the satisfied wife game."

When I left Lodz, at last, for the final time, Ola insisted on seeing me off. It was a warm, sunny morning—unlike all the routine mornings I'd ridden the express to Warsaw and the embassy. I fortified myself against effusiveness, remembering how as I bid farewell to my gathered friends in Changchun, I had suddenly embraced Xaio Wei, my assigned maid and odd intimate, stunning her into a distressed solemnity and giving myself another lesson about presumption.

Ola shored up her barriers as well. On the platform, we crushed each other with a quick, tearless hug, and flew apart like exploding bolts. We joked. We shook hands. I promised I'd keep in touch. She promised as well, her eyes rolling back into their habitual furtiveness. As usual, the departing train rumbled past my apartment house on Tuwima Street, past the park where I'd jogged daily in archless Polish track shoes, past the red-brick clothing factory with the huge sign *Ariadne*—Ariadne who gave Theseus the idea of unrolling a ball of thread to mark his way in and out of the labyrinth.

Two years later, Ola managed to acquire a temporary visa and a scholarship to graduate school up East. She also had a new lover, Linda, a wry and sturdy woman from Dublin who accompanied her to Florida to visit me and my new lover, Lisa, and Disney World, and to further review the country in which they were seeking permanent residency.

"Poland has changed fast," Ola said. "You can make your peanut butter and jelly sandwiches there now. You can get your Perrier. It used to be that connections mattered. Now it's money.

"But in many ways, it's the same old shit. Worse, even. People there still say, 'Let's be friends but settle like Jews.' Someone burned down a home for AIDS children outside of Warsaw, twice. And, of course, the Catholic Church is in power now.

"It's no place for me, just like Ireland is no place for Linda. Even my colleagues back in the university there don't know I'm divorced. They don't know me at all. They ask, 'Is Marek a feminist?'"

I drove Ola to an immigration attorney's office in one of the glass towers in downtown Tampa, passing on the way *The Church of the Avenger*, which advertises nightly seminars on how the Holocaust is a Jewish fabrication. She came out of the interview with the same look she'd had after our demeaning visits to the Polish officials at the passport office in Lodz.

"He told me that if I hoped to get a green card, I would have go back to Lodz and apply for the immigration lottery.

"I didn't tell him this, but it seems I'm ten years too late to be a refugee from the Commies and ten years, or more, too early to seek asylum on the basis of sexual orientation."

Later, she gazed bitterly out the car window, at the waters nuzzling the sea wall along Bayshore Boulevard. I had no idea what next to suggest. Her expertise in slaying bureacratic dragons exceeded mine enormously. "I'm not going back to Lodz," she said, "I'm never going back to stay."

The next morning, just after dawn, she and I and Linda and Lisa canoed down an upper portion of the Hillsborough River, which flows into the Bay not far from where Lisa and I live on Albany Avenue. There, it is a mazy, shallow watercourse through cypress swamps where a whisper equals a shout—a remnant of the Florida before theme parks and retirement villages. Myriad bugs breaking the water's surface flash like bulbs at a rock concert. Pearly ears of split oyster shells glimmer among the lettuce on the sandy bottom. In synch with the clouds, alligators and turtles sun themselves, and timid snakes writhe across the water.

Ola compared the cypress knees to fairy people, the cypress roots to fluted Russian rockets. "The current," she said later, "doesn't seem like it's moving, but it takes you somewhere."

For three hours we passed gently alone under fallen trees and high canopies of branches, some with berries remaining on their most inaccessible tips. Afraid of the water since nearly drowning in a childhood accident, Linda clenched the sides in the front of Lisa's canoe. After a while, she relaxed and finally relinquished her grip to the sights of anhingas clustering on perches, their wings outstretched to dry after a swim.

The moment reminds me yet again of how wonder moves on and makes us dumb enough to speak.

Once in the Treehouse, Later in the Garden

When I returned to the U.S. in 1989, I gathered the few possessions I hadn't liquidated before striking off for China four years earlier, and I moved into the only pleasant place I could afford, an efficiency above a double garage one block from Bayshore Boulevard. I foresaw a long season of enforced parsimony, but my desk in "the treehouse" overlooked my landlord's small swimming pool secluded from the world by congested flora. In the mornings, sea air pulsed gently through my rusted screens, and the languorous, stifling afternoons provoked me to brood and try to settle my soul on a new, worthwhile course. Then the phone rang. It was Sawyer.

"I've been keeping track of you these past few years," he said, "and what I've seen has been pretty impressive."

Sawyer and I hadn't talked since graduate school. In those days, he walked tall, locally, among the fledgling Marxist/Deconstructionists, having already won a prestigious fellowship to study with theorists in Germany. In spite of this, even his peers regarded him as the archetypal *nice guy*. We became racquetball friends, playing once a week and finishing each session with a congenial beer or two.

Sawyer told me that after graduation, he'd turned down a teaching job at Columbia for other ambitions. At present, he worked as an image doctor for a public relations firm in New York that operated discreetly among the highest echelons of American management. "Advocacy," he called it.

"Are you happy with teaching?" he asked. "Are you happy with your life?"

The company had an opening, and he said I was the first person who came to mind. "You're glib," he said, "You can quote things. You're a quick study. You're a natural for this."

How often does that nagging platitude, "It is better to try and fail than not to try at all," spill from those who have succeeded in their endeavors and, most often, remarkably? I hear them and wonder why they do not reveal their failures—for they most certainly have failed somewhere, sometime. I would like to judge how much they really know about risk and perseverance. I want their wisdom for overcoming apparent defeat. I want their insight, not their inspiration—since inspiration, in these instances, is the handiest product of retrospect. The achiever looks over his shoulder and sees most easily his doggedness, not his bewilderment and fury at the debacles that his eventual triumph has transformed now into mere setbacks. Thus, to the listening wanna-be and wanna-do, the achiever can most quickly prescribe further hard work and continued allegiance to dreams, and be done with it.

I speak here, of course, of failure that shapes a life, of deep aspiration and long labor. This is not failure which the painter has in mind when, in an interview, he observes that all paintings are failures, but the failure of the painter, perhaps, to show his life's work, bad or brilliant, and to gain the platform of an interview. It is the agony of the entrepreneur who mortgages everything on his belief in his idea and who sees the whole shebang vanish into the debit column. It is the athlete who submits himself completely to a future in the game only to be jettisoned by the team in the final cut. Such failure, it seems, silences various rooms of the soul, of the mind. The rancor it spawns comes down on the imagination like a drowsiness. All the world's attempts to rouse it into the wakefulness of full life and wide feeling—intentional or otherwise—seem to one in this dozing state a kind of harassment, answered with narcoleptic sarcasm or a lame swat.

I think now that Sawyer considered me fit material not because I possessed the talent, but because I had been ferocious on the racquetball court, lunging for each point, most inspired by a need to rally. It wouldn't hurt him, either, to have a friend from his old life around the office.

Sawyer had discovered that he liked power, that he wanted to be an insider. This hunger opened the door of his imagination as university life had not.

"In this business," he said, "I often get to see tomorrow's news today, which is kind of exciting." And, of course, there was the money.

So I sat across the vast, black desk from Sawyer's boss, Mr. Influence, in his nineteenth floor office with two corners overlooking Madison Avenue. Mr. Influence chatted on the phone for several minutes, his expression like that of a beagle with a bad back. I suppressed my urge to grin at the wonder of the moment, which seemed a parody of a parody of the American success story, "a made-for-TV movie movie," my friend Ola called it.

I was flattered and out of my depth. Years before, I had rejected the corporate route, the life of "getting and spending," according to Wordsworth. The conventional wisdom of youth rebellion in the late 1960s—which I had largely witnessed on television—impelled me, like so many, to fly from the complacency of the dreaded status quo. I also sought to avoid what seemed the equally compromised—though far less lucrative—life which I believed spawned the regret suffusing my parents' tone.

Once, some friends were showing me the ruins of a large garden in the glen behind their new house near Atlanta. As we walked through the thick wet grass, the sweet odor of rotted blueberries issued forth on the slightest breeze—berries fallen from the previous summer and scattered somewhere underfoot. We stepped and sought another sugary waft, and just as suddenly met the searing, acrid aroma of spearmint, a harsh, almost sharp taste that hung on, that caused one to spit. On occasion, the breeze would bring the luscious fruit chased by the obliterating herb. At other times, the scents entwined. Hope and resentment: the blueberry and the spearmint. This is the garden of a certain suffering, a certain ruin. The failure walks here, wherever he walks, and talks and tastes the sweetness in his bitter breath.

As of this writing—1995—I am a failed author. That is, I am a writer in middle-age who has published none of his books. One of my closest writer-friends tells me that this notion of failure is destructive and nonsensical, that it is male and enmeshed with skewed American notions of success. After all, I am a tenured professor at a university, healthy, delightedly married, and these things do, indeed, make me grateful to fate. She is right, as one is who has wisely devised clear boundaries of care. But I am not wise. "If your books were published," she observes, "they still might be ignored, or dismissed by critics. This way, you write as you please, for your life. What's a book, anyway? A pebble tossed into the ocean." Again, she is right, and, again, I am unwise and enmeshed in my garden.

It was one thing to reject money, to lodge myself in graduate school and mutter in moments of doubt, "You could succeed at that other kind of life, if it were really worth pursuing." It was quite another to have That Other Life unexpectedly offer itself. Embarrassingly, some early, long-banished wishes responded to the call.

I discovered that I wanted to sit across the desk from Mr. Influence and not be found wanting, and that in this desire I was like
Lance Correard in China, whose frustrated lunges at such tradi-
tional success in the U.S. and then Asia had seemed pathetic and
destructive and unworthy of respect.

So while Mr. Influence talked on the phone and looked me
over, I sat impassively like old Mr. Xu during salary negotiations at
the Foreign Affairs Office in Changchun, proud that my experience abroad was proving useful. I had already testified before a
dozen desks behind which my future colleagues measured me
as I tried to measure them—future allies and enemies, nearly all
sheathed in the determination to appear tough enough. With Mr.
Influence, waiting seemed the main test of the interview, since he
chatted briefly with me after he hung up, and I was offered the
job a few days later.

When I accepted and told people that I was moving to New
York for "another foreign adventure," some coveted my opportunity. In many eyes, my new plans commanded a legitimacy not
available to my aspirations as a poet. For some, I was advancing
beyond the schoolmarmish underemployment of trying to convince well-to-do, neglected, poorly prepared college freshmen that
writing was an instrument useful to their futures. I was at last taking up a career, and not just the dubious kind which my old department chair excoriated when he counseled me not to go to
China. Proud, my Grandmother Morrill swore I was destined for
the Senate.

In failing thus, I am certainly an American. "How will I know my
limits," a friend says to me, asking an American question, "if I don't run
up against them?" The American is most defined by the No he, or she,
cannot surmount or undo. If there is wisdom in this, it is in learning
that—no matter your effort—you cannot buy into the good neighborhood

*or ascend to the corner office, cannot throw the touchdown pass or alter
the face that has smiled approvingly in the mirror at the belief that it can
become more beautiful or loved. This is one significant way that the pure
products of America go crazy, slowly, minutely—by discovering what is,
simultaneously, most craved by the individual and most unattainable.
Perhaps that is the ultimate discovery of America.*

"You won't be corrupted," a friend said, softly, when I called
her long distance and begged her to assure me all would be well,
"just changed."

During my interview trip to Manhattan, I had scrutinized Sawyer's life futilely for the worm of change. His wife stood brilliant
and lovely and affectionate still, though her computer business
burgeoned. Their apartment, while expensively large, remained
a cheerful, graduate student jumble. Their daughter, already bi-
lingual and attending a good preschool in midtown, seemed to
mesh happily with their continuing manner of achievement. And
Sawyer . . . Sawyer was nice, still a nice guy.

The City offered its insults and inspirations, its symphonic tab-
loid of office-shrines and inadvisable alleys. Dressed like mythical
upper-management dads, Sawyer and I looked past a paper cup
held under our noses in a subway car—that cup dusted with the
gray film rubbed from silver coins—while another man screamed,
"Don't ignore him! I'll rip your faces off," and my gold cuff links
glowed in shame. I also attended a few fundraisers for my new
company, one under a full moon at the zoo: tuxes and gowns
bending toward the seal tank, professional couples cruising for
introductions, the meal served by unemployed actors. Right
away, even casual social occasions with new friends and associates
always included a successful, unmarried woman in her mid-thirties
carefully pleased to meet a single, straight male with excellent
prospects.

To some, my failure—or my sense of failure—is, no doubt, ridiculous. Defeat of one's aspirations is, at least, an embarrassment for those who witness it as well as those who suffer it. Yet, at its worst, the recognition of disappointment devolves to absurdity and horror. It reminds us that wishing can be treacherous, and it questions the whole enterprise. Ability, to be sure, ordains a dreamer's prospects. A doer writes, operates a company, performs as well as he can; and he or she works at it, hard. But luck is often the shadow of talent and means. It stretches from the dreamer's feet in the sunlight of both accomplishment and debacle—a presence to be acknowledged but just as conveniently undetected among the other shadows of things. All aspirants believe in that accomplishment to which they aspire; they sanctify it with their fealty to their potential. They do not live life according to their own terms but according to the terms of their hope. And they believe that their deepest dreams—the ones for which they sacrifice themselves and others—are not wholly of their own choosing.

The ultimate *NO* to all this ascended a column of tears from the gut as I stood at 10th St. and Broadway, out for a walk while the lease for my new apartment was being drawn up by a stooped, pomaded real estate agent in penny loafers and no socks who resembled a young Richard Nixon. It rose to shatter my fidelity to a reemergent former self and prevent that betrayal before it became entwined with legal commitments. Just before I felt the *NO* climb and spread like a silent yowl across my face, I remember thinking, "I'll never write another poem. I'm going to become everything I hate." Such a prophecy is impossible to fulfill, of course. Had I been 25 rather than 35, I might have been able to ignore it. At a certain point, however, you can't really go back to who you might have been, or were once supposed to be—though you can always assent to the attempt, and the sun still will arc. *YES* and *NO* fail us, as we fail them, equally.

When I was seven or eight, my school, St. Joseph's, held a student fair to raise money for the poor. Among the activities was the Penny Walk. Along the outer walls and in the corners of the school gymnasium, nuns and lay teachers bore hefty glass jars. All those competing marched in a single file counterclockwise around the gym, dropping a penny in each glass they passed. The last student walking—the student with the most pennies to give—received an enticing prize, though I cannot remember now what it was. I joined the line, imagining that I would win. I marched and doled out my pennies. My pockets hung fabulously with them, at least a hundred, perhaps more. Soon, of course—or, more accurately, too late—I began to realize that my resources lacked the necessary, obvious amplitude. Yet I walked and spent my pennies. Each clinked in the jar, a fading echo of hope.

And then I dropped out of the loop. I watched the older students, whom I somehow did not perceive at the start, lobbing the change earned from paper routes and part-time jobs and yard work into the jars. This was how it was to be—from the beginning.

Desolate, I drifted over to the auction stage. Above a mass of my jangled classmates, a nun held one toy after another for shouted bids. Among the extended arms shaking like a cluster of angry pikestaffs, I thrust my arm up suddenly.

"Four cents!" I yelled in the middle of the clamor. "Four cents!" Toy after toy was presented and sold, and with each new item, I cried out my bid: "Four cents!" Until, at last, I heard among the voices only my own voice, hoarse and distant and strange.

The failure finds himself in a similarly childish role—with a similar level of understanding. He has his four cents—however much it really is—and he bids strenuously, pathetically, to get the prize, perhaps ultimately any prize. And then he sits jingling his coins in his ruinous garden.

Sawyer hasn't spoken to me in the years since I left New York to return to Tampa, and only occasionally can I indulge in the illusory comfort that this shunning is the worm revealed at last. Most likely, he merely sees me as weak and the judgment of his aspirations, implied in my withdrawal, worthy of his derision, or erasure. Yet when the oil tanker spews its cargo into the harbor, and Sawyer—or someone like him—talks to the media for the shipper, not exactly lying about the damage, just "advocating," I am grateful to the *NO* for its timely ascent. When the jets depart hour after hour from MacDill Air Force Base at the south end of Bayshore Boulevard, bound for some imperialist task posing as a mission of liberation, it is the job of some Sawyer, somewhere, to sell Garfield Avenue on the nobility and necessity of the enterprise. It would have been my job, too. Now, he and I seem like those classmates in an Eastern European novel from the Cold War era—or like students I knew in China—one of whom joined the Party for its privileges and its pay, and the other who could not.

I haven't regretted forgoing this adventure. At the time, it seemed clear I was choosing freedom over power. I also believed that even the wrong choice, as long as I made it, acquitted me from the mirror's charges of complacency. Yet I sometimes wondered how lazy or cowardly I was in returning to the sequestered backyard dramas of a frog, for instance, struggling unsuccessfully to escape the swimming pool into which it had fallen, while a cat with eyes the color of the water approached it; or the landlord's son and daughter trying to seize the perfect soap bubbles of childhood they had blown into the evening light.

When I seek my way out of this garden—which I do over and over— I tell myself that the point of failure is transcendence, to discover that our true failures are the vain conceptions of our original ambitions. I assert that failure is our general condition—certainly our individual and collective destiny—and, as such, it suggests a common bond. I laugh at my envy's pitiful compass and realize that the expectations which produce it must be equally narrow. All of this helps but does not lessen the distress as much as wondering whether I just need to work more on my prose, train harder, refinance the company.

For a while after I returned, Bayshore Boulevard seemed ruefully small. The gambling ships steamed toward their usual evening of tourist intrigue on the cusp of international waters. Dolphins, which rarely venture far from their place of birth, swirled languidly in the milky shallows. Even the same blind power walker called out, "How's it goin'?" to me like an old friend as I jogged past him, usually near the Academy of the Holy Names. Eventually, I decided that fear of this shrinkage explained why so many people I met in New York who professed to despise the city could not bring themselves to leave it; they believed they would be diminished without it. Though temporary, the shrinkage also showed how much I already enjoyed what I was becoming in New York, how good I would be at it, and how unsettling that potential remained.

At such moments, that other nagging platitude, "Don't wish, you may get it," rises into view, and reminds me how little I have considered the demands which achievement makes of the achiever. Obviously, success of any sort after long failure cannot be the same as triumph without previous defeat. If my four cents were to garner its little prize, I would be cast from the drowsy rancor of my garden. I would be forced to walk in an atmosphere composed of more than the odors of blueberry and spearmint. No doubt I would want to cling to the knowledge they have given me—so loyal they have been, for so long—when I should be asking who planted them there in the first place.

"The One Strong Flower I Am"

They are runaways, throwaways, "problem" teens; culls from meager schools and emissaries from questionable homes; bearers of "emotional disabilities" and lurid autobiographies for which they are medicated elaborately and counseled when possible; products of biology, family, community—of fate, impure and hardly simple.

They have landed here, in the group home school—where Sarah, their instructor, and Bob, her assistant, try to give them enough structure and knowledge to function in the working world beyond graduation. In the middle of this task, for two hours each week, I am to teach them to write poetry.

Poetry: a marginalized art form for marginalized people, I think, as I pull into the school parking lot on the day of our first session. I've taken this assignment because I am a poet and have lived into middle age believing the golden assertions of poetry's proponents: that poetry matters because it somehow enlarges the individual imagination, it articulates the life of the soul, it makes the world cohere. I have believed this because I love poetry, but now I suspect my love is rather effete. What place does poetry really hold in this culture, when advertising is the current school of eloquence, and the metaphor of the marketplace devours all other figures of thought? If poetic art is supposed to be so fine for the soul, I wonder, why don't more people care about it, and practice it? Only the fierce grandchildren of the Beats—who dominate poetry slams and spoken word performances—and coteries of university professors seem interested in it. What would a group of hardening and hurt kids think of a poem? The implication in hiring someone like me is that poetry is, more or less, only self-expression, and self-expression is therapy—something the suffering and disenfranchised need.

I enter the front door of the school—a seedy starter house from the 1940s in a scruffy neighborhood across the bay from Tampa. The organization that operates the school and several runaway shelters in the area subsists on government grant money; thus, the facilities are humble and the salaries slight enough to attract only the professionally transient or morally committed. Once inside, I see that many of the inner walls have been removed, and all those remaining have been painted a calming pale mauve. I'm introduced to a dozen students or so spread strategically across desks and tables, a map of emotional nation-states, I will learn later, alliances and betrayals.

Frankly, I'm scared, accustomed to the hierarchy of the college classroom where no matter how antagonistic or aliterate a student, the professor is still endowed with enough symbolic power to merit general compliance with the day's agenda. But what do I do here if these kids merely sit before me, a Mt. Rushmore of indifference?

I keep the formalities short, and the explanations. This is no land for lecturers. Activity—the pen chasing the completion of the assignment across a page—is my hopeful lubricant. And I have assignments—exercises gleaned from the cottage industry of textbooks on teaching children to write poetry, from my colleagues and friends who have taught for years in the Poets in the Schools Program. All assure me that these teens will want to write about themselves, so we begin with a poem by Donald Hall, "Self-Portrait, as a Bear." Though two of the students, boys, refuse to write, they do so out of a sedate shyness, preferring to sit quietly while the others work. In minutes, the rest of the class produces self-portraits as manatees, junkyards, great white hummingbirds. It seems simple, natural. Each wants to read his or her poem, and it thereafter becomes our custom to "read around" the room after each writing session. Often arguments and fights erupt over who will read next, though some of the students struggle to articulate their words when their turn arrives. One of them, Becky, becomes so overwrought by the wall between her ability to write words and read them that she throws herself down in her chair and shrieks. Seemingly oblivious to her torment, the room explodes into a flurry of waving hands.

After a while, the group senses it is break time, and they scatter into the backyard to shoot baskets while Bob monitors them. Hoping to gauge how I'm doing, I remark to Sarah that the kids seem talented and excited. She is a matter-of-fact woman in her fifties, who will prove wonderfully enthusiastic, but today she is tired. "These kids are worse off now," she says, "than a couple of decades ago. They've got dysfunctional *extended* families. And it's difficult for us to deal with such a mixed bag of students. Some of them are brilliant but emotionally troubled, some are just dull. Others are needing a lot of repair. Some are, I'm afraid, certifiably loony."

The students return, careening and sweating from the court, and it takes a few minutes to settle them. Lee Ann, a glib powerhouse of 16 is "cracking" on Jed, a short, doughy boy who is clearly an outcast of the group. All the ridicule is sexual, and Bob tells me later that my sway as the stranger in town helps him cut off the teasing sooner than usual. I then continue with another exercise, using Larry Wiowode's poem, "A Deserted Barn," which begins "I am a deserted barn." They are to replace the barn with their own metaphor.

They write and then read—"I am a VW van," "I am a brain in a jar"—and when it is time for me to go, I'm elated. Though two boys have shied from writing, the rest of us have begun, successfully. The group wasn't so threatening, I tell myself. I want to thank them, but a number of the kids have already preoccupied themselves with other activities, peering into a workbook or a computer game. There is no ceremony of parting, as I'd like. I want copies of their poems, but I'm unsure about how to ask for them. I'm afraid of these kids still, afraid to pry and uncertain what proximity is allowable. I depart feeling as though I've given of myself honestly, yet I peer back at myself with some unease from the rearview mirror.

The following week I arrive with poems by William Blake for Sid, whose writing from the previous session sounded a little like some of the *Songs of Innocence and Experience*, but Sid has been removed from the program, no explanation given. In his place, I find Charles, who has a history of glue-sniffing and marijuana use. He's reentered the program, arriving from his family home infested with so many lice that his head has been shaved. He looks a little like a detention camp internee but wears huge, cascading shirts and vast shorts the crotch of which arches just above his knees—a surrounding intentionally too large, I imagine, so he can never grow into it. Over the coming months, he retains a stupefied gentility, and though I ask him frequently to participate, he declines. Closer to graduation than the other students, he sometimes leans over workbooks he must complete to gain his high school equivalency certificate. Often, he stares absently into space. Sarah tells me that Charles "has come a long way" from being the feral thug who ranted and slugged any face he didn't like. I wonder what he will do after graduation, what kind of clothes he will be able to wear in the world. There is hope, Sarah says, to get him into a trade right away. In the meantime, he becomes a spirit of absence that hovers over the room, the available noncontact.

On this day the talk turns to issues of racism. I've learned already that I must be willing to forgo any lesson plans and adopt some scheme that coopts the mood of the room, so I decide that we shall read poems by Langston Hughes and Lucille Clifton—which receive only mild interest. All present declare discrimination criminal. They know about being outcasts. And though everyone in this class is white, they know something about people of color since the group homes in which they live are run by two black couples with a loose religious affiliation. Still, the kids line up against each other on the slightest pretext—often based on adolescent sexual cliquism—and they think nothing of verbally stoning one of the group. Of the greater world of issues and movements, of ideas and possibilities and socially approved ambitions, they are mostly ignorant, corralled by their age and circumstances into a self-involvement at once crucial and, it seems, stunting.

To shift the tone of the session, I have them write their version of Wallace Stevens's "Thirteen Ways of Looking at a Blackbird." Sibyl, the 15-year-old daughter of recovering heroin addicts, drives into the page as she writes. Bob tells me that she has composed many poems on her own. She struggles with her studies and her moods, damaged by her parents' self-abuse. She bragged one day when members of the class boasted about how young they were when they first smoked crack or dropped acid, "Hey, I was born an addict." Still, unlike Charles, she generally exhibits a sturdy work ethic, probably because her father has been pushing her in that direction. He counsels recovering addicts and knows the value of discipline. So, today, Sibyl is eager to achieve and move on, diligent no matter how wavering her course. She writes:

Five Ways of Looking at the Left Hand

1.

Plump, the shortest
of your kind.

2.

Who are you?
Why do you point
so rudely?

3.

Bad, Bad, Bad!
Keep yourself down
you are not wanted!
Don't express yourself.

4.

To be or not to be,
Will you or will you not,
that is the question.

5.

Baby! Baby!
So you are the baby.
Oh, how you depend on your family,
the four of us!

During the read around, the group begins to unravel. Sarah sees it long before I do, and as soon as possible, she intervenes. She directs the class to a video on the life and poetry of William Carlos Williams. On the stand below the television, subject titles of cassettes outline the agenda of warning and reform—AIDS, Understanding Your Anger, STDs, Contraception, Gangs.... Sarah says she needs the television to draw the group together. The light of the screen, the action, focuses their attention as no other force can. "It tames them," she says. Though its effect is temporary, they behave better under its watchful eye than under the policing gaze of the institutional point system, an economic paradigm in which instead of money, one earns points and, thus, privileges, for good behavior. As the video concludes, with long passages from Williams's later work—quite beautiful but complex and abstract—I assume we will hear the kinds of remarks sometimes uttered by certain students at my university: "boring," "kinda long." But there is an amazed silence, some of it emanating from visual sedation but some from another source. "That was gorgeous," says Jed, the group pariah, almost sighing, "really, awesome."

As the weeks unfold and spring bursts forth with the purple blossoms of the jacarandas near the school, the sessions assume their individual shapes yet evolve into a single drama of manifold relations. Each time I approach the house, I look toward the front window to gauge the conditions inside, hoping for a wave or smile. I am met at the door with poems—assigned and written privately—by Jed, Sybil, Tommy and others, and I begin collecting them, though I'm hardly up to the students' enthusiasm, the neediness that is flooding my way. Jed, for instance, begins each session with the question, "What shall I write?" and he lavishes whole hours on the first subject I suggest. Bob says that Jed's family scattered and his grandmother cares for him on the weekends, which amounts to her locking him in his room because she fears his rages. Jed tells me that he writes because he plays guitar and wants to start a band. On the computer's auto design game, he fashions a racer for me. It brakes well but is endowed with so much speed, he can't control it. He takes me aside to say he remembers a movie about Walt Whitman, *Beautiful Dreamer*, starring Rip Torn.

Clearly, he craves any kind of male attention, and I try to balance his attachment against the demands of the group and my own desire for emotional elbow room. One day, he notices the fountain pen in my pocket and asks if he can examine it. The pen was moderately expensive, a gift from my wife. I had been advised at my orientation to the program not to bring valuables into the school because they could be stolen easily. "These kids are survivors," the case worker said, "they can be savvy about getting what they want." This is the first day I have forgotten to leave the pen in my car. I hand it to Jed, and he uncaps it with his thick hand, touching the nib to the tip of his index finger. I cringe inwardly, fearing that he will somehow damage it, ashamed that I'm seeing him as some kind of ape holding a glass egg. But he writes his name slowly, delicately. "Boy, I'd sure like to have a pen like that," he says, passing it back to me. He generates poem after poem, probing himself, and I encourage him, undeservedly proud, wondering where his words will lead him, and us.

> When I take off,
> I have a secret place to stay,
> I have a big bush that totally surrounds me,
> I made a bed out of straws,
> I never was seen by anyone,
> I always saw them,
> I sometimes spent all day there,

It got lonely and sad,
I had no one to talk to,
Just like everyday of my life,
I can smell the leaves and straw,
I can feel myself get pricked by the straws,
I get bitten by spiders and ants,
This is how I feel everyday of my life,
When I wake up the next
Morning I feel in pain and sad;
I feel dirty as a bum,
Everytime I see a cop car,
I dive in the bushes,
I hate that feeling
of not being liked everyday of my life.

More and more, I try to avoid gestures that mark me "the teacher." As often as the group can sustain it, we read from Walt Whitman, Elizabeth Bishop, Etheridge Knight, Joy Harjo and others. But I want to help open whatever gates are possible into the group's most pressing experience and crucial perceptions, and I want to strip poetry of the institutional authority employed by countless bad teachers to unknowingly humiliate and alienate their classes. I think of the middle-aged woman in the post office at my university, who one day picked up a book of poems I received in the mail and, upon learning what it was, still opened it but asked, "Are these poems I can understand?" Whatever power poetry has, I think, must be for the students to grasp. It cannot be delivered by dictum or hearsay.

So I ask them to write narrative poems based on postcard images I bring in, and later they draw maps of their houses and neighborhoods, composing from the details they unearth there. The exercises migrate from the ostensibly impersonal to the intimate and back again, seeking to extend both territories. Sybil, Lee Ann and Teresa drift onto the subject of drinking. Teresa doesn't finish her poem. Instead, she is eager to tell me that she got drunk first at 13, with her father, and did a striptease for him with two other girls that evening. She then tries to retract the statement as her initial pride fades. Lee Ann recommends Advil and orange juice for hangovers. She, too, struggles with finishing her exercises but not because words elude her. She pours forth increasingly monumental monologues, sometimes captivating the group, especially the females. She bounces into an admirable impression of Lily Tomlin as Edith Ann. She declaims television ad copy and reproduces the chatter of emcees, pitch men, news commentators—becoming a parodic oracle mouthing the detritus of public expression, the most expensive phrases engineered. Part of her, I think, wants to *be* television, to possess its power to command attention. The daughter of a single mother who is a stockbroker, she offers tips on mutual funds and smart buys, all tinged with a sweet, manic loathing. Inside her notebook, which features Einstein on its cover, she has written in hundreds of lines the words "shut up!"

During one of her performances, Tommy, who is usually unable to focus on any task for more than a few minutes, bends unwaveringly over the postcard he has selected and the dictionary he has taken down from the shelf. I leave him alone, not wanting to stem what will be his longest period of work in my presence, hoping he will produce more than his usual ten to twenty slim lines. His poems invariably begin with "I am a . . .," as if each of his poignant, dashed-off compositions were another attempt at initial self-definition, a first level of naming he can't transcend.

While he labors, I think of the map he drew of his house, and his explanation of it.

"This is Dad's room, I'm not allowed to go in there. This is

Grandma's room, I don't want to go in there because she smells. This is the porch, where I go if I'm allowed out."

Earlier, Sarah told me that Tommy's dad is, in fact, his gay uncle who "rescued him from the West Coast." Tommy's map was little more than a sketch, a cluster of blank squares. I encouraged him to elaborate, but he froze before the prospect.

Eventually, Tommy presents me with the piece that has so preoccupied him. No poem this time, but a rough translation of the caption on the back of the postcard, a Russian postcard, which he has executed by replacing the Cyrillic letters with Arabic, aided by the dictionary. So smart, so truly beautiful, he possesses many of the qualities which our culture rewards richly, yet his meteoric application, his constant fidgeting, cast his future in doubt. Were he considerably duller and plainer but steadier and driven toward advancement, there would be more places for him.

Laughter turns us toward the room at large. Sybil, Lee Ann and Teresa—sometimes buddies, just as often mortal foes—have put their hair in pigtails, and are hamming it up. I capitalize on the moment, put all to work on poems about them. Lee Ann writes:

> *I like pigtails. They make me remember.*
> *Remember what? Well, I never*
> *wore pigtails as a child. I never*
> *was a child. I was reading Forbes*
> *magazine by the time I was 9.*
> *A childhood is what I've always wanted.*
> *So if I'm crazy like a kid, just*
> *take it in stride. Accept it. I enjoy*
> *acting like a 3-year-old. Pigtails*
> *are not part of me. They are me, free,*
> *flowing and sometimes hard to tame. . . .*

Sammy, a cute, wispy boy on whom Sybil has a crush this week, writes a rap about pigtails, which he belts out, and the room roars. At this moment, R.J. rumbles from the bathroom. Immense, stereotypically doltish, he can be violent, Sarah tells me, but I have only seen the gentle side, his pathetic confusion once when he sniffed his armpits not quite furtively after he had been teased by the girls about smelling bad. He calls me "sir," and says about his compositions such things as, "this doesn't suck too much, does it?" The map of his house and neighborhood is a lattice-work of thick, layered walls, perhaps as invisible to anyone else as the myriad emotional walls in this classroom. In two weeks, he will be removed from the program suddenly, his foster father collecting his articles, placing them in the car and then telling R.J., "You, you can walk home." But now R.J. lumbers into the middle of the class, into the spotlight of attention, grinning triumphantly, his hair rubber-banded into three prongs. The group erupts gleefully, and soon all the boys with hair enough are wearing multiple pigtails.

A month later, I hear, in passing, from one of the administrators that a group performance has been scheduled. Perhaps it has been on the calendar since before my arrival, but the sidelong quality of the announcement makes me wonder why anyone thinks a public reading by these students is possible. The sessions in the previous weeks have grown more chaotic, reflecting a partial decline in the power of the point system to encourage compliance and an increasing strictness at the group homes, where chores have assumed a boot camp magnitude. Lee Ann has tried to smuggle marijuana into the girls' home, inside a teddy bear. She has run away with Sammy, and both have returned after ten days, Lee Ann slightly droopy from medication, Sammy still clinging to his repugnant "gangsta" persona. Becky, who still labors to read her writing aloud, is back also, having been committed to the local psychiatric unit for depression and suicidal inclinations.

Anger tinges the insistent calm of the mauve walls, and its colors stain the atmosphere suddenly, repeatedly—a kicked desk, a thrown book, an uprising of insults. The seduction of "acting out" gathers momentum, and Sarah divides the room, drawing boundaries like an imperial arbiter. One of the administrators tells her that all the talk of suicide is just a form of manipulation, though she *should* respond to it. The kids seem black-eyed with exhaustion and an unwilling resignation. "They've taken all my points," says Teresa, "and how many more dishes can I wash?" I look on the board which displays the total points earned by each student. Level 7 is the top. Two students hover at Level 4, two at Level 2. The rest lie at Level 1.

More than before, I confront the emotional tone of the group and improvise, fashioning individual assignments on the spot with those willing to work. In this, I'm like that man on the old *Ed Sullivan Show*, who kept a dinner plate spinning on each of a long row of flexible poles, dashing up and down the row, swirling now this pole, now that one, hoping to keep the whole shebang spinning. And there are crashes. One day, I shout at the class to force its attention into some kind of consensus. At the break, Sarah asks me how I am, a little nervous about my having yelled. I tell her that I'm probably just tired. "Doesn't it get to be a bit much?" I say, "Doesn't it take more than it gives back?"

"I get money," she says softly, flatly. And I think of the wife of one of my colleagues, who admired me for my work with troubled youth, until she learned that I was being paid, though modestly. Somehow, that fact shifted my labor into another realm and reduced its worth—probably because, in this culture, most artists are expected to adore their calling so much that they are grateful to tender it any time free of charge, while a few of their number generate vast wealth, and concomitant awe, by inventing mass entertainments.

Still, in each class session, small rewards offer themselves. Sammy smiles slightly when I compliment him on one of his lines. Each time I arrive, Jed greets me at the door and asks to borrow my pen, and I always give it to him, though it is not my beloved fountain pen, which I leave in my car. More than once, I witness a light in a face, a flicker of recognition and pleasure in being a maker, and my eyes water with the sentimentality of a childless man. Those who continue to write believe in words as action with an almost fundamentalist zeal. Like some of my more passionate students at the university—students often neglected and abused by busy, well-to-do parents—they sense how many forces have conspired to cut out their tongues, and they hunger, however remotely, for the power of intelligent articulation, the grace and intricate fury of words arranged like a feast to honor that which is humanly true. And this drive fosters a range of dangers, absurdities, triumphs. R.J., for instance, asks me how to write a love poem, because he is swooning with a crush on Sybil, encouraged by Lee Ann who knows that R.J.'s longing, if expressed, will result in his humiliation. Later, I find his attempts abandoned, mercifully, to the wastebasket. At the conclusion of a brawl between Tommy and Becky, which Bob breaks up, there is sudden, vast silence and Jed shouts, as if having an epiphany, "This calls for a poem!" and plunges into writing. At last, Becky breaks through:

Walking Boys

You see Tommy talking, being
by Sammy, following Sammy,
copying Sammy. Tommy, you
get on people's nerves. You
try to show off at the computers,
in your school books. And how
you piss people off.

You see Jed talking, yelling,

shouting. Jed sits and tries
to get you in trouble. Some times
he acts out and does stuff and
blames it on other people.
Then he kisses butt. Jed,
you need to get a life.

You see Harry wearing cross
colors trying to be like this
kid that was kicked out. Harry,
before that kid came you were
nice, fun to be around. And
treated everyone . . . well, almost
everyone . . . with respect. Stop
trying to be like that kid. Just
be yourself.

For a while, I withhold from the students news of the performance, seeking to maximize its impact, since attention spans are
often short and the attraction of newness ephemeral. I browse
through my file of their poems, deciding which I will "suggest"
that each read, uneasy at the notion of a show which is supposed
to give them a "positive experience" while providing good publicity for the organization. During a class break, one of the administrators appears and discusses with Sarah the need to transfer Becky
to a facility with more supervision, but neither she nor Sarah have
reviewed Becky's file because it has vanished in the labyrinth of
social service offices. Acronyms pass between them, part of the
language of agency-world, with its metaphysic of concrete goals,
incremental achievement, measurable processes. Over and over,
the students are, to me, amorphous, and this quality, for better or
worse, collides with the hard surfaces of method. They are being
dealt with, even if they do not, or cannot, fit their spirits to the

system—which makes me wonder how much my file really differs from the one lost.

One day I arrive to find the blinds drawn on the classroom—a strategy, I later learn, imposed by an administrator to sedate the group by reducing outside stimulation. When I announce the performance, most of the class remains impassive, rumor of it having already visited them. Others seem stricken with delight, or terror. All are accustomed to reading aloud, but for many the prospect of their words striking the public air transforms the room from an everyday prison-house into an exceptional haven. For the first time, they recognize the security in their intimacy with their classmates, however painful. I pull up one of the blinds and point to the jacarandas across the street, which now rain their purple blossoms on a battered, gray Mazda parked at the curb. "That's poetry," I say, hoping to encourage them, "the blossoms and the heap." Teresa rolls her eyes and a derisive giggle or two percolates from the group, and we are underway again.

The evening before the performance—which will be part of a volunteer recognition dinner—we hold a rehearsal-picnic at the boys' group home. An old, well-kept dwelling spawned by a vision of large middle-class families residing in ample rooms, its gables project over the live oaks in the backyard. The sight of the kids in these comfortable surroundings seems incongruous, almost inappropriate, but I remind myself that this *is* where they live, the males, at least. The students and the half dozen adults on hand sit quietly at the tables, or banter, or take a second burger off the grill, and the ordinariness of it all both shocks and reassures me. In recent months, the class has been tutored by a dancer also, so it has been decided that the group will read its poems—all on the theme of "my neighborhood"—while enacting a series of choreographed moves. In the driveway, the kids practice their routines, some slightly gymnastic. Paul, the choreographer, has arranged the work so that at various points each of the participants will drift into the foreground of the stage and read a poem. He believes the body contains its emotional history, and movement can retrieve and express it. He knows also the emotional demands required of one who must hold another, or trust others enough to be held, and he has created a piece that encourages the group to confront itself as never before. Thus, the kids will measure a frontier with the various weights and pressures of their words *and* their bodies.

They tumble, they squabble, practicing in small groups. Jed takes Sibyl's hand, tentatively, to execute a turn; her touch is offered like a dark, velvet bag into which he reaches. Becky performs her slow flip aided by Tommy and Teresa, tossing herself backward, turning the world upside down again and again with greater confidence. Even one of the sideliners, Bill, decides he wants to be in the show, though he has written no poem, and Paul devises a place. I chew on the tip of my pen as everybody tries to meet their cues, mum so as not to further complicate the instructions. When we adjourn, at last, for Teresa's birthday celebration, they have walked through the entire program once, a halting jag about which they seem generally elated. The administrator on hand, the woman who had ordered the blinds drawn, appears grateful for their solidarity and bewildered about how to transport it to the school. Teresa grins over her cake. "C'mon, hurry up. Cut it," says the woman who oversees the girls' group residence, "because you all got to get home and have community time."

The next morning, at our usual session, I have the kids rehearse the program once more, but they seem to have forgotten most of their cues, even the order of their readings. Lee Ann leads the disintegration, reconfiguring it into her brand of improvisational nonsense. Jed fumes at what he perceives as limitless irresponsibility. Tommy decides that he will probably make a mistake during the performance and so must withdraw. Everyone seems to be locking themselves in the bathroom and kicking chairs. Yet that evening, they are all veiled in an immense propriety around their dinner tables abutting the stage. Always, they lust for attention, but the kind they will receive tonight—so different from the usual therapeutic regard, or the glare and thump of trouble—cows them. Also, their performance is already underway: each starring as his or her best behaved self. Again, their game faces remind me how much I project onto them my desire for them to be "normal," conventional—generalizing to that end repeatedly from even their smallest gestures.

I introduce them to my wife Lisa, about whom the girls are especially inquisitive. A hundred or so guests arrive, and we eat dinner and hear a few speakers and many thanks, and then it is time. The room darkens. Into a wan spotlight on the stage, Teresa steps sheepishly, perfectly, and begins to recite, "If you walked down my street, you'd hear a cat crying for food. . . ." Most of the kids have not memorized their poems, so they will read them from a typescript. I've made several photocopies of each for the group, especially Tommy, whom Bob has convinced to stay with the program and who has kept trying to sabotage himself by misplacing his copies.

Other spotlights pool on the stage, and several small groups mill with a haunting slowness. Somehow they are transformed by the moment. They are clumsy, bored teens on a street corner of the heart, children fallen from a jungle gym composed of human bodies. Their faces tilt downward, lift wearily to the spotlight as though to receive admonishment from the gods of all that is older and more powerful.

I look out across the audience—an appreciative assembly of volunteers, who know these kids well—and yet I wonder what they hear in these poems. There is in such public presentations an unspoken demand for adequate—*moving*—content. We want these young people to write about their broken homes and wretched parents—their slings and arrows—poignantly, so that we can be moved by their trials and perhaps glean satisfaction at what help we've offered them. Any furious pride and rebellious dignity they might possess, any ferocity they might direct toward us is not allowed. Anger of this sort is rarely recognized as art. There are acceptable confrontations and others which are dismissed as bad manners, rant, or cant.

The program continues, unbelievably adding one small triumph to another. Becky reads for the first time without stumbling on her words. Delicately, with the restraint of one who has almost forsaken explaining, Sybil delivers her poem in which a love "potion" becomes a "poison." Jed lumbers forth, thumbs in his front pockets, a wizened man in a boy's body. The group shifts like a smoky constellation. It jumps and shouts. It leans and stands, a larger unity. And then—partly to show off, partly in genuine good will—Lee Ann, the last reader, offers an elegant impromptu thank you speech on behalf of her classmates, and the show is over.

As the group bows to the generous applause, I wonder about the people beyond this audience—citizens in a culture where pain is quickly sentimentalized, where the suffering of one person is witnessed by millions through media that divorces witnessing from feeling. What would they hear in the words of these children? No doubt it is easy to forget how much these kids are responsible for the current state of their lives. In my months around the group school, I have seen parents frightened and confused by their children, as well as parents brutish and criminal. But in a time of reduced governmental commitment to social programs, where "personal responsibility" is becoming the newest device to relieve us of the reality that we live with others, shouldn't we also ask: How responsible can a child be? If he can't learn responsibility from his parents, if she can't learn to care for herself from them, where will he or she learn if the doors beyond family are shut by a callous society?

Poetry won't save these kids, if it is that kind of saving they need. Still, they recognize that it offers a form of salvation in a culture itself starving for poetry as it accepts weak substitutes and tries to destroy the poetic spirit. Various believers in their voices, these kids will need their belief in order to be heard, to make a better way, even by themselves. Of them all, I think most often of Tommy. During that vital performance, he didn't sabotage himself, and, later, he had to admit to his success, an action he found exceptionally difficult. In the spotlight, among his classmates, he had read his poem with a sad, clear song in his throat, unhurried, his free hand hanging motionless, for once, at his side:

> *I am a rose*
> *my stem is*
> *strong I am*
> *in a field*
> *of daisies*
> *I have*
> *strong roots*
> *I have to*
> *fight for*
> *water my*
> *spirit is*
> *strong I*
> *have delicate*
> *petals I*
> *will always*
> *be the one*
> *strong flower*
> *I am*

Shoes
at Giverny

Lisa and I sat on a low stone bench beside a pebbled pathway, weary and glum. Here in Monet's famous garden congregated the vistas and hues and reflections which the master had transformed into his great canvases, his impressions. Here stretched the grounds which he expanded and tended with immense dedication for over 40 years, making them part of a most enviable residence. And yet, we wondered wordlessly, how could we appreciate his art and life; how could we relish, as he had, those pink tulips or those purple irises redolent beneath a May sky—with all of these people around?

Though the tourist season had not officially begun, gawkers jammed the grid of paths ringing the flower beds. They choked the walkways which circle the famous lily pond and populated every square foot of the house not roped off. We, of course, had been among them, had *been* them, yet our respite on the stone bench seemed to separate us from those other selves and provide us with a momentary purchase on pilgrim desire.

Presumably, these mobs who trudged past, glancing down at us, knew better than we why they had come, for it seemed their numbers testified to a passion for celebrated places which Lisa and I only marginally share. Yet that fame had drawn us from the train at Vernon six kilometers distant and massed us at the stop for Giverny buses with brushed Pennsylvanians and prim Londoners, cursing them under our breath as our hopes for boarding a cheap ride were gently elbowed aside. Why, I wondered, would anyone bother with such struggles when one can see the paintings and gardens in books or on video? Why continue, as we did, suddenly determined by our exclusion from the bus to offer ourselves to the vulturine cabbies perched patiently, eternally at their stand nearby?

According to Claire Joyes in *Claude Monet: Life at Giverny*, the artist "had to garden so as to have a garden to paint." Joyes tells of Monet's deliberate search for a location in which to make art. Monet liked to work *plein air*, close to his subjects, finishing the canvases later in the studio. When he settled at Giverny—a widower with children, accompanied by his lover Alice Hoschede and her dependents—he had already glimpsed a moment of early fame and since then had faced the long stare of poverty, frustration and personal loss. Supported by Alice's modest dowry and advances from his agent, Paul Durand-Ruel, he began by painting views of the neighborhood. This aspiration sometimes met with resistance from locals, who suspected such activity. Several times his studio-boat, docked on the Seine, was set adrift when its moorings were cut mysteriously. On another occasion, apparently out of gleeful malice, peasants tore down the haystacks he was turning into the canvases that would shock Paris and yield his first enduring success. Later, he was forced to purchase the stand of poplars which he transformed into a second celebrated series—because the trees were ready for harvesting and the owners would not wait. Such incidents, Joyes implies, encouraged Monet to fashion a literal landscape removed from external controls.

Before coming to Giverny and afterward, Monet traveled, and it often affected his work. There was the light of Algeria during his early, brief tenure in the military, the canvases of Turner and Constable seen in London during the Franco-Prussian War. Yet at Giverny, the artist founded a world he could discover. It was, in fact, a fortunate retreat *into* the world. Over the years, power lines and poles appeared in the surrounding countryside, the little islands in the Seine vanished when the shipping channel was widened, but Monet's garden became an object of his will, a tool he employed and by which he was fortunately used. As Joyes notes, "When Monet created the water garden, he most likely did not suspect that it would become an inexhaustible source of inspiration for over thirty years. . . . So intimately did Monet become bound up with his lily pond that it would be impossible to say where the gardener's work stopped and the painter's began."

The artist and his subject. Monet tended his garden, his vision, quite literally. For instance, he tarred the road through Giverny because dust from it settled on the water lilies—unhealthy for the plants, no doubt, but also a distortion of their natural color.

Seated on our stone bench, low to the ground, Lisa and I began to notice the shoes of the throngs passing before us: pumps with little bows, penny-less loafers and X-buckled sandals, deck shoes, wing tips, clogs and flats, black boots and pillowy crosstrainers. Some brandished petroglyphs of scuffs; others, the curling tongue or toe. White shoes passed, their wrinkles like those around the eyes of an overpowdered face. Leathers appeared, richly oiled like antique armoires. There were grubby polymers, humbled straps and reknotted laces, sloping soles of obscure age and means, gorgeous designs manufactured only in the smaller sizes. There were sensible and sentimental shoes, delusional shoes, frayed, thonged, with heels to elevate, balance, pitch a body forward.

Spawned by our verticalness, our evolving form, shoes take our weight, our coming here and going back to the lives we've sought to escape or enhance by traveling in the first place. At each step, they represent yet again culture's struggle for dominance over nature, and its compromises. They protect the feet, direct them, tyrannize or flatter them—until the feet wear them down into that brief paradisal agreement, that period when the shoes are broken in and not yet ruined.

"Shoe," derives from the Old English, *scoh*, which in turn developed from the Latin word *obscurus*, meaning "hidden or covered." Neither Lisa nor I am a foot fetishist, but we *are* fetishists of the concealed elements of life, of obscured states and feelings. What seemed sequestered beneath the blank, milling faces at Giverny, we believed revealed itself in the footwear and limbs— the lives—that met below at gravity's behest.

Thus, we witnessed the drama of lining up, pausing, the frustration of bumping into shoes ahead or behind, of being stepped upon. We considered the gait of a pair, momentarily synchronous. A dirty, wrinkled instep passed, the color of wax on certain cheeses. Phalanges aimed ahead, outward, inward, one bearing a broad nail painted metallic pink, extending like a headlight. Matronly pegs labored forth and weaselly tarsi, prudish male hooves cloaked in black socks, harnessed by cheap sandals. The manifold wounds and wear of the supinating and pronating universe displayed themselves: a bunion bulging against a narrow vamp; a band-aid, like a thin slice of ginger root, peeling from a heel or bunched beneath hosiery. Swollen and callused pads

abounded like mobs of hapless immigrants jammed into diminu-
tive holds. Fluted ankles poured like good wine into better crystal.
Amid these, the raised sole and the cane presented itself, as did
the narcotic tread of a group tour, the gargly drag of plastic on
pavement. We watched the pathetic attempt to stop and go back
against the traffic—and the 360 degree scan for misplaced com-
rades or a rendezvous, the decision, the indecision, as to which
direction now.

Sites such as Giverny today provide distinctive bulges on the
relief map of destinations. Specific elsewheres (which one can approach prepared by anticipation and slight study), they invite one
closer to historical personages, perhaps even humanizing them
for the imagination that savors recognitions such as: "He gazed
out this window," or "He, too, admired these Japanese prints and
actually ate from this china." Visiting in the flesh expands the
range of the photographic image and the descriptive sentence.
And who would contend that such museums—such amusement
parks of culture—mean more to the pilgrim informed about, say,
the details of Monet's daily life at Giverny than to the casual
observer who notes with pleasure the hollow squeak there in the
stairs?

The sight of the shoes encouraged me to pull out the notebook I carry in my back pocket, a tough, cheap thing made in
China, with *Little Black Book* stamped in gold on its plastic cover.
When I travel, I keep a different journal than at home. On the
road, my pen sketches others and forgoes the personal yellow jour-
nalism of my usual entries. Writing of travel, if spurred by spirit
and not merely an editor's assignment, is a gesture of hope, of
youth or the youth that remains to us. It dotes on ruins, is a kind
of rhetorical brag. Its personae are showoffs, stoics, plucky blokes
with easy edges, endearing sourpusses. It is a search for a way to

be still. Weariness rarely figures into such literature as a primary theme, though it is a significant element of travel, as is boredom. In our age and under our economic conditions, the great proponents of travel literature champion the antipicturesque. They seek to enumerate defilement, especially the defilement of their dreams. All travel writing, they imply, is about lost Edens, about peeling away illusions, and it conceals its nostalgias. Travel is an industry, like education, and can only be authenticated now by some wickedly clever subversion or irreverent, credible tone.

Unlike browsers swarming the museum store installed in Monet's studio, writers of travel literature are shoplifters. Rather than purchasing coasters and stationary and refrigerator magnets festooned beyond banality with water lilies, they pilfer personal images, anecdotes, perhaps insights. The shoes of the travel writer are not those of the traveler, since travel literature is, ultimately, more about literature than travel. Surely the advent of virtual travel will alter the aesthetic further and cause us to ask, "What qualifies as a journey?" in more than a metaphorical sense. By then we will be entering, in effect, sites—or sights—like those paintings and photographs which now draw us partly by the limited admission they offer us to the worlds they represent.

Of course, Giverny today offers us limited admission as well, since it is not actually Monet's work, but rather a loving restoration, spawned by philanthropic forces, from the untended state into which the gardens lapsed in the decades after his death. It is, then, also a display of resurrection in which we might admire the impulse to remake and keep.

The years at Giverny constituted nearly half of Monet's long life, a period of exultant artistic triumphs and increasing wealth and prestige, as well as myth-making. In his biography of the artist, however, Charles Merrill Mount devotes most of his attention to the first half of Monet's life—where exorbitant human prices were paid by ambition, talent, and arrogance in the hope of acquiring glory. While Monet's eventual marriage to Alice Hoschede proved serene and supportive, it was preceded by a union with Camille Doncieux, whose family banished her from its bourgeois graces for her association with the penurious painter, and whom Monet married, under some duress, after she bore him a son. Camille, according to Mount, was devoted. During their 14 years together, she modeled for him. She shared his sufferings at the hands of derisive critics. She endured his erratic financial fortune and died at 32 of illness brought on by a bungled attempt to abort her second child.

Such sorrow undoubtedly hovered near Monet at Giverny, along with the scourging memory of his years as an outcast desperate for acceptance by the Salon, the institutional arbiter of art. Mount portrays Monet as a remarkable talent who undid himself early by his refusal to submit to the usual art training. For years, Mount says, "he wasted his genius by not disciplining his style nor acquiring real craftsmanship, and the paradoxical conclusion was that when he made discoveries of magnificent and shocking power, public and critics alike were unable to distinguish between them, and the crudities of his personal style."

Yet the artist and the public came to terms at last, and Monet, also a master marketer and salesman, knew how to guide the new momentum this understanding spawned. During his lean years, he had repeatedly, exhaustively begged from friends and acquaintances, forcing his pictures on unwilling buyers, wresting advances. The lessons of this period never left him. When the opportunity arose to capitalize, he pitted agent against agent. He engineered his shows for their maximum sensationalism, making them into early forms of media events, powered by elite gossip, the aesthetic conformity of collectors invested in the fashionable. In this, he surpassed his contemporaries and made way for the collapse of the old system of artistic credentialing. *Impressionism*, a term coined in derision, became the epithet for the greatest creation of nineteenth century French art, and Monet was credited as its creator. According to Mount, the painter's shock tactics, his economic drive, his genius with color, and the development of new chemically treated hues made this possible.

And so—keeping his family greedily close at hand—the artist built his garden. Aspiring Monets jammed the garrets and cafes of nearby Vernon. Luminaries, such as John Singer Sargent and Theodore Butler, paid their homage at Giverny. In later years, the prime minister Clemenceau sat beside Monet at the lily pond during his Sunday visits, talking of the past. Through it all, including the death of his son and, later, of his beloved Alice, Monet continued to work and grow as a painter. Joyes and Mount both describe a household conforming to the artist's regimen—whether Monet rose before dawn, as he did for many years, or at midday, as was his wont later. In his triumph, Monet made of Giverny a place for the artist's fruitful solitude, for the art of staying put, and this—however selfish—was ultimately a group project. Never reluctant to portray the pleasures of bourgeois life, he sometimes employed family members as models, at leisure in a boat or around a lush, sunlit lunch. In later years, his stepdaughter Blanche painted side by side with him, changing his canvases as the light changed. As he labored on his last great project, the water lilies—his gift to the French nation—she retrieved the brushes he had hurled into the pond, stricken by doubt about the value of the work, frustrated, an old man who, despite three cataract operations, remained nearly blind.

"The long years of patient exercise . . ." writes Mount, "had borne fruit. Poverty and death had been no wasted ordeal. His absolute unshakable confidence in himself had prepared him to reveal poetry in every triviality." It is this power of perception that every artist seeks. Monet painted surfaces, aware that they obscure and reveal. It is difficult to imagine him—or any artist—reviling the adulation which fortune granted him for this feat. He constructed his garden, his vision, as much to draw the larger world to him as to keep it at bay. Wouldn't he now relish these shoes beating a path to his gates?

Seated on the bench, Lisa and I realized that, though we could not have known it, we came to Giverny for the shoes, for what their unexpected appearance would urge us to consider and seek to know. This seemed in the spirit of the place, for, after all, Monet's art implores us to see anew. The shoes were another series of impressions—variations on a theme of wandering. And each made us vulnerable to an epiphany, that pebble waiting to get underfoot.

We chastised ourselves, a little, for the desire to walk alone in another's garden. We remarked on how the grounds shared the same sunlight and air with the countryside beyond its walls, how the city park in Rouen seemed equally, though differently, beautiful, and yet remained nearly bereft of admirers. We rose and rejoined the procession, then, suddenly back among faces most elated by flowers they recognized from home.

Hitchhiker's
Hat

SOUVENIR

Twenty years ago, Rick and his lover—both just out of college—stopped in Las Vegas on a U-Haul move from New Jersey to California. They wanted to play the slot machines—part of their desire to experience everything. And they won a pile of silver, which they then lost in 20 minutes of trying to replicate their initial excitement. In the parking lot outside the casino, they met a young man who was also chasing dreams to the Pacific Coast—a hitchhiker whose last ride had just let him out after robbing him of all but the clothes on his back and the hat on his head. Though Rick's car was topped out with boxes, there was room in the trailer, if the hitchhiker wanted to climb in. Hours later, Rick left him, at his request, sprawled for a nap on the first ocean beach to which they came. Two days afterward, while unpacking the trailer, Rick found the young man's straw Stetson.

As Rick tells this story, he rings the sweet chimes of nostalgia for youthful adventure, remarkable trust in strangers, enduring love. And his listeners hear the undertones.

One difference between the traveler and the homebody is that the former is constantly reminded that much of his experience falls to him like the hitchhiker's hat. He puts it on when he tells its story and hams it up. Sometimes it's the right size. Then he hangs it back on the rack. What else to do?

I think of Rick holding the Stetson, wanting—as he said— to return it but not even knowing its previous owner's name. I imagine the hat hung above his desk in the cheap apartment he and his girlfriend rented, how it was their hat by chance as it is mine, and others', now.

ATMOSPHERE

I stop at Candy's Angus Barn in Wentzville, Missouri. A sign within declares *Good Cookin _and_ we got good Leggs*. A wide-eyed sun, drawn in erasable pen, gazes at curvaceous gams.

Two men sit at the counter, to whom the waitress talks of her divorce. Three men chat at another table. A large photograph of the Empire State Building hangs in the corner. Why?

"Don't know," says the waitress, as she puts a glass of water in front of me.

The front page of the *Wentzville Journal* tells of gang activity— vandalism—in the area; there is also a call for tomato growers to bring their hugest fruits to be weighed for a contest; a doctor testifies that a local infant, dead, shows signs of "shaken-baby syndrome"; beside this story is a photograph of a mother and daughter on a sunlit swing, the mother's arms wrapped around the chains holding the swing, and then around the daughter.

After tolerable bacon and eggs, I pay, and the waitress, who has noted my out-of-state license plate, asks me where I'm headed.

"Family reunion?"

I mention that my niece is getting married for the first time, and that she has two children.

"Yeah," the waitress replies, "my daughter's getting married, too. She has a child. It's the '90s. She says she wants to get married before she gets too fat to wear the dress."

RUINS

Late in the evening in Valladolid, Mexico, a keenly beautiful boy selling flowers appears at our dinner table.

"How are you, lovely lady?" he says, his smile resplendent.

Ralph decides to buy a blossom for his wife, and the boy tries to cheat him out of his change. The boy laughs as though it is all a joke.

Once the transaction is complete, the smile vanishes from boy's face, as though he has been instantaneously lobotomized.

The restaurant allows these children here, though it has posted pleas to us not to patronize them. Our purchases, the signs repeat, only encourage the adults who exploit them.

Later, Laura—slowly rolling the stem of the purchased blossom between her thumb and index finger—will tell us about driving over the border from Texas with her parents, to visit relatives.

"There were always children begging on the Mexican side of the bridge," she will say, "and one day, I got so worked up sitting there in the back seat, wanting to *do something*, I wadded up my raincoat and threw it to a girl as we passed. My father whipped me extra hard because it was a new coat."

As the boy moves off, he bumps Ralph—almost accidentally—with his tray.

"Smell my lovely flowers?" he says, approaching the next table, reigniting his beauty.

NOWHERE TO GO

On the grounds of the Taihu Hotel spreads a huge garden which houses a lotus pool and a small pavilion with a blue ceramic table. I nap near this table for two hours one afternoon of a rainy day—my only day in Wuxi, China. Thus, for me, always, the rain there dimples the pool. The wind rises occasionally, but it rarely chills. The lotuses are trimmed back into rounded clusters, so they resemble giant floating saucers. A distant horn yaps. Cuckoos cry.

OPINIONS/DEFINITIONS

"If a thing doesn't fold flat, I don't want it."

In a foreign land, you soon discover that not everything is different from the ways of home but that some things are, and the next thing might be. We are constantly troubled and enticed and bewildered by how people of another country are like us in that they want the same things we do—sustenance, security, love—yet they are not like us at all.

"I really like him. He's the kind of person I might write to when I move."

"Being unhappy is more interesting in a distant land than at home, though it is also more like being sick alone."

We experience each thing only once in this life, but who can operate daily under this exquisite duress? As sojourners, we can recognize the unique intricacies of a day because there are more, larger one-of-a-kind events in being a stranger in town and more recognition of them: I'll only be here, now, once—this once.

FACES

At a bus stop near the Park of the Revolution stands a man whose flesh hangs from where his left eye should be. It tumbles over his cheek nearly to his chin, in the shape of a flaccid, uncircumcised penis.

After we pass, I mention this to Mitch, who keeps walking and does not peer back, and I am left alone with the man's face which frightens and intrigues me. Mitch says it is a sad case because, most likely, minor surgery could have corrected the horrific condition—were the means available in such a poor country. I wonder about the childhood of the deformed man. Did it hurt him to run? Was he married?

Mitch recalls from his childhood a legless man, callused all over, it seemed, who moved on his hands along walkways between cages of monkeys and toucans at the zoo.

"He spent most of his life looking up, I imagine," Mitch says.

Christian, a Dane, resembles Dennis, an American, who died two years ago of melanoma at 33. The wide sideburns, the boxy jaw and modest manner—Lisa sees much of Dennis in these features, still grieving for her old friend.

And so, as we journey down the coast toward Nicaragua, we repeatedly meet up with Christian and Dennis—or they with us—on set days in particular villages. As the time for each rendezvous approaches, Lisa grows more anxious and excited.

When, at last, Christian and Dennis miss their date with us—for good—Lisa and I sit in the shade on a dusty square, staring glumly at a brown pigeon stalking a gray pigeon among the foot traffic on market day.

On the express train from Rouen to Paris, a young man slouches in the area between cars. He stares at me through the tinted glass, smiles slightly, almost dreamily. A moment later, he turns, showing me his ass. Then I realize that he is displaying his reflection to himself.

RETURN

Just after I unlock the front door and step into my house in Tampa, I'm touched by a coolness, an uncomfortable lack of presence, as if a burglar had just fled through the back window. This ambiance dissipates quickly, like the air in an opened time capsule.

I am grateful to be back. Yet how long ago did I flee this same set of rooms, and the small, grieved life I believed I inhabited here? I am anxious to resurrect my old order. I feel fragile and superfluous. I wonder, fleetingly, foolishly, what those mirrors have been reflecting while I've been gone.

STAMINA

In the Lama Temple in Beijing, we stand before a painting of hundreds of characters (both human and spirit, we decide). One rides a blue bull and one a white beast. One releases a dream cloud by extending his index finger; another leaps in ecstasy; still another pours fish into water cleaving rock. Myths? At the center sits the Buddha.

We are tired and hungry from hiking around a maze of streets in the heat. Both conditions can be easily vanquished. For the moment, however, they dominate us and the painting. We have not come especially to see it. Yet we cannot study it, or feel it, as we might if rested, fed, and less ignorant.

Outside, at dusk, flocks of swallows swirl like gnats around the remains of a city gate.

A TRAVELER'S NOTEBOOK

On the balcony, its owner smokes a cigarette and thinks how lonely Athens has become after three days.

Every two hours a platoon in full gear marches up the beach where it lies among coppery shoulders.

It is abducted in Lisbon and later found in a dumpster. It cannot identify the perpetrators.

"Here," it says, offering an autograph from a child in a truck-stop, a hand-drawn map, words about the conversation and not the conversation itself.

You can see how little time it had to think.

In its pages, the proprietor of the hammock rental says meaningfully, "You can be who you are, here."

A man in Old Cairo kisses his palm before he reaches to shake the hand that holds it. White space.

Like everyone else, it tries to say something sophisticated about the outdoor coed showers.

Its author is ready for a drink. It pretends it is interested.

How much of the special medication beside it in the back pack can be offered to the sick stranger next door?

It contains a list: Dawn dip, breakfast, midday nap, swim, dinner, lounging, swim, beer. This is what it can do to a day.

It contains a list: St. Mark's remains returned to Venice packed in bloody chunks of ham; an outhouse in the Polish woods with a heart carved into the door; the price of admission to the Alhambra.

It holds no one's memory.

DEPARTURE

I step onto the portico of the Foreign Affairs building and look at the sky framed by treetops I will soon only see in memory.

Days numbered. And this small approaching death separates me a little from my fellows. Suddenly, people on the street seem distanced by two or three powers. My students seem more "Polish" than in recent months.

But departure, unlike death, does not relieve us of all undone and unrealized. We do what we can, see what we can—we try. And we may repudiate an adventure in the fear that it will loom and overshadow all future endeavor. Better to take its measure . . . again and again, if need be.

I wish to note all around me, but it resists my attempts because no "interesting" words impress these objects, panoramas, odors, harmonies. The street. The room. The pink apartment house. Red folding chairs. Snow in the crotch of a cottonwood tree. The common surfaces cry most for a place on my manifest. The telling details retreat. . . .

UNANSWERABLE LETTER

It arrives laden with descriptions of markets and cafes and graves which are really meditations on the wandering correspondent—who, undoubtedly, has made a copy of the letter before posting it.

Or it is brief, "fine" and "beautiful" marching hand in hand across the pages of polite—insulting—observation.

Or it is from a marginal acquaintance. How bored—how desperate—he must be at such a distance from his usual self!

Or it appears, in a plastic bag, the envelope slit open quite deliberately by censors. It is stamped *CAUGHT IN MACHINERY.*

ONE-WAY TICKET

On the boardwalk leading into Corkscrew Swamp, Florida, an elderly woman pushes an elderly man in a wheelchair. They ask if this is the way into the wood stork rookery.

"Yes," I reply, adding in my stupid enthusiasm, "and there are alligators—large ones—sunning just a few yards from the walkway!"

The old man peers up at me and then ahead where the walk vanishes into the green tangle, trepidation passing over his countenance. A road map and a bird guide hang in a pouch at his side.

HOMESICK

A delicate evening rain warms Suzhou. Bats flitter about the rooftops lining oil-spattered canals. A woman standing in front of a shop full of the usual tourist ceramics says, "please come in, take a look," each time I pass, and I have passed often on my way to the main section of town.

The cricket vendor hoists his shoulder pole loaded with hundreds of softball-sized bamboo cages, and I remember withered sunflowers in a far corner of Kansas, buried by a sudden spring blizzard that stranded me there.

SNAPSHOTS

Tereza and I sip coffee in her office and watch the Cairo traffic push through the heat on Talaat Harb. She says she views a photograph of home as a portion of that place removed from time and brought forth to her. I say that I treat it as an icon of that moment of world it represents, and I'm drawn to it. I move toward it, not it toward me.

Recumbent on a dock floating in Virginia, Cheri swears that she takes no photographs of her travels. She wants only memories—though she accepts some reprints.

There are those who take photos of themselves in various foreign and famous places, and those who take pictures of those places without themselves.

The photograph is a spiritual space—even commercial photographs, where the spiritual is forced out conspicuously beyond the frame. And, of course, the viewer *becomes* the viewer by pouring spirit into the image, which is a plunging into the three-dimensional world beyond its surface. We have an abundance of spirit for photographs. By drawing it from us, photographs demonstrate to us our general spirituality, our need to plunge.

Years later, I find a photograph I took of the entrance to King Tut's tomb. There is no notation on the back of it. So, I'm still necessary to the picture, part of its documentary aspirations. At least I long to be necessary.

MOMENTUM OF THE PICTURESQUE

A man with thin, bad legs and a cane makes his way ahead of two female companions down a steep, cobbled lane in Dinan, France. His knee buckles. He has recouped himself many times before, but now the pitch of the earth and his own weight force him out of control. The women scurry as the man goes down soundlessly. Another pedestrian, trudging up the hill, races and catches the falling man before he hits too hard. And the dazed man thanks him.

We watch from a slight distance, where we happen to be. And now the town is moving on with its past-ness, its battlements towering around us, the porn magazines in the tobacco shop window, the restaurants serving this lovely Sunday in May.

How will the fallen man get the rest of the way down the steep street to the famously charming river? It is clear that we are not allowed to feel sorry for him—or ignore him—for his sprawled eyeglasses have been retrieved and he is already taking another step toward his destination.

CURFEW

Arthur tells of visiting his parents back in Sierra Leone, which has recently undergone a military coup. Each night, he says, gunfire kept only him awake, his family having grown accustomed to it. When he was socializing with friends, he would get nervous about 9 P.M. and suggest that they might go to the safety of their homes.

His friends would reply, "Relax. Have another drink. The shooting doesn't start until after midnight." At 11:30 P.M., they would laugh at him, "Relax. Have one more for the road."

THE COMPARISON

In a field in central Spain, a tree trunk lies, sliced into pieces resembling the vertebrae of some mythic beast. I have encountered that creature elsewhere, but where?

HOSPITALITY

In the Detroit bus station, we sit next to a woman on her way to meet a man in Pittsburgh, with whom she has been sharing a romantic correspondence.

"I told him," she says, grinning to herself, facing the floor, "that I would stay in the guest room. But he said that the bed in there had been repossessed yesterday. So I told him that I would sleep on the couch. He said that the Goodwill people took it the day before. . . ."

George is having an affair with a woman from Worb, a small town not far from where he has been working in Switzerland. Over the course of several weeks, he has spent the night at her place six, perhaps seven, times. This morning, at his apartment, he discovers a note on the windshield of his car: "If you are going to be living in Worb, you had better pay the garbage pick-up tax."

I enter Club Ginza. A topless bartender nests on pillows at the top of a round bar. She used to run with a motorcycle gang in Jakarta, but Hong Kong is much cleaner, and the work is steady. Our group, encircling her, is international—businessy, maritime, touristic. Next to me sits a burly Texan, drunk, accompanied by a brittle, pretty woman.

"How does it feel so far from home?" I finally ask him, hoping for a little common ground.

"You," he replies slowly and from the vast gut, "say another word about my wife, and I'll hurt you."

I enter another club. It's empty (because of the holidays?). Three semi-nude women and their boss appear like a magician's puff of smoke. Yellow feather boas swirl around me with the female hands that entice the thighs of battalions on leave. The women chatter. Shots of whiskey arrive without an order. The boss scribbles on a pad couched in his palm, like a caricature of a cub reporter. As fast as he can, he tears off the sheets and stuffs them into a tumbler on the table where I've just seated myself amid the fray. It's my tab, and the meter is running. I've been in the place two minutes at the most, and I already owe $200. I move toward the door. The women harp and chase and grasp, swatting each other like scarecrows on fire. The boss tries to block my way. I dig a five-dollar bill from my front pocket and hold it above my head, like a dog biscuit, and shuffle Jimmy Stewart-style sideways past the boss and the women who are now leaping and swiping at the bill. As I back out the door, I release the money.

We stay the night at a posada in Cobá, which seems utterly empty. The proprietor is unnervingly solicitous. He assures us, repeatedly, that our belongings are safe and the room will be clean when we return from a hike to the lake. That evening, we enter our room and find that it is, indeed, in good order, though we are struck by an odd smell. Stains on the pair of shoes Lisa left at the end of the bed provide the evidence: the walls and ceiling have been whitewashed.

FURTHER OPINIONS/DEFINITIONS

"In a large city in your homeland, you can refuse to recognize other people, as a defense. In a metropolis abroad, you can overlook them through fascinated attention, by transforming them into an exotic street scene."

Videos of other lands offer stimulation but no disorientation, no dream-like envelopment of noticing. A skilled, savvy ignorance—that is what the traveler needs. (As opposed to the deigning, debilitating boredom cultivated by some who have "seen a lot" at a young age, who have the privilege of their displeasures and lack of curiosity.)

"It's unconscionable to visit suffering places. But those whom we believe are suffering there do not suffer as we think, if they believe they suffer at all."

"Everywhere is an exotic elsewhere to someone somewhere."

"If I could be as forgiving about my day-to-day life—if I could be as fascinated and patient as when approaching a remote border crossing where the officials have a reputation for capriciousness. . . ."

A NARRATOR

Past the video parlor in a tin shack marked "Elvis," a man pours various substances into glasses (one of the glasses already contains a ten peso note suspended in brown liquid). He walks the circle of witnesses—mostly Indians from the Mexican countryside—with a small amber pyramid pitched on the back of his hand. He asks for a coin at each juncture of speech, and he usually gets it. As he speaks, everyone's attention is divided between his actions and the blue cloth bag beside the playing cards fanned out in the dirt at his feet. The bag undulates, the coiled snake within pushing outward, making the cloth look like some tortured muscle trying to unknot itself.

TOUCHING

Molly and I hiked up the steep hill to the Buddha Temple. In its dim inner chamber, crowds of visitors tossed coins at the Buddha's cup, hoping to get one in and make their wishes come true. Molly tossed a coin, and just after, turned and shoved a young Chinese man across the chamber. He looked astonished and perplexed and embarrassed—and he immediately fled.

After a few minutes, we descended, and among the milling masses at the bottom of the steep steps, we spotted that man, the groper. He didn't seem to see us, or wouldn't acknowledge us if he did. He approached his wife, who was clearly tired and who'd waited at the bottom of the hill with their little girl. The man scooped up his daughter, hugged her, and the three strolled away.

RETURN

I'm back in Tampa—this journey is suddenly gone—and wonder how much money is in my bank account. I knew when I left, precisely.

I put the money belt away. The money belt, which has been the center I've protected—not a nostalgia piece.

This is what my wallet feels like. I forgot that I had a wallet.

Here are the wet wipes I didn't use, the shirt I didn't wear, the coat that I needed but didn't bring, the small scissors I could have used on nose hairs.

"Sorting our bones," Lisa says.

How much should I put back in place? What place is that?

LOST

A young woman rides an exhausted horse up and down the beach between the banana palms. I'm out snorkeling along the edge of the reef, dipping my face into the salty surface to watch schools of glistening fish turn this way and that, like fans at a stadium concert. A young man, a local, trudges up the sand toward my few possessions—a small backpack bearing some clothes, money and a notebook—stacked on the shore. I'm too far away to stop him from stealing it.

I'm also far from home. Yet now I pretend that it doesn't matter what happens, that it would be perfect to have him break my tie with all I've left behind. Why not be forced to dress in what I can borrow in the village? Why not be forced to get a job in the ramshackle restaurant to earn the fare out of here?

The beach is empty in all directions, except for the woman whipping the horse into the distance and the young man who stands over my pack and looks out at me.

I try not look to at him. I go under. I come up, wanting to be free. He flags down the young woman on the horse. He talks to her a long time, ever so slowly taking hold of the reins, as if to keep her from riding the creature to death. Hesitantly, she dismounts, and they sit beside my pack and talk, the horse's head looming over their shoulders.

Salt sears my eyes, and my mask fogs. I tread water, weariness burning my arms, razoring coral below my bare feet.

Then they rise. Through my fog, the young man waves, as if to motion me in.

They walk off, slowly, he holding the reins of the horse with his hands folded behind his back, she with her hands over her face.

I paddle ashore, toward my undisturbed things.

ARRIVAL

At the door of the airport terminal, a young man wearing a tattered pullover waits in the tepid florescent light swirling with insects. He holds a hand-printed sign that seems to have my last name on it. He speaks no English, and I no Chinese, and somehow I expect this, hoping to be "aware." I get into the car—a new Toyota—with him and a driver. In a city of ten million, we hurtle down dark lanes nearly vacant except for an occasional horse-drawn cart on truck tires. The driver does not honk, instead flicking high beams on and off in warning. On the radio, strings whine and coo in an almost country and western plaint. Almost.

Was that really my name on the card?

A Stranger's Neighborhood

1. AT FIRST

On a Saturday near the end of my one Little League season, my father came to his only time at bat in the Father/Son All Star game. A production to foster family unity, the game hardly involved only stars, since several good players on my regular team, the Indians, did not come out that day, and my father, among others, knew practically nothing about baseball. He never watched it on television, never peered into the sports pages. In fact, my mother had taught me to throw. My parents had attended only one of my games that summer, since my father worked at the factory most weekends building earth mover tires for the Aswan Dam project in Egypt.

Because the number of participants exceeded positions on the field, squads from each team were substituted every two innings. I had started the game at my usual position, first base, and then rotated into the dugout, where I sat nervously as Dad, at the plate, swiveled the bat stiffly, shy, improvising.

Somehow he made contact with a pitch and the ball dribbled across the infield. The third baseman, assured that he had plenty of leeway with such an obviously inexperienced player, loped lazily toward the grounder—but he mishandled it. By the time he had recovered and flung the ball toward the outstretched mitt at first, Dad was closing in on the bag. Runner and throw converged. Then Dad made a decision which mortified me and made me oddly proud.

He slid.

He knew next to nothing about such a base-running technique, or that while it was legal to slide into first base, local custom prescribed that one overrun it. A little dust billowed, and he sat in the dirt, astonished, anxiously looking around for some purchase on what had happened, his jeans and blue tee shirt spattered black by rubber from the factory, the soles of his steel-toed oxfords flush against the bag. Safe.

I was elated at his—at our—success. And yet something in my boy's heart grieved sweetly at the recognition of his clumsiness, his obvious ignorance of the game, at his willingness to expose himself not only to humiliation but to physical injury. Several years before, he had severely fractured his right leg in a drunken fall at home. A thick track of crosses extended several inches down the outer side of his knee—carved by a suture of shoelace gauge which he revealed to me, during his recuperation, by unlatching a small hinged hatch cut into his cast.

When I told the story of first base at my father's wake nearly three decades later, I didn't mention the scar, or the fall. At the mortuary chapel, his body lay in the open casket behind me as I spoke to the mourners, many of whom I did not know or whom the years had made barely recognizable to me. I spoke because when the moment in the service arose for those present to share memories of him, a comfortless silence edged in from the walls.

My brother Mike eyed me over his shoulder from the front pew—
a younger brother's command to the oldest.

I spoke because, as much as I wished to hear what others recalled of my father, I wanted him eulogized, however briefly, by
someone who actually knew him. In the mazy hours after his
final heart attack, it had been decided that the monsignor from
St. Joseph's would offer the official remarks, though Dad hadn't
attended church in years.

I think I also spoke out of vanity. As an estranged and then
reborn son, I had imagined my father's death long before the first
heart attack bore down on him like an unsought epiphany three
years earlier. In my first manhood, I had assigned him to the circle
of the spiritually dead, and, later, I had killed him off in poems
and stories—in order to mourn him while giving those scant works
some emotional heft. During his wavering decline, I had fortified
myself for *the* phone call, somehow certain, before I lifted the
receiver on that Sunday, that it had arrived.

I was the child who had moved far away, for good. I had acquired more formal education than anyone on either side of the
family, ever. I had fashioned, I thought, a life preferable to that
on Garfield Avenue. And I wished to be viewed, as I spoke, as an
executor of the word, one groomed for something more than the
wholesome, grubbing futility of pot roast Sundays, doorbuster
sales at Kmart, two weeks of vacation each summer.

I had tried to move away from my family years before I actually left the house, withdrawing into books and escaping into the
households of my friends. And after I did go, literally, I returned
to Des Moines repeatedly, a famished prodigal, relishing the
plangent—and convenient—sadness of each approach to all I
believed I had so hopelessly lost. Those poor people—my family
and friends—how pathetic they were! Such was my little theater of
reassuring sentiment. In the mortuary chapel, I saw, at last, that I

had struggled to free myself from home only to discover that it had left me before I could finally leave it. I had come back again, a body seeking its ghost.

To the gathering, then, I asserted that our parents provide crucial clues to our identities. I claimed that the story about first base illustrated what kind of man my father was: one often out of his element in public, timid even when gregarious, a loving parent who was sometimes willing to tempt the foreign and the foolish. I supplied this meaning because it was true and because I wanted to conclude my remarks by declaring that I was lucky he was my father. After all, I had received his blessing as others have not from their fathers. Perhaps I had always had his blessing.

"Forty is the old of age of youth," wrote Victor Hugo, "and the youth of old age." Feeling myself at that glibly intermediate point, I remembered that Dad was slightly older than I on the day he slid. That had been 1967—the golden year of overtime pay, the year he bought his only brand new car and the lot on which we would build a lake house. . . .

When I sat down after my homage, I peered toward him, proud of the room's hesitation following my remarks. I had stood over him repeatedly all afternoon, approaching in curious charges, retreating when it seemed forgivable to do so. My eyes had been scorched by the peppery onset of tears, but no more than that; rather, I'd tried over and over to clear my throat—an inconsolable dryness. Clipped and tailored and handsome as she had been on only a handful of occasions, my mother had lingered nearby, at one point talking of buttered bread at breakfast. Briefly, Mike had wept, turning to me afterward and whispering, "This place smells like night."

My brother Greg, kneeling, had cried into an unresolved estrangement from Dad that was at once more ostentatious and secretive than mine at its worst, and more immense. We'd all waited for my youngest brother Aaron to appear, furious at his evasive absence. I'd hugged my little sister, already then a grandmother, who had wailed, "My daddy! My daddy!" in the emergency room.

During the two days that had elapsed between my father's death and the display of his body, I feared my first sight of it, assuming that his corpse would exhibit some exorbitant trauma. I found myself remembering him with dark hair and long sideburns, as he had appeared in his late forties and early fifties—when I was in college, my last years before leaving Iowa. At the casket, I kept thinking that his eyes would flash open, and he, startled by my presence, would growl and curse, as he had when, as a child, I had awakened him by accident.

His cold, bald dome seemed to draw no heat from my hand, as a stone might, and it seemed harder than stone. His cheeks were solid and cold, and his ears cold. His white beard had been clipped nattily. He looked as he did in his obituary photo, which had been cropped from a picture taken on a Caribbean cruise with Mom several years before. Mike and I peeked to see that the undertaker had, indeed, dressed him in his suit pants. The broad, hopelessly loyal bruises on the backs of his hands from dialysis needles had been buffed into invisibility. Mike, a nurse, worked the small finger on Dad's left hand—his bass hand at the piano—to demonstrate that even *rigor mortis* was short-lived.

Later, he and I undid one of the buttons of Dad's white shirt beneath the loud necktie, both purchased the day before. I told myself that I wanted to see if he was wearing a tee shirt—which he was—but I think I wanted to touch the scars on his chest from the heart operations. I rebuttoned the shirt and pulled my hand from his chest—afraid of him differently than in life. Then I returned it, let it lie there, gave it the permission he most likely would not have granted it. I thought of how thick he had felt when I hugged him, how he smelled of tire rubber, and his whiskers rasped my cheek. Now, he felt narrow and brittle, and hollowed like rotted kindling. The dense hair in his nostrils had been completely cleared. A tiny moth floated above him.

Aside from the wooden pews, he was the only thing in the room that had once been alive, and he was the only matter that had once possessed identity. This would be my sole time with him as a body—so briefly was he this new substance, since he was, of course, changing still. Older now in my form than he in his, I might accustom myself to him dead, but not as this object before me.

Fewer mourners than I'd envisioned rose and reminisced, and the monsignor offered generic passages of consolation in which I sensed his condescension and the effort to overcome boredom. Mike reminded me that Dad would probably have countered my crabby observation, as he often did in later years, with a shocked and indignant, almost matronly rejoinder: "Why! . . . I think it was lovely!"

Immediately after the service, an elderly, somewhat homely woman approached me.

"You know," she said softly, leaning toward me for emphasis, "I was in love with your father. When I was 21. He was new in town . . . and single. I'd skate with him sometimes at the big parties in those days. . . ."

I thanked her for this, for choosing a memory she believed deserving of some modesty, for giving it away now that only her portion remained.

On the patio of my parents' house that night, one of Aaron's childhood friends stood up from his beer to offer a belated eulogy. A substance abuser since adolescence, marginally educated and infrequently employed, he declared with unfathomable solemnity: "Dean used to get after my ass just like he did his own kids.

He used to yell and raise hell with me, and lecture me. I can't say it did any good. But I didn't have any father . . . or anyone like that . . . except him."

The next morning, he and five other pallbearers—all under 35 and volunteers—lined up in their suits, or denims and neckties, at Laurel Hill for the last lowering. At the funeral, Mike and Greg had sought to throttle their laughter at the monsignor's poor but proud singing—their bodies shuddering as though lashed by sorrow, their faces covered. Now they sat blandly as the monsignor strewed some dirt across the coffin which the family had selected two days before from the basement showroom at the mortuary, the one with a Last Supper in relief on each of its corners.

I imagined Dad in the chapel the night before, after the undertakers had turned down the lights and locked the doors and gone home. There he lay—he and the old woman in the adjacent chapel—alone. They were like those quarters of the world which pass most of their existence empty of human inhabitants. During the day, en route to the bathroom, I'd looked in at the woman, growing anxious somehow that she seemed to have no visitors. I was beginning to understand the comfort in what had once seemed to me programmatic gestures—the arrival of flowers, for instance, with a condolence card. So, eventually, I went in and spent a few minutes with her. She appeared well-to-do. I pitied her loneliness, forgetting that it was my own. Later that evening, her chapel teemed, but they—we—could never be with her and my father enough to populate their vacancy.

In the amiable sunlight, the monsignor blessed everyone. The crowd dispersed across the modest hillside of stones with surnames familiar for generations on the east side of Des Moines and new, strange immigrant names from Asia and the Middle East. Relatives who had taken a day from work and driven from Nebraska and southern Iowa offered their sympathy, and then headed back to their own. Cars crawled away. The limousine awaited us patiently, no doubt scheduled for other journeys like this one. The burial crew lounged discreetly in a blue pick-up truck under a regal oak in the distance. I plucked a petal from one of the sprays of white roses. Its delicate veining throbbed between my thumb and forefinger.

Later, I asked Greg why neither he nor my other siblings had spoken at the wake.

"You spoke for the family," Greg replied.

But, of course, I did not speak for them, just as now. I told the anecdote about the slide into first base partly because it was about me, and I was not wholly spontaneous. In the afternoon, before the wake, I had scribbled a few notes about the incident on the blank lines of a gift contribution card from the mortuary guest registry. I had wanted to make *some* sense during my moment of public attention.

Dean Morrill is dead and with him the Morrill family, my family. Both have become the property of tellers, of which I am only one. The Morrill family born with his passing was immediately caught by its new life. My mother might have died first, or any of us children, but it was my father who ended the family—an actuarial cliché, presaged for decades in his furious response to existence. Yet our significance swirls around a cliché like gnats around that summer nothingness in the backyard. His absence had finished the family, as his presence had shaped it—a prime mover.

Children comprehend their parents on an oddly middle ground—not quite as intimates, since parents present themselves to their children, however poorly, as moral personae, to set examples; and not quite as public actors, since children rarely witness their parents in much of the wider world, which children variously discern. My father, a monumental presence to me, was only a man, of course, and I was fortunate enough to learn that fact while he still lived. But as Greg and Mike and I sifted through his things, I wondered yet again what kind of man. In the room we called "the front porch," where he had slept alone on a twin bed for nearly three decades—a room I entered cautiously even as an adult—we took inventory of some late evidence. Among the grime and salts of years of stock and stash and misplace, there were plastic bags jammed with stuffed zebras and horses bought for future birthdays of grandchildren. There were bags of unused colored balloons, knotted palms from distant Easter seasons, yarn dream-catchers spun in grade school art classes. Secreted beneath his bed were instant cocoa mix, petrified divinity, canned beets, and maraschino cherries. A ventriloquist's dummy slumped on a bookshelf, and hanging above, a purple plastic octopus, a metal owl wind chime, a bird cage containing two ceramic doves. Scattered Kleenexes abounded, and here and there, a fallen Q-tip, amber-ended. Minute drill bits, two cans of ceramic tile adhesive, the tattered blue and yellow cloth bathmat emblazoned with *The Morrills* removed from my grandmother's house after her death, duck slippers, a plaque: *Once a king always a king but once a knight is enough.*

"It's a guy thing," my sister Peggy had contended, retreating from our archaeology.

Aaron appeared briefly, at the urging of his wife who openly announced that she wanted him to get his share, since she perceived us as ravaging some treasure trove. Her rage reminded me of a line from a poem by Richard Shelton that a man who can divide his possessions equally among his children has nothing to give. Hoping to encourage Aaron's involvement in at least this family activity, we passed to him one of Dad's jackets and the enlarged, legendary snapshot of Dad presenting to the camera a catfish the size of a six-month-old baby. One summer at the lake years before, Aaron had anchored his rod, drunk some beers, and gone to bed. Dad had checked the line the next morning, thinking it empty, only to drag forth the spectacular creature, exhausted from struggling to free itself.

After trying on the jacket and staring at the picture for a few minutes, Aaron slipped away, leaving both.

"It hurts him too much," Mom explained. Greg rolled his eyes at the old excuse, and pulled news clippings and thank you cards from the terraces of cobwebs, setting off a mousetrap.

We stacked and bundled the magazines and other publications: *REC, Union Plus, The Catholic Mirror, Hooked on Crochet!, How to Install Chain Link Fence and Pre-finished Molding, Smith and Hawkin Bulb Book, Colombian Mission, Smithsonian, The National Enquirer, The Farmer's Almanac, Enjoy Your Aquarium.* There were also *National Geographic* maps of the Arctic, the Amazon, the Pacific, and China. Dad had tried, absurdly, to forbid my going to Asia ten years before, but after a while, he romanticized it into an adventure.

"I'd get your postcards," he would tell me over and over, later, "and think of that old song. You know, 'far away places with strange sounding names.'"

It was during those years abroad that our relationship was transformed and deepened. In the middle of a north China winter, I had written a pair of extravagantly long letters, one to him and one to Mom—hard and frightening letters, it seemed, about the past, letters dubiously motivated, a child's indulgence. I'd asked them to exchange the letters if they wished but to respect the other's right to privacy if he, or she, declined.

"You remembered a lot," Dad said later, with a warmth that somehow brought me onto equal footing with him, "a lot."

He had shown his letter to Mom, but she had not replied in kind, nor had she acknowledged to me that she had received my correspondence.

Dad had loaned me the money for airfare to China, and after I'd returned, he had refused to let me repay him. When Mike and I sorted through the last effects and documents in his safe deposit box, I learned that he had raised that gift by cashing in one of his life insurance policies.

In the front porch, Mike and Greg and I spoke in lowered voices, asking quietly for permission to keep an object. My hands moved over his possessions, and sometimes I watched them, the fingers growing gummy with the traffic. Mom shuttled unobtrusively to and from the kitchen, not really comfortable in Dad's room.

"I don't know what's out here," she said, anxiously, "I had my stuff and he had his stuff."

Just then, Greg brought out plaques bearing the names *Greg* and *Karen*, each with a history of the name, and misted with paint splatters. They were the kind of item found new on racks at low-end department stores and shop-o-ramas. One day, Dad had spotted them at the neighborhood Goodwill store. Since Greg's wife is named Karen, Dad saw the plaques as a message from fate, though he couldn't quite discern what it was. He bought the plaques and presented them, only to discover that they were same ones Greg and Karen had donated six months before.

"He brought home so much junk like that from Goodwill," Mike laughed, "and now all of it will go back."

Early on, I had defined myself by attempting not to be like my father, or my mother, or nearly anyone of my acquaintance in Des Moines. I knew what I was rejecting, but not much more than that. Perhaps there is an evolutionary logic that urges us to forget the painful and to focus on the sweet—a selective pressure for nostalgia that inspires us to go on, reproduce, build for tomorrow. I resist that impulse, as I resist the impulse which insists that suffering is truth's core. Both are the wandering rocks between which memory must navigate.

"Glad to have you back," one of my colleagues said when I returned to Tampa from Iowa after the funeral, as though I had nearly been lost to my present life. But, indeed, I had been on a faraway journey, had been a foreigner again—on the street of my childhood. A few years before, my father had purchased the burial plot at Laurel Hill. My mother refused to visit the site, but Dad showed it to me one winter afternoon as one might a new real estate development. For him, the place was "lovely," tranquil, with just enough exoticism in the wail of an occasional freight train from the far margin of corn fields. That day, he installed me as his headstone and then, measuring from the road below, decided how large a monument he needed to purchase. I disliked the idea of buying a grave (still in my thirties, it seemed ridiculously negative), and I told him as much. He laughed and remarked again on the beauty of the place.

"I might string some up Christmas lights here," he said. "I think I might even come out here in the spring, stretch out on a deck chair and sunbathe. . . ."

My father stayed put for all but a splintered fraction of his life, and while this was his choice, it was not always his first choice. The day after his funeral his family made pilgrimages to his stone in small groups and alone, our separation and our revelations of that fact typical of us. That has been my only visit to him there, though in bed in the middle of the night, I sometimes try to envision him beneath the earth and the screwed-down lid, quite something else again now. I think, too, of the last moments before they closed the casket. For much of the time I knew him, Dad seemed, at heart, an unhappy, troubled man, sensationally tormented, mostly by regret. From this, I surmised, as a child, that regret is a great, avoidable evil. I sought, and still seek, the path which leads around or away from it, though I am foolish enough sometimes to wade straight into it. That seeking spurred me away from home and back. It has invested my life like little else. It was regret and the wish to defeat it that brought my lips to his lips there in the casket. I feared his kiss and needed it terribly—that last kiss, these words.

2. WHITE HORSE FLAME AND SHADOW

Dad lived in the house—our house—on the corner of East 34th and Garfield Avenue for 48 years. At the time of his death, my mother had lived there for 41. The place began as one of a row of two-room, asphalt-sided tract homes constructed after World War II on what was then the east edge of Des Moines. The sun rose in dense woods beyond the kitchen window, and paved streets and sewage lines lay several blocks—and years—to the west. Dad had moved to Des Moines from his hometown of Omaha after the war, to build tires at the new Firestone plant, and he was the first resident of the house and something of a pioneer on Garfield Avenue, one of its original settlers. Thus, initially, the house featured a chamber pot, a gas heater, yellow and white checkered linoleum—and a Baldwin Acrosonic piano which Dad had purchased after moving in.

Many of my earliest memories of the house and the life within it are not my own, but rather those of the three-minute super-8 films Dad shot with a side-winding Bell and Howell. From the early fifties to the early seventies, he documented holidays and trips and rites of passage. Sixty-seven reels survive, half of them transferred now to videotape. Within their elegiac frame, Mom sits stiffly as she models a black Easter hat that looks like grackles in a whirlwind. I march off to kindergarten, refusing to be accompanied, though Dad sneaks along behind me. The infant Peggy claps and laughs at a birthday cake just before she pushes it from her highchair onto the grass. In boring closeups, summer blossoms float, and cousins, and uncles and aunts, shuttle to and from an outhouse, toss a baseball, rip open Christmas gifts. Many of these romping and waving and shying away are dead now, of course, and the rest ancient or dispersed; but they still perform their eerie feats of ordinary life, just as on the nights when Dad would pop corn and I would prop the front end of the projector on two volumes of *Funk and Wagnalls*, thread the family epic through the gears, and everyone would sit facing, with some delight, the same direction.

Dad appears, briefly, only once in this production—seated in a sleeveless shirt at Christmas dinner—though he is ever present in being constantly behind the camera. The lens may show more than he perceived, but it is through his eyes we see. It is his attention and energy, partly, that is on display. Thus, for years, my brother Greg—out of embarrassment and as one more skirmish in the war he waged with Dad—suppressed the famous reel of himself as a baby in the bath. Likewise, Mike still comments, with minor bitterness, on how infrequently he appears and Aaron almost not at all. Behind the camera, Dad was a judge and a maker, and this was a fundamental emanation of his character. The most profound embodiment of that fact was the house itself, which in the movie metamorphoses with each new addition to the family, each alteration of the life. Just as the family often comprised the content of his films, it inspired and supported his drive to make a place. His house—our house—involved us all.

Over 25 years, the place on Garfield Avenue acquired ten new rooms, a full basement, an upstairs, an adjoining lot with garage, and various landscaping improvements. We children grew up pulling nails from used lumber and bracing studs while Dad toed them in. Mom shoveled sand for hand-mix concrete, and, in lots of four, hefted three-tab shingles to the roof. During most of these years, Dad worked the 3-11 shift, so he devoted his mornings and weekends to the hammer and tape measure, the pant of the rip saw, plastering, fixtures. I often stood with him as he took a number in line at Sutherland Lumber, and we loaded rafters free-for-the-taking from countless houses condemned by freeway construction. I still see him in our new addition, whichever one it is, a blurry silhouette behind visqueen tacked over windowless openings cut into a wall, there amid the tang of sawdust.

With the exception of one moment when my parents nearly purchased another house on the east side, they never talked of moving. Instead, we lived among pallets of cement bought on sale, stacks of doors waiting to be hung, dishes and pots exiled from cabinets by the eminent domain of improvement, items of all sorts that had no immediate application but which might prove useful someday. And we were not alone in this. Our next door neighbors, the Pauldings, and their next door neighbors, the Olivers, struck out on construction projects of similar magnitude. Here, then, stood a row of private designs made public—three youngish couples with children, each family inhabiting an unfinished contrivance, an improvisation of wood and would be, and, in later years, a symbol of ebbing energy or catastrophe.

While being drafted as a laborer on our place interfered with my desire to loll and roam with my friends, it instructed me in other satisfactions and more. I despised starting to work, but once I did, a general hypnosis ensued, and hours could pass before I would come to and beg Dad to cut me loose for play. In these trances, existence seemed wonderful, harmonious. I remember, for instance, tearing out an old brick chimney—this during the biggest addition, begun in the mid-sixties. He crowbarred the bricks free and tossed them into a pile. I, about ten years old, stacked them in my arms, and hauled them to the back door and dropped them into the pit dug for the new basement. I lugged three, perhaps four bricks at a time, but I was secure in what I was doing, and my diligence pleased him. I see now that the job allowed congruence between him and me. It could be completed, and I brimmed with pride at my ability to carry and dump bricks.

On an August day a couple of years later, Dad anchored the sheeting for a sub-floor and set the lines for Greg and me to hammer the remaining nails into the floor joists. Broad-headed and stubby, the nails sank easily, and we made no muss, finishing after sunset. The pleasure of swinging my own hammer, of mastering the nail in two or three blows, became almost a form of meditation, a keeping company with the self and my brother and father. Afterward, Mom brought us lemonade, and we sat on the floor and appreciated our pains. Just then, Aunt Eva and Uncle Johnnie arrived unannounced—almost magically—from the farm. They had come for one of their rare visits to the state fair nearby. So they served as our surprise admirers.

Dad schooled Greg and me thoroughly in the useful ethos of *One more section, one more board, one more nail, and then we'll quit.* But more often, his impatience and capricious temper—his anger—offered its puzzling lessons. As children and teenagers, Greg and I and, later, Mike and Aaron, were no doubt impediments to efficient carpentry. We lollygagged. We misplaced tools. We let a two-by-four slip from its penciled mark before it could be nailed. We fought, brother to brother. But Dad seemed sometimes to treat us as if we were an extension of his mind which would be apprised of his thoughts. He erupted when we stood bewildered at his sudden commands, though he had not bothered to explain what we were doing, and we had not surmised his objectives independently. On occasion, I could sense trouble approaching, and I would try to study him. He roamed around his current project, stalked it, whispering to himself in broken phrases, whistling softly on intakes of breath. Sweat shone on his forehead like mercury and dripped from the tip of his nose. His hands, as he labored, shook in frustration and fury, as if some core tension was vibrating outward on its release—except there was no cessation to that release and no end to the vibration.

My study usually failed to prevent strife. Dad roared often. He seemed, at times, intent on only that. While I met his wrath frequently, he reserved an exceptional heat for Greg, who in those years was clumsy and quick to cry and reluctant to get dirty. An introvert and the artist in the family (he had won a scholarship to the Des Moines Art Center), Greg stumbled over things. Thus, he became Dad's verbal whipping boy on the construction site, and, perhaps, a scapegoat for Dad's own mistakes of carpentry.

Greg usually responded to Dad's ire with tears and a twisting down into himself that encouraged me to pity him, while I also voicelessly sided with Dad because I wanted to avoid his gun sights. Fifteen months separate Greg and me in age, and adults assumed that we should be friends. In our earliest years, our parents dressed us alike—in fedoras and bow ties for church, or matching Perry Como jackets—and we were often given the same kinds of toy trucks and such. But we shared little, constitutionally. He was, in the terminology of the time, a "sissy," and, as I developed friendships beyond the household, commerce with such types blighted one's reputation. At work on the house, I first learned contempt for his kind, and it blossomed. Many times, he attempted to follow me to my friends' houses—to be part of my group—but I drove him away with oaths or fists. Eventually, he stopped following and stayed home, playing with the girls next door and drawing.

Grandma Morrill chastised Dad after he yelled at Greg and swatted him for knocking over his glass of milk once at Sunday dinner. It was obvious, she said, why his grades had plummeted: he needed glasses. Typically, Greg had said nothing about his vision problem, though it proved substantial. When he got the glasses, it wasn't long before he fell and broke them, and then walked through the world with lenses perched askew and surgical tape wrapped like a cast around one of the bows. Not long after this, he and Tangie, one of the girls next door, were frolicking among the bushes and lumber piles between the houses. Greg stumbled onto an old board, driving a rusted nail through his palm. Its point did not break the flesh on the back of his hand but raised it like a big top. Dad, of course, blamed Greg and berated him to and from the emergency room. In simplified retrospect, that nail symbolizes the relationship, from Greg's perspective. Grandma insisted that Greg and Dad resembled each other physically as well as emotionally—both effeminate and nervous—and that Dad was somehow trying, foolishly, to change Greg by "toughening him up."

Decades later, after our reconciliation, Greg told me that he often thought of suicide in those years—one of the reasons he later embraced a fundamentalist faith. Eventually, he went into therapy, and as part of his personal work, he confronted Dad with their past, telling him, "You were a bad father." Evidently, Dad was astonished by this declaration, partly an indication of how much his anger had normalized violence in the family, making it invisible, or forgettable, to him. As Greg told me of this late and unresolved confrontation, I thought of how often I had pounded him—I who, afraid of entering our dark bedroom, surreptitiously paid him a penny to climb the stairs and turn on the light.

At the runaway shelter where I sometimes conduct poetry workshops now, I ask the kids to draw maps of their houses and list what has happened in each room. This is not such a simple task, as I discovered when I finally tried to do it. In our house, a number of rooms changed identity, a bedroom becoming a hallway, a kitchen becoming a den, and territories sometimes migrated with people. Any accurate cartography, then, really requires a set of maps, layered one over the other, like transparencies, and each person in the family possesses his or her own set.

One of my enduring memories, for instance, lives in an area which was not yet a room. When I was about 11, a doctor diagnosed an injury to my left arm. The atrophying muscles, he predicted, would cause it to wither and become shorter than my right arm— unless I undertook an exercise regime to reverse the process. For weeks, I marched around with a beach bucket of sand strapped to my left wrist. From the ceiling joists in the unfinished kitchen, Dad hung a trapeze. For an hour a day, I hung and swung dutifully from it, my arms aching therapeutically, the sunshine through the joists open to the sky laying down ribs of light and shadow. Early on, Mom and Dad and my siblings took a great interest in the activity, but soon wearied of it and resumed their involvements elsewhere. So I taught myself tricks, spinning with limited ability around the bar, trusting the creaking joists of the house I was helping to build, but not trusting myself enough to hang upside down.

Mostly, I think now, I taught myself the trick of being alone (a trick I would relearn over and over, and come, sadly, to perfect and rely on), my hands blistering and then healing unmiraculously. I taught myself a form of trust which allowed distrust of others. I was a boy extending his arms toward a mirror, not quite able to touch even his reflection, fudging to achieve the desired symmetry.

And there was also the living room which was first a bedroom, where I, at three or four years old, slept in a bed with high, barred sides. I have only one memory of this room from that time—a room which would later provide the setting for many public events. One night, my Grandmother Marshall brought me to that bed. She persuaded me to lie down and go to sleep. And then she walked toward the light in the doorway leading to the kitchen, a light casting a white parallelogram against the far wall. As she reached the doorway, she paused and leaned against the parallelogram. She slid down it then, sinking, it seems now, into her own shadow.

I stood up in the bed, and leaned against the bars, curious, most likely, at her odd behavior. The house was very quiet. Dad was at the plant and Mom somewhere beyond the room, probably where the light for the parallelogram originated.

After a while, she called out from the source of the light, "Mom?"

No answer.

And then a rising tone. "Mom?"

No answer.

A testy anxiousness. "Mom!?"

I could hear footsteps approaching.

And then a gasp and sob.

My grandmother had suffered a cerebral hemorrhage from which she never regained consciousness and died three days later. Her dying is my only memory of her in motion, except for some footage that Dad shot of her eating corn at a family picnic.

That quiet after she collapsed, and then my mother's sob, which remains one of the saddest utterances I've heard—both are unmappable.

"A good carpenter hides his mistakes," a man who would know once told me, and Dad was a better-than-average carpenter. I was 12, perhaps 13, when I learned of Nancy, his first wife.

"Yes," Mom said with a sour matter-of-factness when Greg brought it up. She cranked a sheet through the wringer of the washing machine, "It was a long time ago."

Initially, this news aroused in me the same puzzlement as on the day Dad told, casually, of a dream he had of us children. Before that moment, it had never occurred to me that he dreamed. Still, I let the matter of the first marriage go, since Mom's tone down-played it and no stepbrothers or stepsisters existed. Only later did I wonder why Greg knew enough to broach the topic and why

I, the oldest, had not acquired this information first. Such was my introduction to history as more than moving pictures on a screen. Among those phantoms of projected light, the past also involved figures visible only to those who could see them there—and actions inscrutable and distant yet recurring, palpable as a hand suddenly placed on a shoulder.

Two weeks before he graduated from high school, in 1943, Dad received his draft notice. He had been planning an excursion to California but instead stood next to a friend at the induction center, both of them hoping to enter the same branch of the service. A man with a clipboard walked along the line of draftees, pointing and announcing *Navy, Army, Air Force, Navy, Army, Air Force*, so Dad's friend entered the Army and Dad the Navy Air Corps. Dad never talked about those times unless asked, and we spoke most elaborately about them only later, when I was in my late twenties and early thirties—particularly on a drive to Omaha to visit Grandma Morrill when she was dying.

Undoubtedly, as for millions of young men and women of the time, the letter from the draft board abruptly concluded one life and began another. Like one of the handful of monumental decisions a person makes, it cast strange and challenging hues over the dependable, familiar world—except this was no choice. He found himself at a naval training station in northern Idaho—a boy who had designed sets for Central High's production of *Death Takes a Holiday* and *The Importance of Being Earnest*; a boy who, when he spied a friend sauntering down the street, ran into the house and ironed a shirt so as to appear impeccable. In Idaho, he underwent training of all sorts, but the memory he most revisited was of his wilderness survival test. Recruits were given a knife and sent out alone in the forest to fend for themselves for 24 hours.

"It was summer," Dad recalled, "and the woods were actually quite beautiful, with the smell of pine and the big hawks swooping.

But when night came, there was no moon, and it got pretty dark."

Every rustle in the brush spooked him, so he decided his nerves would be soothed best if he settled in one place. He sat down on the pine boughs and leaned against a tree not much wider than his back.

"I fell asleep," he said, "and some time later, I don't know when, a rumbling woke me up. It almost sounded like thunder, far off. I was groggy and stiff, so I got up and stretched. Suddenly, I realized that the thunder was getting louder and louder, and closer, too."

He had just enough time to press his chest against the tree trunk before the herd of wild horses roared past him on both sides.

The navy sent him to radioman's school and stationed him for the duration of the war in Trinidad, where he crewed 18-hour missions, hunting German submarines on a flying boat up and down the coast of Brazil and Argentina.

"I used to hang out the hatches," he remembered, smiling in astonishment at his former self. "I wasn't scared at all. But it was a dull business. We napped in hammocks strung up inside the fuselage—unless we were dive-bombing sharks."

In his navy trunk that lay undisturbed for years in our attic, most of the wartime photographs are either official group portraits or individual snaps taken on leave, in various USOs. At the piano, for beers, he played requests from the hit parade. He looks jocular in those pictures—his face now forcasting the features of Greg's face, now Mike's, now Aaron's—one of the guys.

It was on those leaves that he shed his virginity with a four-dollar whore at the Mayflower Hotel in Panama, and met the man from Brazil who played matchmaker.

A number of his fellow crew members visited prostitutes regularly, and they became determined to get Dad to go with them. At last, they convinced him. In the reception room, he sat nervously with a woman, perhaps in her mid-forties, after the rest of the crew had retired with their selections.

"I've never done anything like this," he told her, finally.

"Well," she replied, "Come on, there's nothing to it. You're not the first."

She put the condom on him.

"It was over that quick," he told me.

Back at his room, he scrubbed himself with shaving cream, fearing the clap.

"I was even more cautious afterward," he said, grinning.

This story emerged in pieces over decades—a reminiscence while he leaned against a sawhorse or while we were driving somewhere—but I remember most how his initial bashfulness at particulars made me, a child of the sexual revolution of the 60's, flush with worldly superiority, even as a virgin.

The man from Brazil, Renato, frequented the same night spots as Dad, and they became friends. They traveled to Carnaval together. Renato, it seems, grew so attached to Dad that he brought him home to his mother and aunts, attempting to arrange a marriage to his sister. In a large interior courtyard, they all sat and sipped tea.

"There was a gorgeous fountain," Dad recalled, "and the old women wore their black lace, you know, with their hand fans going. They were congenial, really. . . . But I just couldn't marry that girl. She was nice, but I didn't really know those people. . . ."

In my adolescence, stories such as these melded with the story of Nancy into a single frieze entitled: *Dad Before My Time.* With the years, of course, that past has proven expandable and nearly as fluid as the present, something that can happen to you again.

Selling magazines, Nancy McAllister knocked on his door at Garfield Avenue on a summer day in 1949. He didn't invite her in because he didn't want the neighbors to get the idea that he allowed strange women into his house, so they sat on the grass. She wore a blue dress and asked for a glass of water, and they talked for a long time.

A few weeks later, he wrote to her in her home town of Birmingham, Alabama, fascinated by her and her accent. A correspondence ensued. Soon, he invited her to Des Moines and flew to Birmingham to meet her.

"We took a bus back," he told me, not long before his death, laughing.

She stayed with his Uncle Hank and Aunt Margaret Morrill, who lived down the hill from Garfield Avenue.

"My parents," he said, "were upset that I didn't bring her to Omaha right away. Dad had even bought a new suit for the occasion."

Not long afterward, they decided to marry. Great-grandfather Gundy told Dad outright that Nancy "wasn't much" because she smoked. Dad wanted to get married in the church, but Nancy was divorced, so no priest would perform the service. He had even sought assistance from a priest downtown, at the cathedral, but the clergyman had advised him against the woman, holding that Dad only had "the hots" and would get over them.

They were married on October 28, 1949, by a justice of the peace. When Dad and I last spoke about these incidents, he couldn't quite recall the date, thinking it was in August, but Mom, passing through the room at that moment, fixed it exactly and with great severity. She and Dad were married in August and, doubtless, she wished to dispel any confusion.

Soon enough, of course, the marriage was in trouble. Nancy, for instance, enjoyed whiskey in considerable quantities.

"Didn't you know this before?" I asked Dad.

"Why, no," he said. "She was just a sweet girl. I thought

everything was sweet. Everyone was good. I loved music and art. I thought it was a beautiful world."

Nancy took a job as a telephone operator downtown, at the Hotel Randolph, and Dad worked 3-11 at Firestone. One day, she told Dad that a friend of hers from Birmingham was in town, and she wanted to see him.

"I told her," he said, "You're married to me now. You're not going anywhere."

She went, and was absent for three hours.

A short time after this, a woman Dad knew from the local Rubber Workers' Union called him. She just wanted him to know that she had seen Nancy "with several men" during a political function at the hotel. She wasn't certain he approved of such behavior.

Here, the history clouds and conflates. Nancy had a lover. Dad stuffed her belongings into her suitcases and stacked them at curbside. He then jumped a downtown bus, in search of a lawyer's office.

"She wanted me to talk to her 'boyfriend,'" Dad said. "But I wasn't having none of it. They were just going to try to change my mind."

The attorney had Nancy sign a warrant for a divorce, so she didn't have to appear at the hearing. The judge, Dad said, was "a fat bastard" who lectured him about the fiasco but awarded him the house and most of the assets, since they were his at the start.

Nancy, if she survives, might tender a different version of these events: Dad as possessive ogre, as short-tempered bully. I also imagine her, in their inevitable arguments, deriding him sexually.

He never saw her again, and she attempted no contact—except, perhaps, 15 years later when Mom answered a phone call from a mysterious woman asking for Dad, who was not home at the time. The woman refused to give her name or number, and simply hung up.

That first marriage endured, officially, three months, but I often wonder how much longer it survived in other forms. Of all the events just beyond the margins of Dad's films or my maps, it taught me that the house that grew up with me, that I assumed I knew intimately beneath the skin of its siding and sheetrock, among its wires like neurons and its skeleton of planking and brace—even that house was mine to know only to a point, and that, ambiguous. As an adult, I finally realized that Dad and Nancy's bedroom, around which the house later expanded, became Dad and Mom's bedroom and, eventually, mine. Did Nancy and her lover lie in that room during the long evenings when Dad worked at the plant? I was conceived there, as was so much else.

In one of the early super-8's, footage of house construction precedes and follows a sequence shot, quite arbitrarily, in the show barn at the state fair. For no more than ten or 12 seconds, among ribs of stark sunlight and curtaining shadow, a white flame swirls partly into view. It becomes a white horse, rearing. Then a horse and white flame and shadow all at once. It finally disappears into darkness. Our house grew to be one of the three largest and proudest residences on a street of modest and lowly homes—a foolhardy prospect, if one assesses property like a real estate agent. But of the three building families, the Olivers moved away early, leaving their upstairs for others to finish. Next door, the Pauldings completed an elegant home, but then divorced, and one winter night several years later, Mrs. Paulding and her son perished in a fire which leveled that house. Mr. Paulding refused to sell the lot to any neighbor but my father. His gesture implied that our household was the sole intact referent to a vanished time, and thus deserving of special status. Even so, privately, something like that white horse flame and shadow had burst repeatedly from between our scenes of daily construction, wrecking the soul of our place.

3. THERE WAS A DANCE

One night at Firestone in 1952, my future uncle, Guy Weldon, told Dad of a dance to be held in Moravia, Iowa.

"There'll be a good-looking woman there I'd be going after," he said, "if I wasn't already married."

In Moravia, Dad and this woman, who was to become my mother, were introduced. They glided across the floor, spun and dipped, as though they had always danced together. They laughed, Dean and Alberta, or Bertie, as people called her. She was quiet, countrified, but attractively square-shouldered and tall.

After this, Dad visited her regularly, riding the bus from Des Moines down Highway 5, getting off at the gravel spur that led to Pershing, sometimes taking a taxi the rest of the way there.

Dean and Bertie dated. Her parents warmed quickly to this love interest. All was cohering.

And then Dean broke off the relationship.

"I just didn't feel right," he told me, vague about that distant interregnum.

Some months elapsed. He fingered the piano in the two-room house shared briefly with Nancy a couple of years before. He went "hell-raising" in beer joints with Marvin and Joe, friends and cousins from the plant. Seeking reasons for the breakup, Guy and some of Bertie's sisters pestered him, encouraging him to talk with Bertie and try again. At last, they convinced him to go with them to a dance the following Saturday night.

There, he and she waltzed and jitterbugged, congruent as always. But he remained merely cordial, so they separated and milled among the others present.

"I guess it was something about seeing her dance with somebody else that did it," Dad told me one night, as we sat on the deck at the lake house. "It got me right in the gut."

I have often lingered on that moment when the vision of another man desiring my mother—and her pleasure at this attention—burst upon my father with a transfixing power. It astonishes me as well, knowing her only as I have. That dance altered her in his eyes and altered the future like that letter from the draft board or Nancy's first knock on his door. Was it merely jealousy which compelled him to take her in his arms and sway and twirl with her the rest of that night? Or perhaps her public regard had unseated a presumption that he was the suave city mouse and she the plain bumpkin who would always be available? Perhaps loneliness had whispered into his ear about time's passage—he was nearly thirty—and that his best second chance for love was dancing away?

She sat through the prescribed catechism classes, was baptized, and married him—all at St. Joseph's. She moved into his house on Garfield Avenue, and they produced five children in the next nine years.

"All planned," he reported proudly to us, again and again.

They honeymooned over a weekend at the Hotel Fort Des Moines.

"In those days," he said, smiling, "your mother was quite eager."

The morning after their first night there, he ate two breakfasts, with a gusto for abundance of which her breasts where the most recent and satisfying manifestation.

This romance report came to me later in my father's life, after drinks, and it has always cheered me with its simple declaration of happiness. My parents had been in love, fucking and pleased with each other. Happy. Yes, they were.

How and why they—such superb dancers—fell out of step with each other and that morning of the two breakfasts seemed to elude them to the end. My mother asserted, with bewilderment, that Dad "turned mean" somewhere between the third and fifth year of their marriage. He said, by the time I was eight or nine, that she had stopped "making a life" for him. Overwhelmingly, their inability to retrieve their initial happiness enhanced their sorrows.

Though I have presented here their renditions of their past— stories with the dire breaches by which children try to judge their parents—my siblings and I had always confronted our parents' versions of each other. They were propagandists, each seeking the self-aggrandizing angle, while jousting with tar brushes. They hoped to explain themselves to themselves, as well as to us, with a flexible allegiance to the truth. Frequently, they starred in an aggressive theatre, their debilitating and very real make-believe an inescapable Punch and Judy show—prodigious because they were also gods to us for so long.

From my earliest grade school days onward, we witnessed their horrific scenes, which assumed over the years a grim predictibility. A broken vase, a sibling struggle, anything loud and close and immediately unquellable would spur Dad's anger. It quickly exceeded the level of rhetorical response and soared into a stratospheric fury. This was not a matter of exhaustion at the end of the day or spent patience, but a more ancient and primitive impulse which seduced him as nothing else. He stomped and shouted and growled, accused and avenged. And the shaking I often saw in his hands as he worked at something that frustrated him snapped through his whole frame in an ecstatic triggering.

Such displays must have begun modestly—oaths over a flat tire, dinner tiffs. And they must have expanded incrementally, each almost a test of what behavior was allowable in the marriage. Since Mom attempted to placate, discuss, and, only later, withdraw, perhaps Dad thought that she wasn't hearing him and so he expanded and increased. My memory teems with images of him in full-force rant, stalking her in retreat through the house, driven to make her listen to condemnations and indictments growing habitual with the years, painful and, eventually, banal. In these tirades, he was everything, she nothing. He had big plans, dreams, friends; she knew no one outside of Pershing and wouldn't make arrangements to go out. He had wanted a house he could be proud of; she didn't care how she lived. He had some college education, was cultured, cared for beauty; she had not finished her senior year of high school and merely existed, a lump, the great undoer of all he had hoped to achieve.

A silent film of these episodes would be quite funny, I think. Dad racing around the kitchen, arms flailing, bumping into the refrigerator, his face wrenched into an impossible contortion, like some villain from the Beijing Opera, his bald head wagging deliriously as though he were some sea creature just hatched and struggling from his egg beneath the sandy beach. Typescripts of these monologues would also garner some amusement—provided one forgot how such idiocy, like local weather, penetrates the bones of those who grow up with it. His anger produced all the appearances of power, and so won my respect, even as I despised it. Until my mid-twenties—when my lover at the time showed me that I needed to reconsider my mother and her family—I had believed much of what he said about her in these instances, though I had suspected his reproaches and believed I had rejected all that were false.

"Get what you want out of life before you get married," he shouted at me one day in the car, after another berating session, "because once you're married, you're fucked."

I also did not perceive how much the general atmosphere of blaming encouraged in me a grave distrust of women and any emotional commitment to them. I remember the father of my college girlfriend arriving home one evening from his factory job. With genuine zest, he hugged and kissed his wife. It stunned me, like some intriguing yet bizarre foreign custom.

At home, the fighting often occurred during the day, we

children scattering for cover but often drawn into the commotion. Once, for instance, Mom retreated outside. Dad attempted to maintain a decorous presence in the neighborhood, so he rarely pursued her into the yard, though anyone nearby would have been able to hear his curses and insults in those months when the windows were open. On this day, he locked the door and sat us children in a row on the couch. On pain of a whipping, he ordered us to stay there, even if Mom knocked on the door to be let in, which she soon did. Shaving in the bathroom, he shouted to us the threat of a beating if we moved. We looked at each other. She rapped again, and again he warned us. Mike, second to the youngest and so small at the time that he doesn't remember the incident, rose characteristically and unlatched the door. Surprised, Dad did nothing.

For most of those years, however, Dad roared even more often at night, and this drama involved us children differently. During the week, he regularly stopped for a couple of beers at the Hilltop Tavern after his shift, and he always brought two six-packs home. The tavern teemed with family connections. A number of the waitresses sent their children to St. Joseph's. Alex, the proprietor, sponsored my confirmation and served me my first legal drink at 19. At the Hilltop, Dad said, he found repose from the machine thunder at the plant. He lounged in a placid, thoughtless zone between work and family.

"Some women," Mom observed years afterward, "say 'My husband was at the bar because of this guy or that guy.' Nope. Nobody makes you go to the bar but yourself. I never begrudged your Dad stopping at Hilltop. He worked, and that was his time off."

Unspoken rules circumscribed Dad's drinking. He consumed beer exclusively, and only smoked when he drank. He never drank and drove with the family. He only drank after work and never missed work because of drinking.

But if he aspired to confine his consumption to a minor, discreet territory, chaos was also loosed within its borders.

Early in their marriage, my parents hosted and were entertained. On several occasions, friends from the plant, like George and Jerri Hood, laughed around the kitchen table and on the patio until dawn. Vividly, I remember wandering among the adult legs and bowls of potato chips and peanuts, enthralled by life beyond bedtime. As a toddler, I had been taken to parties in my pajamas. When I was older, my parents would return from a night out at a union dance or at the Hilltop, and Mom would present us children with miniature scimitars and parasols gleaned from exotic cocktails.

But socializing of this sort ebbed, perhaps because of the demands of a growing family—certainly because of the bitterness and shame in a faltering marriage. On ordinary work nights, Dad drank alone because Mom, while she consumed coffee round the clock, consented to only one or two highballs a year, at Christmas or on New Year's Eve. His first two beers, and sometimes his third, bestowed upon him and his surroundings an immeasurable grace.

"That was the one sure time he would be sweet with you," Peggy observed.

Unlike his explosions during the day, his more commonplace and damaging rages emerged somewhere after the first six-pack. They began with scattered comments, small, snappish statements and challenges. They rumbled, seemingly distant, like an inferno behind a hatch about to blow off its hinges—a loathsome tone. Immediately, Mom would seek to diffuse matters by caressing his sense of reason. Occasionally, she would venture to point out a contradiction in his thinking. He viewed any response from her as a riposte.

The alcohol and his anger swirled and formed a new being. It was impossible to say the booze, or the anger, was shouting. The new being railed, a thing unto itself, with its own logic—or illogic. And my father was this thing. He became it, later punishing himself with remorse.

Well after 1 A.M., that voice of the thing-he-became often awakened me. On other nights, it cried out through the piano, elaborate, weeping melodies. "People" was a favorite song: *People who need people are the luckiest people in the world.* . . .

Mornings bore the astringent odor of dregs, his fuming empties jammed into a stained brown bag. I once rose for breakfast and found him passed out on the kitchen floor, to my distress and shame, though no one else was present. And, of course, there was the fall in which he had broken his leg. Daily, while he labored on the house, he also toiled through a hangover. No matter how racked his body, he kept appointments, taking Greg to art lessons, Peggy to ballet. In winter, if he was not still up and flush, he would rise at 3 A.M. and drive Greg and me on my Sunday morning paper route. The Sunday edition abounded with ads, so it was huge and heavy. Once, the temperature plummeted to 24 below zero, and the car wouldn't start. He carved two holes for handles in the ends of a cardboard box and hauled the papers on foot as Greg and I delivered them. This definition of responsible action was part of his unspoken rules for drinking; perhaps, he hoped it exonerated him for his less worthy performances. The sizzle of Alka-Seltzer tablets in water accompanied so much of his waking, then—a parodic echo of the general burning.

At some point during this time, out of negative pride, I computed how many cans of beer he had consumed, averaging a dozen a day for 25 years. That he imbibed was well established among my friends in adolescence, yet this carried some cache with them, since their first notions of manhood resided in shoplifted quart bottles of malt liquor. He charmed them with grilled cheeseburgers on sleepouts. When we were in college, he bought them rounds at the Hilltop. Still, I tried to keep them clear of him and our place.

While Mom often sought refuge from Dad's ferocity, she retaliated against him in other ways. During these years, however deep my belief in Dad's condemnations of her, I remained closer to her than him. As the oldest, I became the first audience in a ceaseless campaign to recoup her self-worth by demonstrating to her children her equanimity, rationality, patience. Thus, in her post-fight monologue, after Dad had gone to the plant or to bed, she would reinterate that despite his awful and preventable behavior, he was a good man who loved us.

"I always say to your Dad," she would begin, "'Why do you have to act this way? Life's too short for this.'"

She sought our allegiance against Dad as much as our love, and rules governed her actions, just as they did Dad's drinking. The most important of these was that she could not appear to wish Dad ill in his children's hearts, could not seem to wish herself above him in our affections. Our love for her over him had to seem a spontaneous vote for her character, a vindication and restoration of the identity which Dad battered.

That identity was not always, and is not often now, clear. To me, she remains mostly anonymous—very shallow or very deep, a cliché-monger or wise mystic. One of my earliest memories is of her and me holding hands among fat snowflakes tumbling, the two of us part of a long line winding toward *The Sword in the Stone* at the RKO Orpheum Theater. On another occasion, when I was small, I gathered gravel from the driveway into a plastic Wonderbread wrapper. I presented it to her as a bag of gems, and she accepted it as such—our alchemy.

With my hand on her stomach, I felt my siblings move inside her, and as I grew up, I measured my height against her shoulder.

She held up ovoid loaves of dough and slapped them hard so I could yowl, gleefully, pretending to be beaten. She chased me with a huge, cartoonish plastic golf club, failing to scare me onto the bicycle I pushed around the yard but could not yet ride. Two times she sat with me in the afternoon until I fell asleep, once terrified after seeing *The Tingler* on my only other movie trip downtown, and, again, haunted by a news story featuring body bags in Viet Nam and my realization that I could be destined for that war. I remember also trying to decide, as an adolescent, how to ask her for an explanation of the brown line around the tip of my penis and down its shaft (my circumcision scar, I later realized) but resolving that it just wasn't something you could bring up with your mother.

She endorsed my adventures, and convinced me that I was her favorite, which I believe I was for some time, despite her protestations that "I love all my children the same." While Dad was moody and monstrously chancy, she remained reliably placid. Her emotions never wrought sensationalistic displays and were thus rarely, if ever, recognized. And she did little to alter this status quo, perhaps not knowing how. Even now when I ask her how she is, her first reply is a bland "fine," which further questioning can sometimes unpack. It is this pacific inclination and verbal leveling which I mistook for a fatal and weak passivity, probably at the point when I tried to rescue their marriage.

How old could I have been? 12? 13? I called the family together for a council one evening while Dad was at work. We— meaning she and we children—*would* pick up the piled clothes clotting hallways, *would* purge the carpets of ancient, crushed potato chips and petrified bread crumbs. We *would* clear the stacked food and scrub the crayola from the walls. We *would* eat at normal times and speak quietly and act like a normal family—like the families of my friends, as I imagined them to be.

I think now I was trying to enforce the suburban suavity which Dad professed to desire. He accused her constantly of letting us and the place go, which she did, partly out of sadness and partly, to be honest, out of a rustic sense of housekeeping. I thought somehow that this regimented renewal would resolve their differences. Certainly, it would relieve my growing shame.

When nothing came of my dictatorial reforms, my strategy shifted. I lobbied her to leave him. This signaled a new phase in our relationship, in which I at last answered all of her speeches. I had gone to sleep countless nights listening to her putter in the kitchen before Dad arrived home from work, her quiet hours. I had awakened to her weeping, the slapped second wife. This had to stop. She could go, and we kids would go with her. We'd all be free.

Dad had shocked us when he had first announced, in one of his harangues, that he was divorcing her. Repetition, however, had consigned this threat to his repertoire of ludicrous gestures. He needed her to abuse too much to leave her. But she . . . she didn't need him, I pleaded. She could establish a new life. Just a little courage was required. Think of it.

She listened. At times, I believed I had convinced her.

Though Dad whipped us children when we misbehaved—and I always deserved it—I have no memory of him physically abusing us. With Mom, he did not check himself. Greg recalls his striking her early, when we were preschoolers.

"I see it just as clear as can be," he told me. "She was wearing a white dress with purple flowers. He knocked her to the floor and threw a glass of water in her face."

Mom had two miscarriages, one between Greg and Peggy and another between Peggy and Mike.

"He caused the first one," Greg said. "He didn't know she was pregnant. About the other one, I don't know."

I cannot fix a particular moment when I first recognized the violence, which suggests how desperately I wished to conceal it from myself. Greg speaks of an Easter at Grandma Morrill's when Mom had blackened eyes, though I do not remember her ever marked in any way. My most vivid early memory of these devastations, however, stems from an incident that could not be denied.

During another visit to Grandma and Grandpa Morrill's house, Dad charged drunkenly at Mom. I stepped between them and screamed, "Don't come any closer or I'll kill you. I swear I'll kill you."

I meant it, 15 years old, standing there with acne cream daubed all over my face. As I told my father in that crucial letter I sent from north China—a letter which contains much of this early history—I had to do *something*.

He and I struggled a bit, a peculiar dance. I felt his strength, his body which seemed, as I hugged it, amazingly larger than it looked. I ached inside, being there with him like that.

Grandma had enough power to call him to withdraw. I shook. Still, I didn't realize until later how much of his anger coursed in me, how much it was his voice stabbing from my mouth—me, who so much resembled her, glaring at him then.

Rugged physically, Mom eventually fought back. I remember another night when Dad locked her out of the house. She slammed her fist through the glass and unlatched the door. He struck her, and she punched him in the jaw, almost dislocating it. More than once she bragged to me how she had repelled him with a skillet. And he had been shocked and temporarily quieted by these defenses which sprang from her tomboy childhood. But somewhere amid the recounted blows, I stopped listening to her. She seemed to lack the ultimate courage to leave because she appeared to be the inert substance he said she was. Stubbornness, perhaps suffused with fear of the outside world, fortified her will.

She became the stone around the sword of certainties which her life offered, and there was no Arthur to whom she would yield it.

Thus, she fostered a considerable inattention to the obvious, wearing inner blinders which obscured her perception and the recognition of her denial. I wore them, too—for years ignoring the ruckus, and later, on my own, never thinking what might have transpired before or after I entered a room. Those blinders delivered me safely into adulthood, and I have clawed at them since.

Many years after, Dad spoke to me, seriously, of divorce. We sat in the Des Moines airport, waiting for my flight back to Florida after the Christmas holidays.

"I've just had it with that old lady," he said calmly, without warning, and went on to explain how he was going to get his own place, start fresh with his retirement.

I encouraged him, thinking how he and she had really separated long before, with his moving to the front porch—his narrow, clotted lair and pathetic refuge.

On a day just weeks before his death, he told me that he had investigated the realities of leaving but decided that he couldn't afford it. He had known others from the plant who had divorced in their late fifties and early sixties.

"None of them had a thing left," he said. "If your mother had worked out of the house, I might have done it. I wanted to leave long before that. I felt trapped."

"You could have left any time," Mom snapped from the kitchen. She entered the room where we sat. "No one kept you. You weren't trapped."

"Of course," I said to her, playing the therapist, "it may be true that he wasn't trapped, but he felt like it anyway, and he has the right to express that."

She looked bewildered by my remark, by this approach to

communication. Thinking of that moment now, I imagine his ill-ness during his final three years as both her revenge, because he was suffering, and her bitter burden, because he often needed her. A tectonic pressure focused on the edge where her rules for hon-orable conduct ground against her desires to punish. She disliked hospitals, but more than that distaste influenced her reluctance, on occasion, to visit him there.

"I just couldn't find the time to go today," she'd say, or, "He'll just be there, sleeping, and I'd be bored."

When he suffered his last attack, she refused to ride to the emergency room in the ambulance, sending Aaron in a car be-hind, and calling Mike to transport her immediately thereafter.

Mom and I rarely discuss her more distant past, though when I spoke to Dad in his last months about his recollections, her memory, so long dormant, flourished in competition and pre-sented its bounty. Prior to this, we had gained our only mutual purchase on that history while driving through the countryside. During one of those meanderings, she alleged that Grandma Morrill was a matriarch, the power of the family, and that early on Grandma had made her vow that she would never leave Dad—probably because Grandma knew how Dad was.

"How could you promise such a thing?" I replied, astonished and skeptical.

"Because I didn't know how he was going to be," she guffawed.

On the day that she and I and Dad talked about feeling trapped, he spoke—the only time in my hearing—harshly about his mother.

"When I got back from the war," he said, "she was changed. She was a drinker—a drunk—and so was Dad. I got out. I couldn't live with that."

A few minutes afterward, he confessed his sorrow at having struck his father—both of them drunk—in a row at a family holiday. He peered at me as he spoke, searching my hunger to know and my capacity to pardon.

He and Mom bickered over her remark that he could have left her any time he had wanted. Their voices spiraled upward, and, again playing the therapist, I relieved them of the old ascent.

"You guys have been married 41 years," I offered, "and you don't have forever. How much time can there be? Are you going to go on like this, finish like this? Is this really the way you want to live the rest together, or are you going to settle up?"

For a moment, a strange and attractive channel opened between them, a pathway apparently unknown to either of them. Puzzled, they gazed at each other as at a foreign landscape, or a new life form. I had introduced them to this possibility, but, of course, I was still thinking of the future, still investing in that hope, and their future was all in the past.

The channel closed.

"It was kind of a blind date," Mom explained to me later that day, as we drove through the countryside, going nowhere.

"What did you think when you met him?"

"He was handsome . . . and nice to me . . . and a good dancer."

I let a few minutes pass.

"How did you know you loved him?"

She paused. "By the way he held me or kissed me."

"Did you ever have any other serious boyfriends, any other engagements?"

"No."

I let a few more moments go.

"When did you know that you loved him?"

A pause. "God, I don't know. . ." She sounded surprised, agitated, embarrassed, "It's been so many years ago."

After some further minutes of silence, she said, "I have always loved your Dad and I know he loves me, but it's a hate love."

4. PEANUT BUTTER SOUP

Mom enforced bedtimes strenuously when we children were small, but as we grew a little older, these curfews, on the weekends, fell away. This occurred as a capitulation to our rambunctiousness but also to allow us more time around Dad. During the school year, the 3-11 shift kept him and us apart most of the week, bringing us together for chores on Saturday, and on Sunday, for church, dinner and, sometimes, *The Ed Sullivan Show*. The conflicts which usually engaged my parents on weekend nights emerged in the wee hours, after their children's magical sojourns in lateness.

We awaited Dad's arrival anxiously on Friday nights because he often called home from the Hilltop and took orders for pizzas, burgers and fries. In my memory, he always enters the house from the winter darkness, a snow king with the cold pouring from him, and we race into the kitchen from the TV room where we had been perched in front of movie Draculas dubbed over Spanish or giant ants ransacking cities. On Saturdays, after the 10 P.M. news, he sometimes popped a pan of corn and joined us to watch Karloff and Lugosi on *Gravesend Manor*. During the commercials, he would recount walking home in the dark as a kid after seeing *Frankenstein* in the theater, his eyes widening as a shadow leapt out in his story and spooked him. Or he would try to frighten us into laughter with recollections of radio shows like *The Shadow* and *Inner Sanctum*, whining the mordant farewell of Digger O'Dell, the friendly undertaker, "I'll be seeing you . . .!"

In such circumstances, his ebullience often bounded forth as it would from a goodnatured child. He sat at the piano in the living room, next to the doorway where Grandma Marshall had collapsed with a stroke, and bit down on a Liberace grin.

"I wish my brother George were here," he'd say unctuously.

We'd call for a boogie-woogie, or "Roll Out the Barrel," or "Twelfth Street Rag"—one of our favorites. With Mom looking on, we'd shamble and shake to his pumping beat, scuffing our socked feet on the carpet and shocking one another with near-touches.

And sometimes he would sit serenely at the kitchen table, smoking a cigarette and sipping a beer, with Harlan Hanna spinning downy melodies from the '40s Hit Parade on KCBC.

Later, when my younger brothers and sister had gone to bed, I eased into my first semi-adult hours with my parents. I would perform for them, entering the kitchen from the hallway as though stepping onto the stage at the Copacabana. I would hop down on one knee and sing "Mammy" like Al Jolson—whom I had seen in cartoon parodies—or stagger under a fedora like Jimmy Durante, barking out in a chalky whisper, "That ain't no banana, that's my nose!" I would improvise melodramas inspired by a yardstick or highchair, or wastebasket, soaking up my audience's attention.

Dad and I would also play simple word games in which there was no winner, merely countinuing rounds interrupted by moments when we delighted at unexpected diction. Quietly, he would lecture me about the need for integrity and responsibility and education, and I would smirk furtively at Mom. Sometimes, often out of his own style of malapropism, he made up words which he then commissioned for his sermons.

"Get some imprenchipios about yourself!" he would command, chortling.

He misnamed the world when he was harried by the moment's demands and his muse could do no more than lunge at the greased pig of sense. Thus, the Shaw family, who lived on the west side of the street, became The Wests, the Roseberries down the hill, the Pillsburys. Instead of a joint, degenerates smoked a "wig" of pot, and so on.

At other moments, however, Dad would break into Shakespeare.

> *O that this too too sullied flesh would melt,*
> *Thaw and resolve itself into a dew,*
> *Or that the Everlasting had not fixed*
> *His canon 'gainst self-slaughter. O God, God,*
> *How weary, stale, flat and unprofitable*
> *Seems to me all the uses of the world!*
> *Fie on't, ah fie, 'tis an unweeded garden*
> *That grows to seed, things rank and gross in nature*
> *Possess it merely. . . .*

My chin jutted forward in wonder when I first heard this passage, which he was to quote most often. His hamminess confirmed my erroneous assumption that he had been an actor during his period "in the theater." With a triumphant puff of mentholated smoke, he concluded and cast me a look that said: *There, you see. And you thought you knew your old Dad.*

The late hours also saw another of his recurring impulses: coming to his children asleep in their beds. My sister, brothers, and I agree on the matter and means of these visitations. His chosen party would be shocked awake, usually by his switching on an overhead light, and more often by his whisking the pillow from beneath the dreamer's head. I remember many rousings that began this way. Dad muttered beery concerns about my health and the need for appropriate rest, furiously clapping the pillow into maximum fluffiness. He clamped a hand where my neck and shoulder met, and hoisted my torso upward, far enough that he could return the improved pillow to its former location. He then, gently, let me fall back supine and began the re-tucking in. This procedure could consume several minutes, with his spooling away all covers and, in effect, remaking the bed with me in it. Finally, he pulled the blankets up to my neck and folded them behind my shoulders, battening me down—choking me a little—in his quest for ultimate snugness.

Often, he left the room after this, shutting off the light. But sometimes, he shut off the light and returned to sit on the edge of the bed and murmur various things which I, hoping to go back to sleep, tried to ignore. I recall nothing of what he uttered in those moments, only that he punctuated his sentiments with the refrain, "And, son, I want you to know it."

Other nights, he sat wordlessly. And, sometimes, he wept. And, once or twice, he lay down beside me and threw his arm over me, and slept, his snoring—which kept me awake—resonant as the hammering of a pileated woodpecker.

On school mornings, we could encounter other signs of his enthusiasms. He sometimes left love notes, in green crayon, on white paper napkins next to our breakfast plates. Regularly, I would find back issues of sports and car magazines he got from a man at the factory, rolled and cinched by a strip of raw tire rubber—my only reading interest at the time. A bulletin board hung near the door and a blackboard was affixed to the wall in the hallway. On the former, he thumbtacked morally efficacious clippings from Ann Landers and the funnies. On the latter, we met protestations of his love for us, or an inspirational quotation, or, in a boozy scribble, a fanfare such as *I've got rhythm, I've got music, I've got my girl, who could ask for anything more!*

On those mornings after report cards had been issued, each of us faced his review. He fumed about my poor grades for "deportment," and he preached achievement as many of his generation did to their children. He admired what he believed was culture and cultured behavior, and he wanted us exposed to it. Thus, the bookshelves abounded with encyclopedias purchased on special promotions from gas stations and grocery stores. I took accordion lessons at Professional Music Center, a two-story house in a ramshackle neighborhood encroaching on the university. Greg took piano; Mike and Aaron: guitar; Peggy: ballet and tap.

Dad adored beauty. He was enthralled by its force—whether he perceived it in an aria by Jesseye Norman on the educational channel or in the kitschy plastic petunias he would arrange on top of the refrigerator. His love-gasp at art works such as the Sistine Chapel and sentimental movies like *Intermezzo* set him apart from Mom—or, at least, he wished it to separate them. He also wanted it to relieve him of the drabness he sensed in ordinary existence. It was part of his attraction, also, to crafts and various tinkerings. While he recovered from his broken leg, for instance, he taught himself to crochet and thereafter produced rugs and throws and sweaters. He also sewed on occasion, turning out the costumes for Peggy's dance recitals. He constructed bird hotels. For the club house I shared with my friend Tom, he fashioned a large fish from brown grocery bags he cut, stuffed and painted. He raised pigeons—white kings and fan tails—for which he won ribbons at the state fair. He planted amaryllis bulbs and morning glories and cosmos.

He also baked. On a Sunday night, he would open a cook-book and begin making divinity, deviating from the recipe as his inspiration directed. And these improvisations often succeeded. Among friends and neighbors who received them as gifts, his apple rings became the paragons of breakfast sweets during Christmastime. His fudge provoked swoons.

I shared his inclination to "improve" upon the recipe or to ignore it completely. I never looked at the instructions that accompanied model airplane kits, choosing instead to figure them out on my own. I have done something similar as a writer, wasting much time, I believe, on avoidable errors. This character trait—which is sometimes a flaw and sometimes a strength—derives not from a lack of respect for expertise and directions, but from a foolhardy impatience to plunge in and get started and make the thing at hand work, now.

This proclivity, which was not a constant, could plague Dad. While building the house on Garfield Avenue and at the lake, he tore down concrete blocks he had misaligned out of ignorance; he ripped out door jambs that he had incorrectly set. I remember once that he decided to save money by installing the new exhaust system on our station wagon himself. His own father had made him tear down a car and reassemble it before he would allow Dad to drive, so Dad felt confident that he could finesse this repair. Beneath the car propped on blocks in the drive, he grappled all day with the long snaking pipes, trying to fit them to the contours of the chassis. No manipulation seemed to work. He bolted them in as well as he could and wrapped the gaps with tin and what he said was asbestos fabric. We drove around the block and arrived back in the driveway with smoke issuing thickly from the flaming cloths beneath. When Dad examined the instructions that accompanied the pipes, we discovered that they were made for a model and year different from our car.

His most famous and farcical debacle, however, was peanut butter soup. One summer, Mom stayed for a week with her sisters in Pershing, and Dad, on vacation, babysat. A woman on a local morning chat show presented the day's recipe for a tremendous soup made with peanut butter, which she avowed her children lapped up like greedy puppies. Dad jotted down the ingredients, envisioning a paradigm shift for lunch. But somewhere in the concocting, he added other ingredients. When he ladled it into our bowls, the dishwatery brew piped forth the reek of peanuts and onions commingled. No one would touch it. He threatened us with a paddling, to no avail. Finally, he turned to me. I was perhaps 11 at the time, by far peanut butter's greatest devotee.

"Go ahead," he said, nodding toward the bowl, though he had not yet tried it himself.

"No, I don't think I want any," I said.

"I'll whip you if you don't eat."

"Whip me, then."

He stared at me, and at the other kids. He was like the oldest kid, trying, and failing, to force the younger ones to play a game he had invented, and we sensed this. He tried to threaten me again, but before he could finish, a conceding smile overthrew his imperious tone. It is one of my happiest memories of him. We all laughed as he collected our bowls and dumped their contents back into the pot. He brought out bread and cold cuts. While we assembled sandwiches triumphantly, he flushed his invention down the toilet.

Such moments—he alone with all of us children—were rare in the early years. More often, we hung around him and Mom while they performed some vaguely ritualized task, like slaughtering chickens for winter. Dad had no stomach for the killing, so Mom worked among the caged birds in the driveway. Without much ado, she, the country girl, placed a broomstick across the neck of each creature, stepped down on it and yanked the body. We children screamed and fled from headless hens dashing across the gravel, crashing down, twitching. We'd bring the corpses to the kitchen, where Dad, somehow calmed by it all, plucked them as they soaked in basins of steaming water.

I do recall one day in my childhood, however, that he and I spent alone together in ways other than at work. Dad decided that I needed school clothes. He took me to McCoy's House of Remnants and bought me new shoes and jeans. We drove across town to Merle Hay Plaza. We ate burgers in the bowling alley there. It was my first time in such a place, and the fluorescent light in the deep lanes and the spectacular roar of tumbling pins entranced me—as did the fact that we were eating out somewhere other than McDonald's, and he was saying to me over and over, "You want anything else? Order whatever you want."

Afterward, he bought me shirts at J.C. Penney's, the ones I picked out. His eagerness for me to try on things and his willingness to spend stunned me; it was as if the momentum of this project had mobilized all his resources. Though I was hardly deprived in ordinary circumstances, he usually lavished such ardor on Peggy, his only girl. In fact, she wielded so much clout in this regard that it was she whom my brothers and I enlisted when we wanted Dad to take the family for a ride to the Dairy Queen. She could crawl into his lap, issue the tender request, and get the job done.

As the afternoon stretched on, Dad and I strolled through Sears. He purchased socks and underwear for me, a sweater and a belt. The day seemed to brim with gifts and his attention. I relished it increasingly, unconcerned about the jealousy that would be aroused in my siblings when I arrived home with so much.

We were preparing to leave the store when I saw it—a single CPO jacket on an emptied rack in the men's section. CPO jackets topped the list of fashionable items at the junior high school that year. It was beyond my hopes.

"Try it on," Dad said, surprising me again. He must have seen the wild want in my expression.

It fit perfectly.

The purchase of that jacket sealed the day's magic. My father had coaxed forth my desires and served them. The world seemed also to affirm my wishes, providing a landscape of ready pleasures. All things awaited me, like that jacket. My father and existence were just my size, just that once.

Dad had no memory of the bowling alley burgers or the

spending spree, or the harmonic convergence in the CPO jacket. But he always laughed over the story of peanut butter soup. That hodge-podge of silliness, incompetence, impulse and imagination—it is the more fitting image of the harmony we knew. During vacation visits in my thirties, he and I spent hours alone together over lunches and while running errands. Often, he collared the waitress or a sales clerk—whatever stranger was handy—and launched into an extended encomium of me, his son the professor in Florida. He knew little about my education or my work—and even less about my writing, since I had sent him only newspaper columns from college, a couple of nonfiction pieces, and two published poems. Yet he never relented from his proud rambles, however much I threatened not to go out with him if he wouldn't stop embarrassing me. I would look at the busy service person trapped with Dad, the customer, by required courtesy, and I would roll my eyes and grin condescendingly toward my father, seeking indulgence for the old man. The complicity in such a scene was like that created by peanut butter soup—except here was a new recipe, and Dad and I were trying it this time, even liking it.

5. MOMENTUM

One day, while Dad and Greg and I were laying the foundation of the lake house, our next door neighbor there, Dr. Fermer, came to the redwood fence that separated his property from ours. Dr. Fermer was a well-to-do veterinarian in Des Moines. He and his wife had purchased two adjoining shoreline lots on which they had constructed a three-tiered redwood house with an indoor swimming pool and sauna. They kept a chic runabout, as well as a paddleboat, tied at their dock. Two tailored Pekingese bounded across their pleasantly manicured lawn. By comparison, our place was humble. Dad and Greg had built a landing from which we fished but at which no boat had ever been moored. The house, when it was finally completed, embodied the typical prairie style found in most working class suburbs built in the Midwest after 1960. Goodwill items and castoffs from the Garfield Avenue house furnished it.

Dr. Fermer balanced his martini glass on the fence and watched. His sons had moved to the West Coast years before, and he made no secret that his relations with them were at an impasse.

"It's wonderful to see you all working together," he said.

I was about 15 or 16 at the time, and I disliked Fermer. He had built a double garage at that point where the frontage road—which served as a driveway for us and several residents beyond—branched from the main road. With easy access to our houses thus blocked, we had to park on the main road and hike down the hill, crossing the unusable frontage road in the process. Dad and some of the other affected parties complained, but Fermer mustered lawyers. The garage was already there. He had the means to fight. Dad resigned himself to Fermer's selfishness and tried to be a decent neighbor.

Dad broke off work and walked up to the redwood fence. He and Fermer chatted for some time, watching Greg and me haul concrete blocks and ready another batch of cement for hand-mixing. Eventually, Greg and I took a break for lemonade and sat on blocks not far from Dad and Fermer. The doctor sipped his martini and then turned the conversation to the large amount of unmechanized labor we relied on in constructing the house. He shook his head in what now seems mock-admiration.

"I just can't believe you do so much by hand," he said. "Automation is the way things have been going for a long time."

"I suppose so," Dad replied, casually, gazing off across the water.

"You work at Firestone, right?"

"Yeah, been out there 20 years."

"Well," Dr. Fermer said, "It won't be long before that kind of work is all done by robots. I mean, it's cheaper to pay for spare parts than for the cost of health care and wages. And robots don't complain. . . ."

Dad smiled nervously and fidgeted a little, trying to find a way to retreat. "Well, I suppose so—"

"And robots are intelligent enough," Fermer continued. "Quality control is better, no daydreaming or extra breaks—"

"Well, yes," Dad said, his head bobbing anxiously. He drifted away from the fence. Well, yes . . . but . . . I . . . I'll be retired by the time that happens. C'mon kids, we need to finish this bit of mixing before dark."

I had never before seen my father so besieged by the assurance—however malicious—of another man, and it stunned me. He looked weak and confused, exposed. The notion that he could be replaced at his job, that his hold on his place in the world was not entirely in his hands, opened beneath us like a rift in our purchased piece of real estate. Jealousy of Dad's apparently good relationship with Greg and me had spurred Fermer's vision of "progress." But my father's helpless retreat before the doctor's onslaught was also one more set-piece in a woeful and commonplace drama. That day, I sensed obliquely that men like Fermer wielded power over men like my father, and money, education and social station made the difference. Fermer's assertions surprised Dad because he had reckoned himself secure enough within. He believed that a man's chance of achieving the prosperity unique to post-war America was wholly a matter of personal spirit and choice: if you wanted to work, and you did indeed work, you would prosper.

What was this job that my father had so invested himself—and us—in? As a child, I identified with Firestone, proud when drivers riding on its tires won the Indianapolis 500. I chanted along with the company's inspirational pitchman on TV: *Firestone! Where the rubber meets the road!* I played with toy trucks bearing the company logo and attended the annual company Christmas party at KRNT Theater, an extravaganza of magicians and glittery show tunes, juggling seals and vast gift distribution according to age and gender.

Each day, Dad readied himself for "going to work" in the same way. He labored on the house, or on other chores, and then he entered the bathroom to perform his ablutions. He shaved and gave himself what he called a "basin bath," assiduously cleansing his torso, slapping on Old Spice and baby powder afterward. He slipped on a dark blue tee shirt. Over this, he always buttoned up a plaid shirt—short-sleeved cotton in summer and long-sleeved flannel in winter—which he kept in his locker while actually on the job. He soaked his comb under the faucet and raked it through the remaining arch of hair on each side of his head. Then he ate bacon and eggs, took up the brown bag dinner either he or Mom made, and drove off with at least a half hour to spare, so he wouldn't have to hurry, he said.

For years, the factory itself remained a brooding mystery to me. It steamed, winter and summer, in daylight and flood lamp, as we passed by it on Interstate 35. "Thirty acres under roof," I'd heard one of Dad's friends estimate. Vast banks of dark green windows lined its sides, open and gasping for relief in summer.

"We're gonna die out there today," Dad would say in such seasons, and remark on how his department lay adjacent to the molds, where completed tires were "cooked" and cured.

I sat before the plant in his truck one January day when we had driven to pick up his strike check at the picket line. The place stood inert and gleaming like a slab of polished onyx, while strikers warmed themselves at fires in rusted drums blocking the entrance. I wondered where he fit inside a structure so enormous.

I was in graduate school when that question finally received an answer. On a winter evening, for the first time in decades, the company opened the plant for tours by workers' families. My girlfriend and I decided to visit. We must have been on our way to a social event elsewhere because I wore a suit and she a fairly formal dress. Once inside, we followed a guide down avenues of booming equipment, through production zones overarched by a sky of cranes and hooks, the clanging atmosphere suffused with fresh grease—all of it populated by the 3-11 shift, each person with a clock number on a card punched twice a day.

The guide showed us the whole process—from raw rubber to showroom tire—but I remember little of it except the stop we made where Dad worked. Behind yellow warning lines painted on the concrete floor, he bent toward his equipment with his partner on this night, Harold Hodges, an old friend who had introduced us to the lake where Dad had bought our lot next to Dr. Fermer. Though Dad expected my girlfriend and me, he seemed surprised at our arrival and a little self-conscious, like a child who looks up from singing alone to himself and finds someone has been watching him. Dad smiled shyly and came toward us. Harold nodded and waved. They were building earth mover tires, big enough that a man could stand inside one. Both Harold and Dad had started at Firestone in passenger tires, moving up to tractor and finally to this most lucrative, and demanding, department. In their mid-fifties, they were old-timers, plant originals, among the lowest clock numbers.

"Well," Dad shouted amid the din, "this is it."

From years of helping build the two houses, I knew about work, and how to saw and hammer. But by this time I also had earned my money for school and supported myself independently by working nights in boxcars and semi-trailers, loading and unloading cement, shingles, batts of fiberglass insulation. For not much more than minimum wage, I had riveted and wired dryers that clung to grain elevators, climbing ladders twelve stories up through their sheet-metal shafts in 120-plus heat. I had labored in a machine shop where the union had been broken and the new hires were novices, like me, or burned-out dopers, or marginally reliable journeymen, and the foreman was alternately lunatic or merely moody. I had lain in the emergency room, smeared with power tool filth, as the doctor plucked twelve metal slivers from my right cornea, suggesting that I always wear my safety goggles from then on. With six others, I had put my shoulder to iron flywheels, hefting them up onto the axles of motors strapped to flatcars, understanding something about the lives of the slaves who dragged blocks up incline planes for the pyramids at El-Giza.

I was well acquainted with the carnival release of quitting time, especially on Friday afternoons, the parking lot clearing instantaneously. And the glory emanating from hot coffee on a break from a frozen freight yard, the oasis in a Milky Way bar and the full 15 minutes at mid-morning and mid-afternoon when you didn't have to move for anyone. I had fought and flowed with the rhythms of repetitive jobs, seeking the interstices and crawl spaces in their routines, where your mind and spirit could nestle and gain a respite from the demanding banality. And I knew the games you devised to help yourself dig in and make your quota for the day, games to invest that number with a heroic, if temporary, consequence.

I had experienced these things—that's why I clung to school and did not get the girlfriend pregnant and made vague plans to leave Des Moines before it trapped me. Though Dad had never pushed me to work at Firestone, where the pay surpassed that of my jobs, he made it clear that he could always "get me on out there," if I wished it. I never countenanced the possibility because that thought terrified me. On the one hand, I didn't want to embarrass my father by proving a washout on his own turf; he had no friends, really, beyond those at the plant. On the other hand, I was afraid of succeeding too well. Several of my cousins and uncles were also employed there. I might prove myself capable, decide I liked it, never leave Des Moines, and end up like them—like him.

I knew work of this sort, but I didn't know a lifetime of this work. I had little intimation of what it took. I was the guy on the production line who was leaving at the end of the year, temporary summer help, not vested, definitely. At the end of the day, I showered off the layers of dried sweat lacquering my body and, drowsy, tried to read Virgil and write the English essays that would help me get out of town.

And so there I stood in my suit, callow before Dad and Harold, this pair of lifers, looking like a tourist in the land of endurance. Dad tried to explain how he and Harold constructed a tire, shouting out the steps as best he could. Then he and Harold went to work to illustrate. I could soon understand why his fingers often ached. He and Harold pulled a black sheet of rubber from a mammoth roll and spun it onto another roller, cutting it on the bias and pouring benzene and other chemicals and adhesives onto this body, preparing it for another ply, which they drew from the first roll. Machine and muscle. No doubt the work required skills which I could not perceive, but I had imagined it involved more obvious craft. I watched his hands, the battered, scrimshawed nails and blackened whorls on fingers which at the piano conjured elegant glissandos and strutting riffs—that black which no cleanser could defeat, ground in until long after retirement.

Dad's aura of violent regret had, by this time, led me to judge him a coward and failure, one who had forsaken the main chance, whatever that was. Besides the theater, he had also turned down offers of promotion to foreman.

"Just headaches," he had said, dismissing the opportunities.

Yet the sight of his hands, and of him glancing up at me to see if I was observing intently—the vulnerability of my father so diligently laboring this way—caused him to shrink into something that could be loved, just as on that day at the fence with Dr. Fermer. I understood that it was the momentum of things—represented by life on the production line—that I feared would sweep my better future away. At that moment, I saw how much of him stubbornly remained, persisted, and how much my prospects had for so long depended upon this.

6. SOMETHING ABOUT YIELDING

At 62, Dad accepted Firestone's offer of early retirement. After 37 years on the line, he was not sentimental about such an opportunity.

"The job was getting harder every day," he said, "hell for an old man like me."

He enjoyed pretending to imminent infirmity and a general ebbing of his powers, though he still worked around both houses as usual, adding another room here, replacing a deck there. He also fought with refurbishing projects at Mike's home and rental properties. He still drank, in hefty quantities—which he partly justified by switching to *Lite* beer. And he still railed, though perhaps less frequently because his audience, and irritant, diminished as we children grew up and moved out of the Garfield Avenue house. During this period of childless quiet, he and Mom discovered themselves alone together for the first time in more than twenty years. I like to imagine that, in this state, surprising pleasure and peace of mind landed on them more than once.

This quiet state, however, proved to be a brief interim. My sister, who had become pregnant at 16, had married, with Mom and Dad's encouragement. But after some time in an apartment, she and her husband—without enough education to acquire substantial employment—found themselves financially strapped, so they and their daughter moved into Mom and Dad's place. With higher hopes and better prospects, they ventured out, only to return when their personal subsistence economy collapsed. Eventually, their marriage faltered and failed. There were two children by then, and they and my sister returned home. After several foundered attempts to gain her financial independence, she remarried and, at last, forged a modest but relatively stable place for her family in the world.

By then, she had moved in and out of the Garfield Avenue house several times, and years had elapsed during her residencies. When she and her children had finally gone, my parents confronted a similar scenario with my brother Aaron and his girlfriend. They also housed my sister's oldest daughter, Elizabeth, after she, too, had become pregnant at 16.

In sum, throughout the time when they might have redefined their lives together after their own children had been raised, Dad and Mom found themselves living with two, and sometimes three, generations of dependents. Imagine an older couple giving refuge to six new semi-permanent guests—four of them under seven years of age—and you can fathom the demand made upon them in the last years of Dad's life.

This state of affairs engendered moments of joy, of course. My parents relished the roles of grandma and grandpa. Dad often passed out candy and savored moments when one of the smaller children would sit placidly in his lap while he watched *Masterpiece Theatre*. Mom bragged about the flowers her grandchildren had planted in cracks in the patio floor. She also chortled at first words and reported proudly on indiscretions—her grandchild of three, for instance, strutting around the kitchen and declaiming, "Poppa's bitchin'!" in response to Dad's thrusting himself into another rage.

But my parents literally became "Momma" and "Poppa" to these live-in families, blurring timelines and former roles. Dad, for instance, sometimes confused his granddaughter Elizabeth with his daughter Peggy, and on other occasions treated them as though they were siblings and not mother and child. Ultimately, my parents existed daily on the border between helping their troubled progeny and being exploited by them, between needing to be needed and making their dependents more dependent upon them. Their days were defined by their children's life mistakes—actions that could hardly be called decisions, more the result of a violent careening through circumstances, a striking out at . . . something.

It can be argued that my parents themselves, to some degree, sowed the seeds of this situation. Their overextended "dysfunctional" family was fate's revenge on them for their own worst mistakes: they had yielded too frequently and too easily to what was least in them; they had given up on trying to create a worthy marriage or a workable divorce; they had worn each other out.

I see now that my siblings and I had each attempted, however unconsciously, to flee this oppressive drama. There was Peggy's pregnancy, of course, and my escape into books and narcissistic remoteness. But Greg had sought asylum in a community of religious rigor; Mike had chased money and consumed material life at high velocity; Aaron had swept himself away with uncontrollable substances. Each of us failed to free ourselves, but the failure of some exacted a higher toll both on themselves and Mom and Dad, and it was everywhere to be seen in the house through the years up to Dad's death and beyond.

Early in their marriage, Dad had withdrawn to the front porch, almost certainly to punish Mom for their troubles. But during his final years, especially in his illness, the front porch became his residence on the outer edge of a dwelling laden with others and empty of privacy, a house less and less his. It became a cell from which he offered himself to his live-in grandchildren and great-grandchildren and to which he retreated, trying to hide from the clamor. To a much lesser extent, Mom's bedroom functioned the same way, yet with the years, it came to resemble Dad's room in its remarkable congestion. There, old crossword puzzles lay stacked on the bureau alongside cans of air freshener and two-liter jugs of Diet 7-Up, bottles of perfume and prescriptions, and ceramic chickens designed to look like rattan. On the night stand: a sequined clutch purse, a hardback children's book entitled *That Happy Feeling of Thank You*, a bride and groom cake decoration, pseudo-marble busts of Jesus and Mary, and a red baseball cap emblazoned with *Sweet as a Strawberry*. On every surface, more and more of the same, and where there was not more of the same, plastic bags, gravid with clothes, sat in extensive, unbudging heaps.

As with these rooms, so with the house. Though it had never exhibited the neatness which aspires to bourgeois respectability, it devolved, gradually, from general disarray into a spectacle of pathetic surrender—becoming a junk shop grotto, a heart occluded with ruin. Whole areas filled up with knickknacks and furniture, boxes and minute detritus—part of it belonging to various temporary lodgers—and these areas were virtually sealed off. If one ventured among them, it was as if into a forlorn storage vault, and one made one's way by sucking in the gut and squeezing between objects that had lost all purpose or worthiness, all pretensions to an orderly future. The remainder of the rooms suffered only slightly lesser encroachments. So, in effect, people in the house operated along pathways through prodigious clutter and in larger clearings here and there where they watched television or drank coffee and read the newspaper. In later years, when Aaron and his family had settled in, Mom and Dad capitulated completely to the general expansion of filth, so one could find, for instance, on the crowded kitchen floor torn pieces of prewrapped American cheese, tossed pacifiers, sticky spills, bags of potting soil, trash tumbled from the waste basket, grit.

All of this mirrored what I have come to call "the falling within." Over a lifetime, the unacknowledged changes of heart and conceptions of self, the unaddressed dreams and lies, the unarticulated wishes and sorrows fell like a lazy, continuous snow in the souls of my parents and us children. At some point in those later years when Mom and Dad faced increasing friction over, and with, their live-in brood, that snow tumbled harder and heavier— the betrayals, the cowardly gestures, the incapacities, the physical defeats, the dependencies, the angers, the follies, the humiliations, the denials piling one onto another, burying that which had amassed earlier before it could be cleared away. Rarely could anyone locate the original pain or problem, or the first sign of a wrong turning. It was lost or crushed beyond recognition somewhere beneath the weight of aftermaths and consequences, blame and counterblame.

Thus, when I came home to visit, I stayed at Mike's house, on the other side of town, stopping briefly "over there" on Garfield Avenue, to spirit Mom or Dad away for a few hours. Though my parents' place deteriorated ceaselessly, a desperate arrest also seemed to encase it. Entering the house was like reanimating a scene in which the action had remained suspended since my last departure. People were still fighting about the same things as before, mouthing the same lines. No insight had breached their habits. Little seemed to exist beyond their immediate crises, which were the norm. In her most bereft years, for instance, my sister stood emotionally and physically encircled by her frenetic children clawing for attention, incarcerated by the destructive solace sought from drugs, alcohol, and the wrong men. In some respect, though she inhabited the room which had been hers as a girl— the room which had been our parents' first bedroom—she lived further away from her people than I did.

Coming home also represented my confronting less polished and sadder versions of myself. I sometimes drifted into the old shouting matches with Dad or Mom, though I tried to walk away from them. More often and more intensely, I realized that I had fashioned out of all I had ignored at home the tunnel through which I had eventually fled it. I began then, finally, to ask of my parents the questions I could muster about the past. The glitter on the fallen snow within me deviled my childlike eyes with the comfortless light of an older mortality. I reacquainted myself with a melancholy I had refused to countenance as a child and young adult, a chilly, tickling tinsel in the blood which I believed, foolishly, bore no relation to the saner, better-groomed life I vowed early to create for myself, later, on my own.

It was not depression that I reencountered in these instances but the first recognition of life's capacity for overwhelming cheapness. It was the voice of futility, a voice embodied for me, literally, in a singer whom my mother had known. When I was twelve, Dad purchased an ancient Wurlitzer jukebox from a garage sale. Shaped like a Tudor arch, vaguely churchy, it smelled of burning dust when warmed up and spinning 45s by Jimmy Dean and Grandpa Jones. Among the records which came with it were several by a man named Jerry Byers. He was from Pershing, Mom said, a fine piano player who had aspirations to fame. He fell ill, however—cancer—and in the months before his death, he made as many records as he could, hoping through their success to support his family after his passing. I remember punching the numbers for "Corinna, Corinna" and "Bonnie by the Sea" over and over, wondering at that honky-tonk twang of the dead—a voice, I hear now, refusing to give in, doing all it can, ultimately to be stacked among other disused objects.

It might have been any of us children, but it was the recurring tenancy of Aaron and his family that brought on the final capitulation. In the middle eighties Dad had gotten Aaron the job at Firestone that had always been available to me and my other brothers. With a wife and children and only a GED, Aaron was fortunate to gain employment this lucrative. He had been a superior athlete—the tallest of four tall boys, strong and fast, a coveted power hitter on several senior league teams. But before even trying out for his high school squad, he cast aside all which his ability might have wrought and roamed with self-styled outcasts, blowing dope and, eventually, dropping out.

Occasionally, we other children contended that Aaron's problems lay in not ever being able to do right in Dad's eyes and not ever being able to do wrong in Mom's. Though hardly complete, this explanation hit on the fundamental fact that, as the youngest, his growing up was the last opportunity for our parents to battle each other through their children at home. He came of age in their crossfire and was wounded, perhaps fatally, by the power he discovered in this position.

After some time at Firestone, he started snorting cocaine regularly. Broke, unable to support the family on his wife's modest salary, he and his wife and children were evicted and moved back to the Garfield Avenue house. He had thinned into a gray, scabrous stalk, short-tempered, often drunk, alternately morose and sweetly sentimental. During this time, Dad remained aloof, when he was not consumed with fury. Mike and I assailed Mom's persistent illusion that all was well with Aaron, until she agreed to convince him to seek help. He did, through Firestone, passing several weeks in rehabilitation. He emerged—having regained some weight and color—with a newly acquired fluency in the language of psychotherapy, self-awareness, responsibility and hope.

Eventually, Firestone gave him a pink slip during a general layoff. He zigzagged, thereafter, in and out of part-time work, the recipient of Mom's relentless exoneration and Dad's alternating support and derision. He also drank, mildly, and flirted with the drugs he had reputedly forsworn. He entered the construction trades, demonstrating admirable skill with a hammer, hanging sheetrock for various contractors. Seeing Aaron's tenuous prospects, self-destructive habits, and multiple dependents, one of these contractors "adopted" him and tried to school him in the business—with the idea that, since this contractor was retiring soon, Aaron could buy him out and begin afresh, on solid ground.

After considerable conflict—centered on Aaron's past unsteadiness—Dad loaned Aaron several thousand dollars to buy the old man's equipment. It was a moment of amnesty for Aaron among his jealous siblings weary of his piteous stagger. Perhaps, we thought, all that had transpired would later seem only a bad patch if he made good at this chance, got a place, paid his bills, fed and actually raised his children.

No equipment appeared, nor did Aaron engage in any activity resembling sheetrock contracting. The loan from Dad vanished, as did later advances from Mike for promised construction work—work often never done. Hundreds more disappeared each month thereafter from Mom's Social Security check, as did further thousands she passed on to him from high interest cash advances on credit cards, borrowing to the limit and concealing it from Dad, until the collection agency called.

"Mom will always be there. She won't let these kids go hungry," Aaron remarked to me, with a handsome smile, one summer afternoon years before—when he had simply decided not to go to the plant for a few days and instead found his way to the lake for fishing. As one fiasco after another unfolded, I often recalled those words, so simple and so true—his defining, and paralyzing, insight.

Over and over, Dad "washed his hands" of Aaron and his problems, and was coaxed back into involvement by his son's nearness and the obvious vulnerability of the grandchildren. As matters worsened, however, the news I received from Mom was brightened, buffed with hope and the wish to avoid my censure: Aaron and his daughters had just returned from a fishing trip to the lake; Aaron had started a new job; he and his wife were saving money and were planning to get their own place again, at the first of next month.

In her desire to sanitize every degradation, to ignore her son's obvious flaws, Mom operated according to her oldest principle: she loved her children and she looked always to their good side, especially when Dad had condemned our behavior. Early in their marriage, being a mother had supplanted being a wife as her preeminent project. Her power, such as it was, derived entirely from that. In those most physically violent years, this role prevented her from abandoning us children, or abandoning herself to alcohol or worse. It permitted her, somehow, to allow—rather than impede—our love for the man most cruel to her.

She defended us, fiercely, sometimes crazily. Once, for instance, when three of Aaron's "friends" pulled up, drunk and spitting threats because they claimed Aaron owed them money, she told Aaron to stay inside while she—in her early sixties—walked out to the street to meet them.

"Why don't you just drive on up the road," she said, "Aaron's not around here."

The driver of the truck got out, tottered over to Mom, and socked her in the jaw. Immediately, she punched the man in the nose. Aaron dashed from the house and attacked the other two, who had jumped from the cab to help their compatriot. By the time Dad arrived at the scene—for he is the source of this story— Mom and the man with whom she had exchanged punches were rolling on the ground, his drunkenness having evened the odds, she clawing and pounding him.

"I'm hurting," Mom said the next day, her face swollen. She held up her fist adorned with ornate, protruding rings. "But he's hurting more."

Of all she has surrendered, Mom has never yielded her principle of positive interpreting and significant omission—her precious inner blinders. Had I spoken to her on the day of this fight—and perhaps I did—she most likely would have failed to mention it and told me things were "fine." If I had learned of it and inquired, she would have offered a stirring version from her own propaganda ministry.

This approach to survival, however—while it served her enough when her children were young—enslaved her in these later years. Aaron had drifted into a new relationship with our parents, his family, and his future. In Mom's belief that excusing encouraged reform, he understood that there lay an irrevocable permission. Pained, glib enough to lie to himself about his heart, sensitive and savage, he gradually released himself from the labor and sacrifice required to be independent in the life he had created. Drugs helped the rationalizing, as did a searingly unhappy marriage. His days became a round of sleeping in—hung over and depressed—and Mom covering for him when an employer called, wondering why Aaron had not arrived on the job. He engaged in petty crime, lifting goods from abandoned houses, selling marijuana and cocaine. His friends grew rougher and more suspect, young men with nefarious backgrounds, eventually prison records, who stole from Aaron and our parents, as easily as he did.

He no longer made any pretense of seeking work or moving out, instead tinkering with the blown engine in his four-wheel-drive truck parked in the driveway, sipping beer and smoking in the shade. Just as Dad had withdrawn to the front porch, he gradually ensconced himself in the garage. In a grim parody of a childhood clubhouse, he held court there with his cohorts—a father of four in his late twenties and then early thirties—lounging and getting stoned on two battered couches on the dirt floor, heavy-metal tapes grinding out fuck-it-alls beneath the lone fluorescent light.

For a long while, we other children pleaded and argued for corrective action, something positive, at least an acknowledgment that the situation might pose horrific problems for the grandchildren. No recognition. Dad's ultimate complicity in these matters puzzled me. Angry, he paid off Mom's cash advances, yet he still sometimes spoke warmly of Aaron, hoping for a reversal. I see now that he refused to force consequences on his desperate and selfish son because he did not wish to be perceived as the ogre-father which Mom had long implied he was. His previous brutality and torment had engendered a harm which he could not stem without confronting the unresolved past as it existed in the present. He treated that past as a spurious former self, as a bad habit he did not want to adopt.

Aaron and I spoke less and less, and when we did, it required that I ignore the obvious, which had become impossible. Humiliation shoved his gaze to the side. Bewilderment and frustration simmered in my small talk. We managed a goodbye hug at the ends of these strained visits, and then we began avoiding each other. Dad became sick and receded from the scene, occasionally reemerging and arguing with Aaron in his better spells of health. More and more, things were happening beyond him then—things involving Aaron and crime and further large bills. Aaron's anger expanded. Over the phone one night in the last year of his life, Dad told me of an altercation between them. Aaron seemed ready to strike him, a man whose factory biceps now resembled shriveled peaches. At the last instant, however, Aaron spat on him.

Dad whispered these concluding details, afraid that his son in the next room might hear him. His fear reminded me of Greg's Saturday morning ritual as a child: get up early, dress, leave the house quietly so as not to wake the dragon who would surely be furious and mean. In that whisper, Dad and his son exchanged roles. My father, at the end, became one of his own cowering offspring.

"I was thinking about Dad," Aaron said softly, the night before the funeral. He leaned over the hood of his truck in the driveway, slightly drunk. I smoked and stood beside him. Young men I did not know shuttled from the house to the garage and back, keeping a respectful distance from us.

"I remember a time at Teachout Swimming Pool," Aaron went on, almost whispering. "I was in the kids' pool and he was in the deep end. I wanted to come in and he said "C'mon" and held out his arms, and I jumped in and he caught me."

He lit a cigarette and blew a smoky sigh into the darkness.

"Why should this come to me now?" he asked.

Three weeks before his death, Dad, Mike and I went to lunch, our last meal together as it turned out. Dad chatted waywardly with the waitress, as usual, embarrassing us. He also had a spell: intense pain behind his right eye—most likely another small stroke. Frail, clearly ebbing between bursts of his old demeanor, he did not, I think, entirely believe time was yet closing down on him. We spoke again about the situation at home.

"For quite a while," he said, with conviction, "I've felt like I'm just floating outside my life. It's not mine anymore."

I thought, at that moment, of a night in college 20 years before, when I cried profusely in my girlfriend's arms—cried and wailed because I could not feel. It was the armor forged by the great falling within that those tears rained against, a steel that had become unnecessary.

I remember now, also, a day just months before Dad's first heart attack. On the only visit he made to me after I moved from Des Moines, he and Mom flew to Florida. We rented a car and, with Lisa—then my lover of more than a year—toured the Gulf Coast and the Everglades for a week. At the end of this trip, I dropped Mom and Dad at the ship terminal in Miami where they embarked on a Caribbean cruise, their first full-dress retirement vacation—which I had proudly planned.

Along the way, we spent a night at the home of Lisa's parents on Sanibel Island. Dad gasped at my future mother-in-law's phalaenopsis and dendrobium—and he and she spoke lavishly about the spring flowers in the North, which she had not seen in years but adored. He and my future father-in-law played the baby grand. At the sumptuous dinner, Mom sat quiet, pleased. Alternately, Dad beamed and chatted, and I could tell that in his eyes Lisa's parents were those "fashionable" or "well-to-do" people with whom some part of him identified and from whom another part shied. I had been lobbying my parents to rent a condo the following winter. Dad had inherited a fair sum from his mother, and he had saved—they could afford it, I was sure. I hoped, ultimately, this visit would inspire them to sell it all out from under Aaron and begin again, laved in this sunshine.

When we departed the next morning, warm goodbyes

abounded. Before we left the island, Dad demanded that we stop at a florist's shop, where he purchased an enormous bouquet of northern spring flowers and had them sent to Lisa's mother. He was smitten with her, I thought, a worldly, elegant, passionate woman, clearly forceful—the kind of woman who intimidated him, about whom he knew next to nothing.

While Dad ordered the flowers, Mom sat in the car, wordless, sighing as though his action was usual and trivial, though I suspect she was peeved. I tried to make a joke of the matter as he reentered the car and I drove on. A moment later, he was sobbing into his cupped hands, and then shuddering, breaking down beneath a sudden, vast weight. Astonished, Lisa and I tried to comfort him.

"She was a delight," he said through his tears, "It was just the loveliness of it all."

7. Quitclaim Deed

Driving through the old neighborhood these days, I sometimes wave to people I don't know standing in their front yards and on their porches. I think *In your basement, I played toy trains with Linda Ackelson* or *In your living room, Mark Hanna and I smoked cigarettes stolen from his mother's purse.* I remember a kid named Troy—whose parents seemed always absent—scorching macaroni he tried to cook on the greasy stove in that white house on the corner. And in that blue one farther on, I again see Jack Huxford's wooden leg leaning against the bedroom wall one afternoon as I pass the door with his son Lenny. On the lawn of that gray ranch house—which was then brown and tiny—I yet rock back and forth as the leaves gust silver and green in the sumptuous, sunlit roar of a spring day muscling in. And there, on that stoop, I see myself lounge briefly with old Mr. Larson, managing the Kansas City Athletics on the radio.

In these moods, I assert a questionable intimacy with strangers by mustering the dead and vanished that surround their lives, ghosts of whom they are almost utterly ignorant. It is a foolhardy, and perhaps hazardous, attempt to fuse a place from another time with the present. Yet it underscores my desire not to be the only vessel for that particular portion of the bygone, though I am, nearly. Only my mother, Aaron, and the Stanleys across the street remain from those who resided on Garfield Avenue in that time. The rest of the current inhabitants are relative newcomers, preparing their own era for its vanishing, with the objects and sites from which memory may one day be released like a secreted spirit.

The houses now, for the most part, seem shabbier. But a number also appear smaller and slightly menial, which suggests that the grandness, the sweep and lush greenness I knew of them as a boy derived from distraction and wonder at my circumstances rather than from outward evidence. This was the gift of the place—that it revealed more of its richness to me than its privations, leaving time and experience to expose the balance. I sometimes marvel, abashed, at the unspoken pride Garfield Avenue engendered in me and which I bore into a world equipped to show me reason for shame at my origins. That shame is a gift as well, but only as a later counterweight to a lucky satisfaction with childhood.

Among the houses and households, ours has continued its irresolute decline. Named executor of Dad's estate, Mike assumed Dad's role as Mom's money manager and presented plans for rebuilding and refurbishing—provided Aaron and his family move out—but none received Mom's support. After Dad's death, she revealed many more thousands in credit debt—funds passed on to Aaron—which she had kept secret from Dad. As Mike and I reviewed the documents in Dad's safe deposit box, we speculated that perhaps Mom believed a large insurance payment would be forthcoming and so she took advances on her cards, hoping to pay them off later. But only a relatively modest policy remained in force—enough for funeral expenses and, fortunately, clearing the cards. The money Dad had inherited from Grandma Morrill proved modest as well. And Mom seemed as ignorant of her situation as she was of the world beyond her house. Mike and I had feared that Aaron might drain Mom financially after Dad's death. In the last year of Dad's life, we had tried to prevent this by lobbying him, without success, to change his will. But Dad's records revealed that Aaron—believing, too, perhaps, that a large and replenishing insurance settlement would be due—had already achieved our worst fears.

Mom's principal assets now are the Garfield Avenue house and the lake house, though the quitclaim deed names us children with her—ironically and appropriately—as "tenants in common." Among the other residents there, her grief and love commingle as never before. Composed by the time I had arrived home on the day Dad died, she had told me that she would manage well enough because she knew sorrow from having lost her parents early. I learned later from Mike that she had wandered through her first hours of widowhood bearing Dad's wallet, repeatedly taking out his driver's license and staring at his photograph. Weeks later, at the bank, she collapsed in tears when a white-bearded customer who slightly resembled Dad said, "Good Morning," and tipped his cap to her. Months afterward, she told me on the phone that she had been sorting the last of Dad's things in the front porch.

"I felt funny there, in his place," she said, haltingly, "I finally just said to him 'I'm sorry. But you know I have to do this.' And I think he understands."

Aaron now substitutes for Dad as her defining impediment and utility. With Aaron's wife and four children, the house again shelters seven lives, as it did when I lived there. Mom is not alone as she feared, nor is she available to her other children's desires to spruce up her grannyhood or introduce her to the new.

But the barrier between public decorum and private mayhem, which Dad attempted to preserve, has been breached. Both Aaron and his wife have been arrested, Aaron repeatedly and on more serious charges. One day, Mom told me, she looked up from the television to find several men standing over her—police, searching for the drugs Aaron is reputed to be selling. Fortunately, they found none, so the house was not confiscated.

Eventually, Aaron was jailed for possession. He called Mom for bail. Finally, she had no funds. He excoriated her, emphasizing her cruelty, and he hung up—and phoned her back with sweet apologies spawned by second thought. Though she insisted on his innocence—"it was those scurves he was with"—she also expressed relief that she knew where he was and what was he was doing. The week before, she had canceled her Christmas trip to Florida because she feared for the house. Toughs had been driving past, shouting threats to kill Aaron, and someone had shot the windshield out of Dad's car.

"I'm sleeping with one eye open," she said.

Aaron's most symbolic transgression, however, was made with the 88 checks he wrote against Dad's account, closed just after his death. On the afternoon of the first great sifting in the front porch, when Aaron abandoned the jacket and snapshot of Dad bearing the catfish, he must have noted Mike handing the checkbooks to Mom with the command, "Destroy these."

The forged checks proceed in numerical sequence from the last one Dad wrote. Ten thousand dollars worth of chicken dinners, liquor, snow blowers, clothes, Christmas toys, gasoline, cash.

A shoe box full of collection notices sits in Mom's room. The State's Attorney says no prosecution is likely; he has other things to do besides redeem businesses that have accepted personal checks without proper identification.

Eighty-eight times Aaron signed his dead father's name, a grotesque parody of the fiscal respectability on which Dad prided himself. Perhaps revenge flowed in that ink, a payback for injuries even Aaron can no longer fathom. Perhaps Aaron felt closer to Dad in those moments with pen in hand, or maybe he savaged himself with every stroke. Maybe the risk excited him. Or he was moved merely by the habit of taking. He also may have savored the attention his actions would earn him from his siblings.

"It was horrible and weird," Mike said, "to see photocopies of those things with Aaron's scrawl around the East Side . . . and that warning, *Don't accept checks from Dean Morrill.*"

Some of the items among Dad's effects offered a commentary I still ponder. In his safe deposit box, Mike and I found the insurance policies, of course, but also a minute gold piece from California, dated late 1800s, wrapped in gray cotton—willed to the oldest son. A glass match case contained a miniature monkey wrench and a note in Dad's hand which said these items had been given as a first birthday gift to his father in 1902. There were Brazilian coins, Dad's retirement watch, a gold chain, a gold ring, two silver dollars, and a clipping of a newspaper column titled "Where's the Fire?" referring to a night in the Garfield Avenue house when the pilot light went out and Dad, then still a bachelor, dragged himself to the door, nearly asphyxiated.

There was Dad's selective service card and honorable discharge. His diploma from the Omaha Public Schools. An Award of Merit from the Omaha police, for "protecting the lives of school children as a member of the school boy patrol."

And a certificate of marriage to Nancy McAllister, October 28, 1949, Justice Bickwell presiding. Three receipts for services rendered by Adelman and Adelman for the divorce, July 5, 1950. Clippings from the newspaper announcing both events.

Nothing of Mom, of their lives together.

Even the deed to the properties lay elsewhere—among papers in the front porch, nested in a white envelope on which Dad had scribbled "In case of (my) Death! Open!"

I learned later that Dad had only changed the deed after Grandma Morrill's death four years earlier. For decades prior to that she had been named tenant in common with him, despite her insistence that the house should be deeded to Mom. My sister also revealed, in passing, that Mom's wedding and engagement rings—so sweetly extravagant and a fascination to me as a child—belonged first to Nancy.

Mom no longer wears them.

Among Dad's other more significant effects in the front porch, Mike, Greg and I found 12 *Playboy* magazines secreted beneath formidable junk piles—a surprise, considering his mortification at the naughty. Closer, more readily accessible to him, however, was an issue of *Playgirl*.

We also discovered six photographs of Renato the matchmaking Brazilian, as well as two brief aerograms and a postcard from him. Why Dad had separated these items from the other mementos in his Navy chest immured in the attic no one knows. Dated from November 1944 to December 1946, they testify to a relationship of greater duration than Dad's brief remembrances had suggested to me. The photographs bear dates different from each other and from the aerograms, perhaps accompanied by other letters now lost.

In the aerograms, Renato's English—easily broken—displays an unremarkable propriety, bounteous with good wishes for Dad's mother and sisters, or calls for quicker replies and longer letters. Yet several of the typed inscriptions on the backs of the photos give pause. "Ren" stands barechested and square-shouldered on the roof of a house: *At Yacht Club. I am not so fat as this photo is showing.* He sits in the cockpit of his single engine wing-over: *Would you like to fly with me?* He smiles suavely, a Latin Gene Kelly in navy whites: *I like coffee/I like milk/I like you/Do you like me?*

These communications invite me to peer more deeply into other, formerly ordinary passages, such as: *I should like very much to shake your hand, as you are the greatest friend of mine. I am very sorry I was unable to say goodby as I wanted very much to do, but I suppose that's the way things must be at present. It seemes we never did get to go swimming or do anything that I would like to have done. . . .*

Why—at the end of World War II—does Ren begin one letter with warm wishes in faulty German? In this same communication—the last in this group—he writes: *I was glad to hear that you are free to make your own choice about a good girl to get married with, if I were you I would choose a beautiful blonde with green or blue eyes, what's your type?* Yet he concludes, as always, with eager wishes to see Dad again and: *Why don't you come down to Brazil now that you are a civilian, and you'll see that everything is quite different.*

"Your Dad didn't say much about him," Mom replied, when I asked about the relationship, "Only that he helped Renato's sisters with their English, and they were a very prominent family. And after your Dad came home from the service, Renato sent him a kind of love letter, and your Dad didn't answer it. He didn't want no part of that."

Though that scandalous letter is missing, Greg and Mike are convinced that something substantial, most likely amorous, occurred between these two men, and it may very well have. They believe that even if Dad and Renato never touched, Dad encountered powerful desires which he suppressed at great cost over a lifetime.

"I feel sorry for him," Greg said. "It was the way in those days, the way he dealt with it. He denied *himself,* but not completely. Why else was he so tormented, so angry?"

Along with the aerograms and snapshots was a drawing of Dad and Ren by Joselito Matos which appeared in a Brazilian publication in December 1945. They sit side by side, in uniform, the wings of their respective services hovering on a cloud over their shoulders next to the frame. Above them, national flags hang from crossed staffs, Brazil's over my father and the Stars and Stripes over Ren. The caption announces that these aviators symbolize the friendship between the two largest countries on the American continent.

Looking at this picture, I understand, in a new way, Dad's enthusiasm for my sojourn in Asia. Brazil was his China. Introducing him to a taboo and, thus, a frightening sense of himself, this experience may have proved too foreign for him. Or maybe he merely was experimenting with who he was in the great fluidity far from Omaha and his parents—a new recruit (only 20) to the legion of possibility. It *is* also conceivable that Dad simply did not perceive the emotional terrain on which he tread, and naively assumed that all Brazilians were as friendly as Renato. Yet his complicity seems everywhere in evidence. Whatever the nature of this relationship, whatever the character of his ignorance, I do not imagine he was innocent. He was alive in that place and time unlike he was to be alive anywhere else. After all, he ordered as his epitaph the inscription *WW II.*

Dad had been moved by the long letter about the past that I had sent to him from China. Though he spoke only once, briefly, about it, from that moment onward, a new force drew us closer. Several months after the funeral, I found among his papers this unsent response to that letter—drafted on the cover of a Ralston Purina Pet Food Coupon Book.

Dear Son:

This writing will undoubtedly be the last letter I will send to you in China. Every man looks for his Shangrila—liken to his first love taken at the banquet of youth, and if he passes by these thoughts I fear he has no creativeness, drive, nor will he set goals in his life. Aloneness is prescious for every individual. Dreams are far more recognizable, and gives an individual far more preception of which direction he wants to go in life. So carefully thought out so as not to make a mistake, yet one makes them, and learns by those mistakes. Moments alone in thought can give you confidence—Too often confusing around an audience of irrational people who care nothing of your innerself.

I have endured a sustained life by being my own man—in thought, word, and deed. I chose my life this way. I believe because I had to early in my youth to make decisions on my own. Some peoples lives were far more wretched than my own. I have had a wonderful experience, and determined as I am, I never missed anything. So you see. I have achieved my Shangrila. This may seem somewhat selfish, but I did not mean this, as a role model. Your adventures accomplished that in your letter, which I might add, was a brilliant biography of someone who missed the point of fatherhood intimately with his children. It couldn't have been better written. I trust the character in your letter could be well-established—as a character in any novel—such a colorful person. "My dramatics always did get me in trouble." But you certainly were an observant child and have carried these thoughts of me for some time. I'm proud of you for coming forth as you said "it's time." You are indeed your own man.

Love Dad

Who knows why he didn't send it? Maybe he allowed it to be lost, until now. Maybe this is how such words are delivered.

Sometimes I imagine him on a lustrous autumn afternoon clacking with red leaves. He is replacing a few torn shingles on the roof of the lake house. It is three years before his death but only minutes before the first eruption of the heart which will send him writhing down the ladder, to the car and the hospital, struggling onward, changed again, forever, to the end.

There are problems in the family. Yes, troubles. But today he is alone. He gazes at geese migrating northward, until they are out of sight. He watches the lake below him quiver as a breeze touches its surface. The sere fields tumble from the abandoned clapboard schoolhouse sagging on the far hill. He is at home. The day is oddly beautiful, and it is his.